CW00951832
NORMAN WILKINSON

# War at Sea
# 1914–45

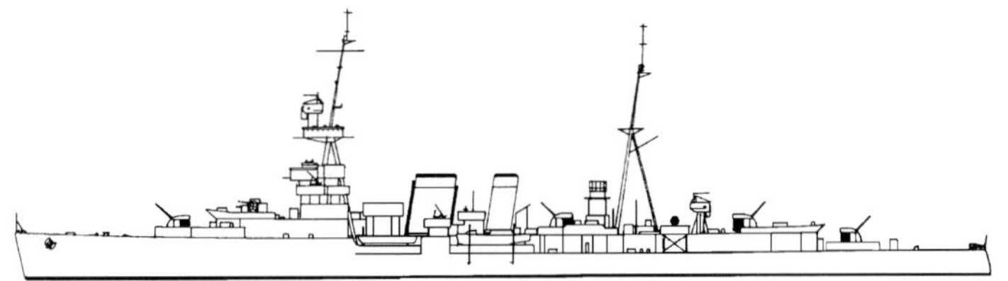

# War at Sea 1914–45

*Bernard Ireland*

*General Editor: John Keegan*

CASSELL

*To Daisy*
*my very first granddaughter*

Cassell
Wellington House, 125 Strand
London WC2R 0BB

First published 2002



British Library Cataloguing-in-Publication Data
A catalogue record for this book is available from the British Library.
ISBN 0-304-35340-X

Cartography: Arcadia Editions
Picture research: Elaine Willis
Design: Martin Hendry

Typeset in Monotype Sabon

# ACKNOWLEDGEMENTS

For their unstinting help in the production of this book, I would like to thank both the staff at Cassell and their associates. Firstly, Ian Drury, for inviting me to participate in the series, and Penny Gardiner, as fair an editor as ever wielded a blue pencil. Then Elaine Willis, who cheerfully scoured the world for pictures with unpronounceable captions, and Malcolm Swanston, whose excellent maps and diagrams materialized from my not over-informative wish-lists.

Lastly, of course, my wife who, as ever, patiently converted my stubborn insistence on hand-written manuscript to one of those magic disks.

BERNARD IRELAND
*Fareham, December 2001*

*The German fast battleship* Gneisenau *with new 'Atlantic bow'.*

# Contents

# KEY TO MAPS

### Symbols on map

battle

airfield

sunken ship

XXXXX army group

XXXX army

XXX corps

XX division

X brigade

III regiment

II battalion

### Name style

**SPAIN** Independent state

**Thrace** province

*Dogger Bank* physical name

### Geographical symbols

urban area

road

river

seasonal river

canal

border

### Military movements

attack

retreat or conjectural movement

# Map list

# CHRONOLOGY

**1901**
Jan — Death of Queen Victoria.
**1902** — Anglo-Japanese Alliance agreed.
**1903** — Cuniberti advocates all-big-gun capital ships.
**1904**
6 Feb — Japan attacks Russia without formal declaration of war.
10 Aug — Battle of the Yellow Sea.
14 Aug — Battle of Ulsan.
Anglo-French 'Entente Cordiale'.
21 Oct — Admiral Sir John Fisher appointed First Sea Lord.
**1905**
Mar — USS *South Carolina* and *Michigan* (all big-gun battleships) authorized.
27–28 May — Battle of Tsushima. Japan recognized as first-class naval power.
**1906**
10 Feb — Launch of HMS *Dreadnought*.
**1907**
13 April — Launch of HMS *Invincible* (first dreadnought battle-cruiser).
Triple Entente of Britain, France and Russia.
**1909**
May — Britain abandons Two-Power Standard as no longer practicable.
**1910**
Jan — Fisher resigns.
14 Nov — USS *Birmingham*: First aircraft take-off from ship.
**1911**
18 Jan — USS *Pennsylvania*: First aircraft landing aboard ship.
25 Oct — Winston Churchill appointed First Lord of the Admiralty.
**1912**
10 Jan — HMS *Africa*: First aircraft take-off from British ship.
**1913**
7 May — HMS *Hermes* commissions as first experimental seaplane carrier.
**1914** — Panama canal opened. Widening of Kiel canal completed.
4 Aug — Britain declares war on Germany.
26 Aug — Intelligence coup when wreck of *Magdeburg* supplies British with German codes.
28 Aug — Battle of Heligoland Bight.
5 Sept — HMS *Pathfinder*: first British warship to be sunk by U-boat.
22 Sept — HMS's *Hogue, Aboukir* and *Cressy* sunk together by U-boat.
27 Oct — dreadnought battleship HMS *Audacious* sunk by single mine.
29 Oct — Turkey enters war on side of Central Powers.
30 Oct — Fisher reappointed as First Sea Lord.
1 Nov — Battle of Coronel.
3 Nov — German bombardment of Yarmouth.
5 Nov — Britain declares war on Turkey.
5 Nov — British force arrives in Shatt-al-Arab. Mesopotamian campaign begins.
7 Nov — Japanese capture Tsingtao.
8 Nov — Battle of the Falklands.
16 Dec — German bombardment of Scarborough, Whitby and Hartlepool.
25 Dec — British raid on Cuxhaven. First shipborne air strike.
**1915**
24 Jan — Battle of Dogger Bank.
4 Feb — Germany declares British waters a 'war zone'.
19 Feb — Naval attack on Dardanelles begins.
28 Feb — First unrestricted U-boat campaign begins.
25 April — Allied military forces landed on Gallipoli Peninsula.
7 May — *Lusitania* sunk by U-boat.
15 May — Fisher resigns over Churchill's 'circumventions'.
21 May — Churchill dropped from Asquith's government.
23 May — Italy defects from Triple Alliance and enters war on Allied side.
25 May — *U21* sinks HMS *Triumph* off Dardanelles. Era of close blockade ended.
5 June — Restrictions placed on U-boat operations.
17 Aug — First successful aerial torpedo attack.
Sept — Tirpitz replaced by Capelle at German Navy Office.
15 Sept — French submarine *Foucault* sunk by Austrian seaplanes. First submarine to be destroyed by aircraft.
18 Sept — First U-boat campaign called off.
**1916**
8–9 Jan — Allied evacuation of Gallipoli.
24 Jan — Scheer appointed C-in-C, High Seas Fleet.
14 Mar — Tirpitz resigns.
19 April — British forces surrender at Kut-al-Amara.

| | |
|---|---|
| 24/25 April | German bombardment of Lowestoft and Yarmouth. |
| 31 May – 1 June | Battle of Jutland. |
| 5 June | Lord Kitchener lost when HMS *Hampshire* mined. |
| 19 Aug | Foray by High Seas Fleet. |
| Sept | Grand Fleet's North Sea operational area constrained. |
| Oct | Germans commence restricted U-boat campaign. |
| Dec | Jellicoe becomes First Sea Lord and creates Anti-Submarine Division at Admiralty. |
| **1917** | |
| 1 Feb | Germany resumes unrestricted U-boat warfare. |
| 11 Mar | British capture Baghdad. |
| 6 April | United States declares war on Germany. |
| 24 May | First ocean convoy sails. |
| 11–19 Oct | Germans mount large-scale amphibious operation against Russians in Baltic. |
| 7 Nov | Bolsheviks seize power in Russia. |
| 17 Nov | Action off Heligoland Bight. |
| 7 Dec | American battle squadron joins Grand Fleet. |
| **1918** | |
| 3 Mar | Northern mine barrage commenced. |
| 22/23 April | British raid on Zeebrugge. |
| 24 April | Last sortie of High Seas Fleet. |
| 10/11 May | British raid on Ostend. |
| 19 July | Shipborne air strike on Zeppelin sheds at Tondern. |
| 14 Sept | HMS *Argus* commissions as first true aircraft carrier. |
| 11 Nov | Armistice agreed with Germany. |
| **1919** | |
| 21 June | High Seas Fleet scuttled at Scapa. |
| 28 June | Treaty of Versailles signed. |
| Aug | The Ten-Year Rule is adopted by the British government. |
| **1922** | |
| 6 Feb | Washington Treaty signed. |
| **1923** | Construction of Singapore naval base begins. |
| **1925** | |
| 1 Dec | Locarno Treaty signed. |
| **1927** | |
| Aug | Geneva Conference. |
| **1929** | Ten-Year Rule made self-perpetuating. |
| **1930** | |
| 22 April | London Naval Treaty begins. |
| **1931** | |
| Jan | Invergordon Mutiny. |
| **1932** | |
| Oct | Ten-Year Rule abandoned. |
| **1933** | |
| Feb | Japan gives notice of leaving League of Nations. |
| Oct | Germany gives notice of leaving League of Nations. |
| **1934** | |
| Dec | Italy engineers hostilities with Abyssinia. |
| **1935** | |
| 16 Mar | Germany abrogates Versailles Treaty restrictions. |
| 18 June | Anglo-German Naval Agreement signed. |
| | US Congress approves Neutrality Act. |
| **1936** | |
| Feb | US Neutrality Act extended in scope. |
| Mar | Germany reoccupies Rhineland. |
| 25 Mar | Second London Naval Treaty signed. |
| 18 July | Spanish Civil War begins. |
| Nov | 'Rome–Berlin Axis' declared. |
| **1937** | |
| Jan–May | US Neutrality Act further extended. |
| July | Fleet Air Arm returned to Admiralty control. |
| | Operational Intelligence Centre (OIC) established at Admiralty. |
| | Japanese Navy's 'Third Replenishment Programme' approved. |
| Dec | Japanese aircraft bomb British and American gunboats in China. |
| | USS *Panay* sunk. |
| **1938** | |
| 11 Mar | Germany invades Austria. |
| April | British relinquish right of access to Irish naval bases. |
| May | WRNS reformed. |
| 29 Sept | Munich agreement signed. |
| **1939** | |
| Mar | Germany invades Czechoslovakia. |
| 1 Sept | Germany invades Poland. |
| 3 Sept | Britain and France declare war on Germany. |
| 5 Sept | US Neutrality Patrol commenced. |
| 17 Sept | HMS *Courageous* sunk by U-boat. |
| 14 Oct | HMS *Royal Oak* sunk by U-boat. |
| Nov | US Neutrality Act repealed. |
| 13 Dec | Battle of River Plate. |
| **1940** | |
| Jan | First attempt at U-boat 'wolf-pack' tactics. |
| April | Germany suspends work on only carrier, *Graf Zeppelin*. |
| 9 April | Germany invades Norway and Denmark. |
| 10 April | First battle of Narvik. |
| 13 April | Second battle of Narvik. |

| | |
|---|---|
| 8 May | British establish Iceland garrison. |
| 23 May | Faeroes occupied by British. |
| 26 May –4 June | Dunkirk evacuation. |
| 3–8 June | Allies evacuate Norway. |
| 9 June | HMS *Glorious* and escort sunk. |
| 11 June | Italy declares war on Britain and France. |
| 22 June | France agrees armistice with Germany. Force H formed at Gibraltar. |
| July | President Roosevelt's 'short of war' declaration. U-boats begin operating from French Atlantic coast. |
| 3 July | Force H neutralizes French squadron at Mers-el-Kebir. |
| 7 July | British begin operation against Dakar. |
| 9 July | Battle off Calabria. |
| Sept | British and Free French operation agains Dakar ends unsuccessfully. |
| 28 Oct | Italy invades Greece from Albania. |
| Nov | British establish base in Crete. |
| 11/22 Nov | British carrier attack on Taranto. |
| 27 Nov | Action off Spartivento. |
| **1941** | |
| 6–13 Jan | Excess convoy to Malta. HMS *Illustrious* heavily bomb-damaged. |
| Jan–Mar | First US–British strategy discussions. |
| 1 Feb | US Atlantic Fleet formed. |
| 9 Feb | Force H bombards Genoa and Leghorn. |
| 14 Feb | Deutsche Afrika Korps begins to land in Libya. |
| 7 Mar | British army begins to land in Greece. |
| 11 Mar | US Lend-Lease Bill approved. |
| 28/29 Mar | Battle of Matapan. |
| April | Coastal Command aircraft put under operational control of the Admiralty. |
| 4 April | Arrangements made to repair British ships in US yards. |
| 21 April | Mediterranean Fleet bombards Tripoli. |
| 24–25 Apr | British evacuation of Greece. |
| 5–12 May | Tiger through-Mediterranean convoy to Egypt. |
| 20 May | German airborne assault on Crete begins. |
| 24 May | HMS *Hood* sunk. |
| 27 May | *Bismarck* sunk. |
| June | Naval support to campaign against Vichy French in Syria. |
| 1 June | British complete evacuation of Crete. |
| 22 June | Germany invades Soviet Union. |
| July | 'Hedgehog' AS weapon introduced. |
| 21–25 July | Substance convoy to Malta. |
| 9–12 Aug | Churchill–Roosevelt conference at Argentia. |
| Sept | First convoys sailed to North Russia. |
| Sept | HMS *Audacity* proves value of CVE in convoy protection. |
| Sept–Oct | First incidents between US escorts and U-boats. |
| 1 Sept | US Navy free to escort convoys anywhere in Atlantic. |
| 26–28 Sept | Halberd convoy to Malta. |
| 13 Nov | HMS *Ark Royal* sunk by U-boat. |
| 25 Nov | HMS *Barham* sunk by U-boat. |
| 7 Dec | Japanese carrier attack on Pearl Harbor. |
| 10 Dec | HMS *Repulse* and HMS *Prince of Wales* sunk by Japanese aircraft. |
| 11 Dec | Germany and Italy declare war on US. |
| 17 Dec | First battle of Sirte. |
| 19 Dec | Italian special forces raid on Alexandria. HMS *Queen Elizabeth* and HMS *Valiant* disabled. |
| 25 Dec | British surrender Hong Kong. |
| **1942** | |
| Jan | Start of U-boat offensive on US eastern seaboard. |
| 12 Feb | *Scharnhorst* and *Gneisenau* escape up-Channel. |
| 15 Feb | British surrender Singapore. |
| 27–28 Feb | Battle of Java Sea. |
| 19 Mar | Japanese carrier attack on Darwin. |
| 22 Mar | Second battle of Sirte. |
| 28 Mar | British raid on St Nazaire. |
| 5–9 April | Japanese carrier offensive in Bay of Bengal. |
| 18 April | Doolittle's raid on Tokyo. |
| 4 May | British landings in Madagascar. |
| 7–8 May | Battle of Coral Sea. |
| 4–7 June | Battle of Midway. |
| 12–16 June | Harpoon and Vigorous convoys to Malta. |
| July | End of U-boat offensive off US eastern seaboard and Caribbean. |
| 2–13 July | PQ17 convoy disaster. |
| 8/9 Aug | Battle of Savo Island. |
| 10/14 Aug | Pedestal convoy to Malta. |
| 19 Aug | British raid on Dieppe. |
| 22–25 Aug | Battle of Eastern Solomons. |
| 7 Sept | Americans land on Guadalcanal. |
| 11/12 Oct | Battle of Cape Esperance. |
| 26/27 Oct | Battle of Santa Cruz. |
| 2 Nov | Final British breakthrough at Alamein. |

| | |
|---|---|
| 8 Nov | North African landings. |
| 12/13 Nov | First naval battle of Guadalcanal. |
| 14/15 Nov | Second naval battle of Guadalcanal. |
| 20 Nov | British take Benghazi. Stoneage convoy to Malta. |
| 27 Nov | French fleet scuttled at Toulon. |
| 30 Nov/ 1 Dec | Battle of Tassafaronga. |
| 31 Dec | Battle of North Cape. |
| **1943** | |
| 23 Jan | British take Tripoli. |
| 2–4 Mar | Action in Bismarck Sea. |
| 27 Mar | Battle of Komandorski Islands. |
| 18 April | Admiral Yamamoto killed. |
| May | U-boats temporarily withdrawn following defeat in North Atlantic. |
| 11 May | Axis surrender in North Africa. |
| 30 June | US landings on Rendova. Pacific debut of LST, LCT and LCI. |
| July | Climax of Bay offensive against U-boats. |
| 5/6 July | Battle of Kula Gulf. |
| 10 July | Allied landings in Sicily. |
| 12/13 July | Battle of Kolombangara. |
| Aug | Anti-ship guided bombs introduced by Germans. |
| Sept | Acoustic torpedoes introduced by both sides. |
| 3 Sept | Allied landings at Lae and Salamaua. |
| 9 Sept | Italians agree armistice with Allies. |
| 9 Sept | Allied landings at Salerno. |
| 9 Sept | Italian battleship *Roma* sunk by German guided bombs. |
| 6 Oct | Battle of Vella Lavella. |
| 1/2 Nov | Battle of Empress Augusta Bay. |
| 5+11 Nov | Rabaul abandoned as Japanese fleet base following heavy US carrier attacks. |
| 21 Nov | US landings on Makin and Tarawa (Gilbert Islands). |
| 26 Nov | Battle of Cape St George. |
| 26 Dec | *Scharnhorst* sunk. |
| **1944** | |
| 22 Jan | Allied landings at Anzio. |
| 31 Jan | US landings on Kwajalein (Marshall Islands). |
| April | U-boats effectively abandon North Atlantic. |
| 16 April | British Eastern Fleet begins attacks on Japanese. |
| 30 April – 1 May | US carrier raid on Truk. |
| 6 June | Allied landings in Normandy. |
| 15 June | US landing on Saipan (Marianas). |
| 19–20 Jun | Battle of Philippines Sea ('Marianas Turkey Shoot'). |
| 21+24 Jul | US landings on Guam and Tinian (Marianas). |
| 15 Aug | Allied landings in the South of France. |
| 15 Sept | US landings on Morotai (New Guinea). US landing on Peleliu (Palau Islands). |
| 17 Sept | US landing on Angaur (Palau Islands). |
| 10–16 Oct | Formosa neutralized by carrier air power alone. |
| 20 Oct | US landings on Leyte (Philippine Islands). |
| 23–26 Oct | Battles of Leyte Gulf. Kamikazes make their appearance. |
| 12 Nov | *Tirpitz* sunk. |
| 15 Dec | US landings on Mindoro (Philippine Islands). |
| **1945** | |
| Jan | First Type XXIII U-boat operational. |
| 9 Jan | US landing in Lingayen Gulf (Philippine Islands). |
| 16 Feb | First US carrier raids on Japanese home islands. |
| 19 Feb | US landing on Iwo Jima. |
| April | First Type XXI U-boat operational. |
| 1 April | US landing on Okinawa. |
| 12 April | Death of President Roosevelt. |
| 8 May | Germany surrenders unconditionally. |
| 6 Aug | Nuclear attack on Hiroshima. |
| 8 Aug | Soviet Russia declares war on Japan. |
| 9 Aug | Nuclear attack on Nagasaki. |
| 15 Aug | Japan surrenders unconditionally. |
| **1946** | |
| 1 July | Experimental airburst nuclear explosion at Bikini Atoll. |
| 25 July | Experimental underwater nuclear explosion at Bikini Atoll. |

INTRODUCTION

# The Nature of Sea Power

*Airships were commonly used by the British to cover coastwise convoys. Their low speed and long endurance enabled them to watch for submarines over extended periods. Few U-boats were, in fact, spotted but the presence of an airship made their skippers cautious in attack.*

# The Nature of Sea Power

For the Lord our God Most High
He hath made the deep as dry,
He hath smote for us a pathway to the ends of all the Earth!

In his 'The Song of the English', Kipling reflected the then-confident national assertion that the seas, 'their' seas, were a natural highway. Beyond this lies the implication that centuries of hard-contested superiority had conferred some God-given destiny. What had ever been, ever would be.

Whether a nation looks upon the oceans as a highway or a barrier, facility or impedance, has little to do with geography and everything to do with the national temperament.

Two centuries ago, when Cornwallis maintained his weary watch on Brest and Nelson kept station off Toulon, both were exercising sea power in its purest form: that of controlling the seas for their nation's own purposes, while denying them to its enemy. Even with the then-considerable resources of the Royal Navy, however, 'command of the sea' was a condition that could be established and guaranteed only in limited areas and for specific purposes. The alternative lay in the expensive and time-consuming destruction of an opponent's maritime capability. As this was implicitly the weaker, it would not sensibly expose itself to confrontation except on the most favourable terms. Its strategy would be likely to be that of a 'fleet in being'.

When 'in being' a fleet is, strictly speaking, assuming a defensive posture until such time as a growing capability will allow it to take the offensive. More loosely, the term refers to a weaker power concentrating its naval assets sufficiently to be able to exercise local superiority, under favourable circumstances, thus obliging the superior fleet to modify its otherwise unchallenged activities by taking due and necessary account. Used sufficiently aggressively, the weaker force may persuade the stronger that a certain strategy may really not be worth the risk. This is one aspect of 'sea denial'.

A long-established and effective strategy for the weaker force is the so-called *guerre de course*, or war on commerce. Trade is extraordinarily vulnerable to interference by predators. The privateers and letters of marque of earlier days have given way to cruising ships and submarines, but the problem remains. Convoy, as a principle, has been exercised back to the dawn of seaborne commerce, but it is a principle that had to be relearned in the twentieth century through hard experience.

'The army', it has been said, 'is a projectile to be fired by the navy.' In the situation of a general war, as opposed to what might be termed a confrontation, the issue will probably be settled finally only through military occupation of territory. To achieve this, an expeditionary capability is required.

*As in the French wars of more than a century earlier, the British fleet was constantly at sea. It wore out ships, it wore out men, but kept morale and fighting efficiency higher than that of the enemy. Here, W. L. Wyllie beautifully depicts armoured cruisers in the wastes of the North Sea.*

The establishment of local, and temporary, sea superiority might be sufficient to conduct raids with limited objectives. More permanent superiority by a hostile fleet, however, raises the spectre of invasion. Thus, even when the shades of Cornwallis and Nelson are enforcing local control, the main battlefleet is held poised to defend home waters against the 'bolt from the blue', for the defence of the realm is its ultimate priority.

The inherent flexibility of sea power facilitates military intervention in areas inaccessible by other means. The naval role does not end at delivery, for a force, once ashore, requires support and supply and, in the event of an unsatisfactory outcome, evacuation. When the going is a little rough it is important to the military to know that this support exists, that the outfield is being held. In 1941, during the bitter days of the evacuation of Crete, Admiral Cunningham was asked if he could go on sustaining the grievous level of loss and damage to his fleet. For Cunningham, the abandonment of the army was an unthinkable option: 'Replacing a warship,' he observed, 'will take three years. Rebuilding a tradition would take three hundred.' The evacuation went on.

His remark underlines the fact that the general principles briefly touched upon here were perfectly understood and exercised in the days of fierce encounters with the Dutch. Ships and weapons, the enemy and the issues, have all changed, but the principles remain perfectly valid today.

The subject of this book, *War at Sea 1914–45*, is vast in scope, too large to compress into a narrative form that could cover everything in the space available whilst still remaining readable. Faced with being necessarily selective, it seemed that the best solution was to identify and amplify the key aspects that decided the outcome of both major wars at sea. The chapters devoted to the two world wars thus begin with these sections but end, in each case, with more detailed accounts of secondary campaigns which, while important in themselves, proved to be less than critical in determining the ultimate result.

All the principles briefly described above will be found, exemplified, in the chapters dealing with the wars. Indeed, they will be recognized in the study of every foreign war and confrontation since, be it Korea or Vietnam, Suez, the Gulf or the Falklands. It remains a matter of controlling the seas for one's own purposes, using them as the highway of opportunity that they surely are.

*Superficial assessments of the major fleets participating in the First World War often overlook the small but capable Austro-Hungarian navy. The dreadnought flagship* Viribus Unitis, *first of a class of four, was completed in 1912 and is shown by artist August Ramberg in review, impressively leading the the Radetsky-class pre-dreadnoughts.*

DREADNOUGHT

## CHAPTER ONE

# Anglo-German Naval Rivalry

*HMS* DREADNOUGHT *stemmed in a partially flooded dry dock. The lack of casemates housing secondary armament is very obvious. That this is an early picture is evident from the 3-inch guns sited on the quarterdeck. Although the 12-inch gun barrels look of impressive length, they are short, 45-calibre weapons.*

# Anglo-German Naval Rivalry

While the so-called 'naval race' was not the cause of the First World War, it was a major contributory factor. Its beginnings can be traced to 1888, when the 29-year-old Wilhelm II became Kaiser of a newly unified Germany. Wilhelm envied the status of his grandmother, Queen Victoria, but disliked her eldest daughter, his mother. His uncle, the future King Edward VII, he despised.

Naval careers and naval ceremonial were interwoven with Victorian royal life, and young Wilhelm's frequent spells in Britain imbued him with a deep interest in maritime affairs. Germany's industrial and commercial vigour were already challenging those of Britain, entitling her, in Wilhelm's words, to 'her place in the sun'. He believed in the 'reapportionment' of colonies from 'dying' imperial powers and, to reinforce his claims, a first-class fleet would be a *sine qua non*. His grandfather and hero, Wilhelm I, had made Prussia a European power through nurturing the army. He, Wilhelm II, would take Germany to the status of world power by the creation of a fleet of which, indisputably, he would be the commander-in-chief.

Britain's main concern was with France, her traditional foe who, together with Russia, was engaged in provocative colonial boundary disputes and expansionism. French naval programmes raised questions regarding the adequacy of Britain's own strength. This was underlined by criticism of the shortcomings of various types of warship during exercises and, indeed, of the cash-starved dockyards upon which they depended and which 'functioned, more or less, like a firm on the verge of bankruptcy'.

*Uncle and nephew. King Edward VII, on a state visit to Germany in 1909, rides with Kaiser Wilhelm II through Berlin, here being officially greeted by municipal authorities at the Brandenburg Gate. Poor relations between the two added significantly to the tensions between their two nations.*

*Typical of a large force of British pre-dreadnoughts,* HMS Ocean *was a 12,950-tonner, completed in 1900 as one of the six Canopus-class ships. She was mined and sunk during the Dardanelles operation but, prior to this, had supported the landings in the Persian Gulf.*

The result was the passing of the Naval Defence Act in 1889. No less than seventy warships, fifty-two of them major, would be built over five years. Britain would also adopt the Two-Power Standard for naval strength, maintaining a Royal Navy capable of meeting the next two largest fleets acting together. This massive plan had nothing to do with Germany but to the young Kaiser, just a year after his accession, it created resentment at his nation's own inadequacies.

Bismarck, creator of modern Germany, had remarked that the state should remain 'a seapower of the second rank', linked to the fact that 'as long as he were Chancellor there would be no colonial policy', and in 1882 had concluded a Triple Alliance with Austria and Italy.

Britain failed really to comprehend that France viewed her as less of a threat than the Alliance. When, in 1890, she embarked on her own ten-year fleet reconstruction, its extent matched almost exactly that of the British, who expressed concern.

In 1891, as a further hedge, France formed an alliance with Russia. Naval exchanges were followed by rumours that a Russian squadron would be allowed the use of a new French base at Bizerta in Tunisia. Alarm in London was now considerable, while in Germany, too, there was unease because France and Russia, both considerable military powers, bracketed her geographically.

Despite Bismarck's misgivings, Germany still acquired a fledgeling empire in Africa, New Guinea and the Pacific. He was proved correct, for the colonies were expensive to administer, generated little trade and demanded resources for their defence; and he was well satisfied when, in 1890, he recovered Heligoland from the British in exchange for Zanzibar. Bismarck's diplomatic skills only made Wilhelm's lapses the more obvious and the latter excluded him increasingly from decision-making. Eventually, as Wilhelm intended, the septuagenarian statesman tendered his resignation, which was accepted. The pilot had been dropped.

Wilhelm's ego was further inflated during 1890 by his grandmother's unfortunate decision to create a sinecure post for him as honorary Admiral of the Fleet in the Royal Navy. It was at about the time that he read Alfred Thayer Mahan's newly published book *The Influence of Sea Power upon History*. Hugely influential, it argued the connection between colonial success and an

*Pre-dreadnoughts of the Wittelsbach and Braunschweig-class exercising on a typical blustery North Sea day, well captured by artist Carl Saltzmann. Ships such as these were built to conform to Tirpitz's 'risk theory' and were designed with comparatively short endurance.*

*The vainglorious Wilhelm II revelled in the pomp accompanying his status. Although much given to cruising the Norwegian fjords, he is seen here arriving to an enthusiastic welcome in Venice, aboard the royal yacht* Hohenzollern. *Italy was to prove an unreliable ally in the trials ahead.*

efficient battle fleet, and effectively debunked Aube's *Jeune École* theories (that emphasized the vulnerability of a battleship navy to emerging technologies like the 'automobile torpedo', torpedo boat, and submarine). For the moment, however, any Wilhelmian dreams would need to remain just that, for all parties in the Reichstag were, for their various reasons, opposed to naval expenditure beyond the modest programme triggered by the Franco-Russian alliance. It was already funding the construction of the Kiel canal, commenced in 1887. This waterway would be strategically important in permitting naval forces to be switched rapidly between the North Sea and the Baltic.

The canal was opened officially in June 1895 in the presence of an impressive international gathering of warships. These included the first four of the British Royal Sovereign-class battleships. Setting new standards, this class of seven was to be followed by nine improved Majestics, funded by the so-called Spencer programme of 1893, the objective of which was to guarantee equality with any Franco-Russian combination.

Also present were several large cruisers, the Russian *Rurik*, French *Dupuy de Lôme* and American *New York*. These represented national interpretations of Aube's ideas on commerce destruction; for Wilhelm their potential paled beside

*Admiral Tirpitz viewed the submarine as an irritating distraction from his task of creating a battle fleet. The first German U-boat, in consequence, did not commission until December 1906. She was armed with one tube and three torpedoes.*

that of the capital ships. Aware of his nation's own modest representation, he felt patronized, particularly by the British.

Large numbers of Germans had settled in South Africa and British attempts to destabilize Kruger's Boer republic created hostility. The spectacular failure in 1895 of the so-called Jameson Raid resulted in the notorious Kruger Telegram, pledging German support for the creation of an Afrikaner heartland. Probably less guilty than his Foreign Office, Wilhelm attracted British fury, fanned by a popular press in full voice. A British naval 'flying squadron' was put on standby and measures were taken to prevent the landing of German 'volunteers' on the South African coast.

For Wilhelm, any difference with Britain was a family affair attracting disapproval from both Victoria and the heir apparent, the future Edward VII. A fleet would lend him authority and gain their respect. Britain, however, was enduring a period not only of German popular resentment but also of diplomatic isolation, with a triple Franco-Russo-German axis felt to be a distinct possibility. Inevitably, demands were made for further naval expansion.

In June 1897 Britain exploded into an orgy of patriotism for the queen's diamond jubilee. At the fleet review a line of twenty-one British battleships lay

adjacent to the foreign representatives, of which the German was the elderly cruiser *König Wilhelm*. Widely interpreted in Britain as a snub, the choice caused Wilhelm further embarrassment.

Rear Admiral Friedrich Hollmann, Secretary of State for the German Navy Office, had announced in the previous March that his increase in naval estimates had been severely trimmed by an unsympathetic Reichstag. His

*A German postcard commemorating 'victory' at Jutland. Seen flanking the Kaiser are Tirpitz, the creator of the High Seas Fleet, and Capelle, who would shortly succeed him at the Navy Office. Below, Scheer would also soon be succeeded by the battlecruiser admiral, Hipper.*

situation already undermined by intrigue, Hollmann was replaced in June by Rear Admiral Alfred Tirpitz. Appointed with the obsequious courtier Fürst von Bülow as Foreign Secretary, Tirpitz came with a clear mandate to create a battle fleet.

He based his plans on a so-called 'risk theory'. Britain (never mentioned by name) would always have the larger fleet, but needed to spread it worldwide.

*A coloured photograph of about 1910 showing a German battleship in a floating dock in Kiel. Fisher's dreadnought initiative resulted in a sudden increase in the dimensions of capital ships, necessitating expensive enlargement of locks and dry docks, and widening and deepening the Kiel canal.*

Germany, therefore, required a force large enough to face that element based in home waters. If not large enough to defeat it, then at least it must be strong enough to inflict unacceptable damage. The strategy, therefore, was one of deterrence, leaving Germany free to pursue a foreign policy without interference.

Using the size of the British Channel Fleet as a basis and estimating British building capacity, Tirpitz calculated that he would need to build sixty capital ships over twenty years. He set to single-mindedly, sidelining any champions of cruiser warfare and submarine development. Well aware that he would have to advance by easy stages, both to placate opponents in the Reichstag and to avoid fatally antagonizing the British, Tirpitz exercised great powers of diplomacy. On 10 April 1898 the assembly approved a naval bill to expand the fleet to a total of 19 battleships, 8 armoured and 42 smaller cruisers, to be constructed over six years. Justified to offset the naval power of France and Russia, the force in no way threatened British supremacy.

During 1898 the French provocatively dispatched a military force into the Sudan. Confronted by British military forces at Fashoda, they refused to withdraw. The use of force by either meant war, and stalemate developed. British fleets were exercised off the French coasts and an expeditionary force overtly prepared. Aware of their own fleet's inadequacy and general state of unpreparedness, the French backed down. It was the last occasion upon which the two nations contemplated hostilities and its resolution gave the British a further boost to naval pride.

Britain's continuing assertion of authority over Afrikaner-dominated provinces in South Africa led to a *de facto* state of war. Mobile Boer columns used ambush and skirmish against British military forces ill-trained for the purpose. The latter responded with harsh repressive measures which fanned German Anglophobia to white heat, not helped by the indignity of German shipping being stopped and checked by the Royal Navy.

As Bülow observed that 'in the coming century the German people must be either the hammer or the anvil' and the Kaiser announced that the navy would be

*Ships of the High Seas Fleet lying off Kiel in about 1914. At the near end of the line, two Helgoland-class dreadnoughts flank an earlier Nassau, all with hexagonally disposed main batteries. Beyond are light cruisers, the near four-funnelers being of the Magdeburg or Karlsruhe classes.*

the equal of the nation's army, Tirpitz had little difficulty in steering through a revised naval bill. On 14 June 1900 approval was given to increase the fleet to 38 battleships, 20 large and 38 smaller cruisers.

British resentment at German opportunism in South Africa turned to anger at what was now seen as nothing less than a direct challenge to her naval supremacy. The death of Victoria in January 1901 did not improve the situation as the new king made no secret of his dislike of his nephew.

German plans were still largely just that, while the Royal Navy had added twenty-eight first-class and four second-class battleships to the fleet between the Naval Defence Act and 1902. More major units were brought to home waters through reductions in the China and Mediterranean fleets, achieved through diplomacy. The signing of the 1902 Anglo-Japanese alliance provided for co-operation with a first-class naval power which, in 1905, eased the situation further by virtually annihilating a Russian fleet at Tsushima.

France, coming at last to the realization that she and Britain faced a common threat, ceased to seek naval equality and in 1904 agreed the Entente Cordiale. A concerted effort to resolve all minor causes of friction allowed British naval presence in the Mediterranean to be reduced. Meanwhile, whereas existing naval bases in Britain were sited for possible war with the Dutch or the French, a start was made in 1903 on a new fleet base at Rosyth, located for control of the northern North Sea.

For the Royal Navy, this era was dominated by the restless genius of Admiral Sir John Fisher. A natural reformer, he swept aside outmoded practices and, as its commander-in-chief, put the Mediterranean Fleet on a war footing, which he regarded as its standard condition. His recognition of the abilities of Captain Percy Scott resulted in a dramatic improvement in gunnery both in accuracy and range of engagement.

Appointed First Sea Lord in October 1904, Fisher applied his 'three R' principles – Ruthless, Relentless, Remorseless – in refashioning the Royal Navy to meet the new challenge. Having brought home a maximum number of ships from foreign stations, he identified 154 others as having little or no fighting power. These were scrapped without sentiment to release resources for reallocation. Ships not required in the active fleet were classed as 'fleet reserve', and maintained in a state of reduced commission by

*Admiral of the Fleet John Arbuthnot Fisher, First Baron Fisher of Kilverstone and Tirpitz's nemesis. Twice First Sea Lord, he brought about the 'dreadnought revolution', championed the steam turbine, the submarine, torpedoes and oil-firing, and transformed fleet gunnery. He resigned over the Dardanelles fiasco in 1915.*

nucleus crews. Some remote commands were abandoned or amalgamated. The Royal Navy's major concentrations were now the Channel Fleet (formerly Home Fleet), Mediterranean Fleet and a new Gibraltar-based Atlantic Fleet that could quickly reinforce either of the others.

Long aware of the potential of the submarine, Fisher believed that, in conjunction with mines, it would make the narrow seas too hazardous for battle squadrons. There were many who feared the 'bolt from the blue', whereby the temporary absence of the main fleet would allow an enemy army to be landed swiftly on the English east coast. Its movements restricted by defensive minefields, such an invasion fleet would now be countered by Fisher's 'flotilla defence'. Harried and attacked by a swarm of torpedo craft and submarines issuing from every minor port, it would be unable to support any military force.

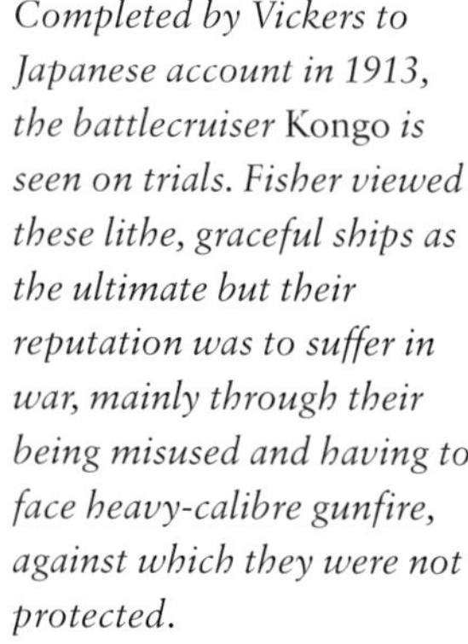

*Completed by Vickers to Japanese account in 1913, the battlecruiser* Kongo *is seen on trials. Fisher viewed these lithe, graceful ships as the ultimate but their reputation was to suffer in war, mainly through their being misused and having to face heavy-calibre gunfire, against which they were not protected.*

Where Mahan espoused the raw power of the big gun, Fisher believed in speed – to run down a reluctant foe, to force or decline an action, to dictate the fighting range. Speed and aggression, he maintained, provided their own protection.

During 1903 the great Italian constructor Cuniberti had proposed in print his concept of an ideal ship, powerfully engined and with a homogeneous big gun armament. Foreign navies were already moving in this direction, as can be seen from the following table:

| Class | Nat. | Built | Main batt. | Secondary batt. | Tertiary batt. |
|---|---|---|---|---|---|
| Duncan | UK | 1903–4 | 4 x 12in | 12 x 6in | 10x12pdr |
| Virginia | US | 1902–7 | 4 x 12in | 8 x 8in | 12 x 6in |
| Benedetto Brin | It. | 1904–5 | 4 x 12in | 4 x 8in | 12 x 6in |
| King Edward VII | UK | 1905–7 | 4 x 12in | 4 x 9.2in | 10 x 6in |
| Lord Nelson | UK | 1908 | 4 x 12in | 10 x 9.2in | 24 x 12pdr |
| South Carolina | US | 1905–10 | 8 x 12in | 22 x 12pdr | – |
| Dreadnought | UK | 1905–6 | 10 x 12in | 27 x 12pdr | – |

The Duncans were the fifth class with virtually identical armament, but the influence of the *Virginia* and *Brin* resulted in the upgunned King Edward VIIs, from which the more logical Lord Nelsons developed. The South Carolinas then

broke the mould with a battery that was not only homogeneous but arranged to give an unprecedented broadside of eight 12-inch guns.

Fisher had no option but to respond, and the leisurely American building rate allowed him to rush the *Dreadnought* to completion first. Although equipped with two more big guns than the Americans, her inferior layout permitted only a similar eight-gun broadside. Her great innovation was to adopt the yet unproven steam turbine and partial oil-firing for a speed of 21 knots.

Fisher's personal ideal, however, was what came to be termed the battle-cruiser, of which the three Invincibles were pressed to completion in 1908. A sustained speed of 25 knots demanded huge hulls with only sparse protection and a reduced six-gun broadside. Like the *Dreadnought*, they could theoretically bring six guns to bear in chase fire; in practice, blast damage precluded this. They proved excellent in their intended role of neutralizing the large armoured cruisers then common, but proved vulnerable to the heavy gunfire of their peers.

In building the *Dreadnought*, Fisher was often unfairly accused of offsetting the Royal Navy's great numerical superiority, which was made obsolete. Tirpitz,

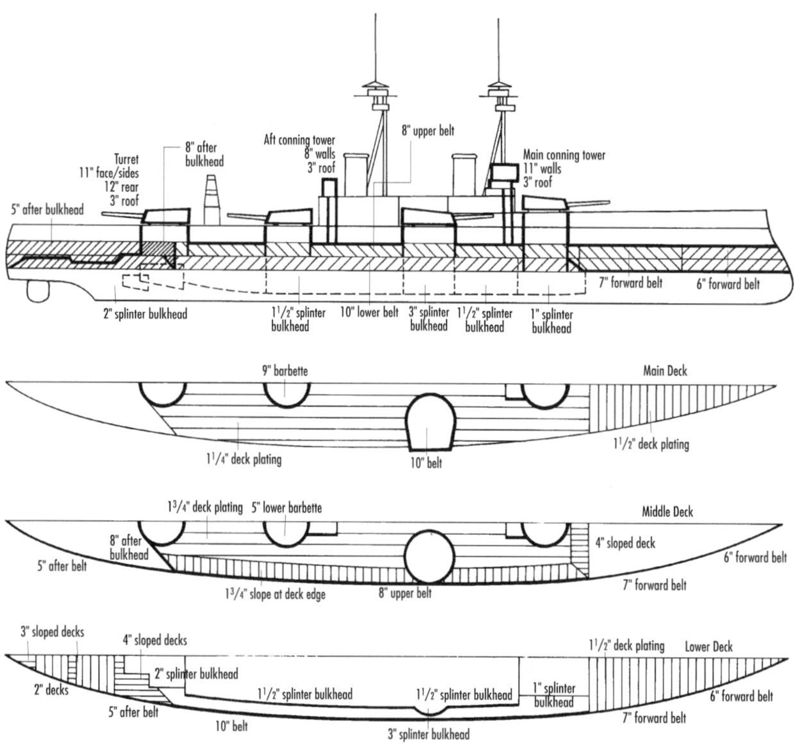

## Armoured deck protection

ABOVE: *The armour disposition of the British Bellerophon-class dreadnoughts shows a continuous side belt, tapered in thickness towards the extremities. Under water, machinery spaces and magazines are screened by inner protective bulkheads. Above the armoured decks only barbettes, turrets and conning tower are armoured.*

## Immunity zone

BELOW: *Long-range (plunging) fire will penetrate a protective deck but not a side belt. Short-range (flat trajectory) fire will penetrate the belt but not the deck. At intermediate ranges there usually exists a band over which neither is penetrated. This band is termed the 'immunity zone'.*

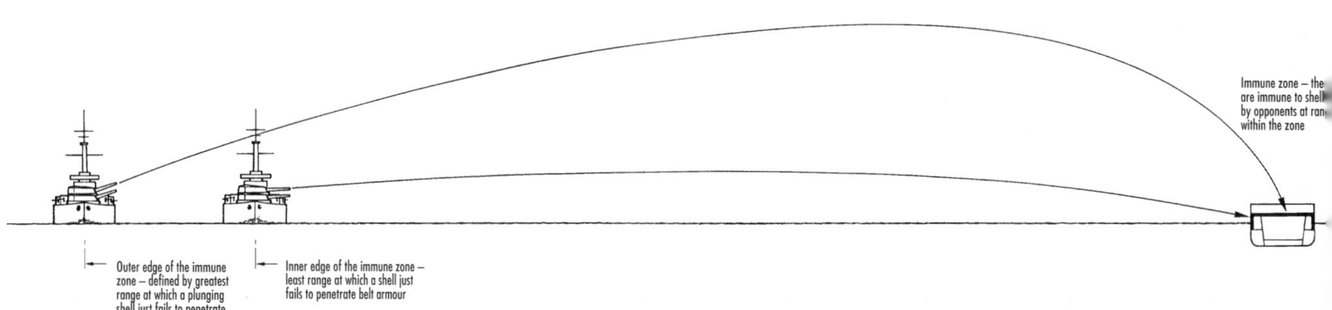

however, was put into a quandary. Not to build similarly would be to abandon the master plan by leaving the qualitative advantage with the British. To follow suit would be to make German intentions clear. Like Fisher, he had no choice. Backed by a threat of resignation, he forced a supplementary naval bill through the Reichstag in May 1906. It approved a one-third increase in funding, not just for six 'large cruisers' but also for necessary increase in dimensions to infrastructure, particularly the Kiel canal. Fisher later claimed that this alone prevented the Germans contemplating a naval war before 1914.

*Resplendent in a Far East colour scheme prior to heading for the China station, the* Fürst Bismarck *transits the Kiel canal. An armoured cruiser of 10,690 tons, completed in 1900, she had a light armoured deck and a shallow side belt.*

Ever controversial, Admiral Fisher made many influential enemies in the course of his reforms. In January 1910, continuous opposition finally brought about his resignation at the age of 69. During the following year, the 36-year-old Winston Churchill took over as First Lord, the Royal Navy's political head. With 'his entire inability to realize his own limitations as a civilian', he rapidly offended everybody from the Sea Lords down.

To anticipate briefly, in October 1914 Churchill was instrumental in the dismissal of the much-respected Prince Louis of Battenberg as First Sea Lord and reinstating Fisher. Within the year, and following Churchill's endless interventions over the Dardanelles, Fisher went for good. Shortly afterwards, a change of administration saw the First Lord follow him.

The German-engineered Agadir Crisis of 1911 stoked up public feeling in both camps, bringing Britain and France closer but also providing Tirpitz with an easier passage for a 1912 supplementary naval bill. The fleet would be able to deploy forty-one battleships and twenty battlecruisers by 1920 including additions and through the abolition of the navy's 'material reserve'. The new First Lord's response was that Britain lay down two for each one by Tirpitz. Germany, unable to match British financial or building resources, was indeed outbuilt by a margin that explains the later strategy of the High Seas Fleet.

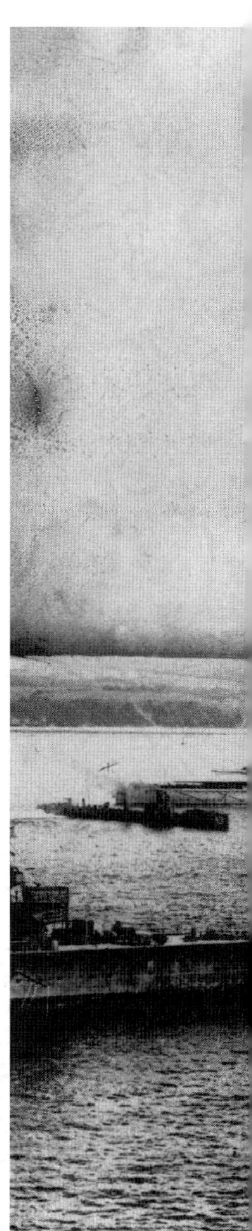

*Between 23 and 30 June 1914 Vice Admiral Sir George Warrender's Second Battle Squadron attended Kiel Week. Here, three of the four King George V-class battleships lay beyond ships of Commodore Goodeneough's First Light Cruiser Squadron. A German Kaiser-class battleship is anchored in the distance, while a Zeppelin carries sightseers above.*

It should be remembered that the Anglo-German naval race echoed significant increases in other major fleets which, however, posed no threat to Britain. If German expenditure in 1899 is expressed as unity, increases in naval budgets were as follows:

| | 1899–1900 | 1905–6 | 1913–14 |
|---|---|---|---|
| Germany | 1.00 | 1.76 | 3.51 |
| Great Britain | 3.74 | 5.12 | 7.10 |
| France | 1.77 | 1.92 | 2.77 |
| United States | 1.49 | 3.17 | 4.44 |
| Russia | 1.40 | 1.89 | 3.74 |

Although the German economy went into significant deficit during this period, the naval budget exceeded that of the army in only one year (1911). The

table shows that, despite their naval vote increasing by 250 per cent, the Germans were spending less at the end of the period than Britain spent at the start. Having begun as the smallest spender, Germany finished in much the same situation, having overtaken only France. Thus did Tirpitz's 'risk strategy' fail, and by a factor that was actually increasing with time.

At the outbreak of war, in August 1914, the capital ship strength of the major fleets was as follows:

| | Great Britain | Germany | USA | France | Italy | Austria | Russia |
|---|---|---|---|---|---|---|---|
| Battleships | 21 | 15 | 8 | 4 | 4 | 3 | – |
| Battlecruisers | 9 | 5 | – | – | – | – | – |
| Pre-dreadnoughts | 40 | 22 | 25 | 18 | 8 | 12 | 8 |

CHAPTER TWO

# FIRST WORLD WAR 1914–18

*AMONG THE MOST EXTREME of warship designs, the British Courageous-class are impossible to categorize except as 'large light cruisers'. Displacing over 19,000 tons and carrying four 15-inch guns, their 31.5 knot speed meant that, other than on turrets and barbettes, they were virtually unarmoured.*

# First World War

## Cruiser warfare

Earlier wars, particularly those fought against the French and Americans, had exposed the vulnerability of British commercial shipping to both enemy cruisers and licensed irregulars. The economy was damaged not only by lost ships and crews but also by huge hikes in insurance and high costs caused by shortages. Captured cargoes also helped the enemy.

The Treaty of Paris of 1856 thus greatly assisted the British by, *inter alia*, making privateering illegal under international law. Henceforth, only government cruisers and auxiliaries could prosecute a trade war.

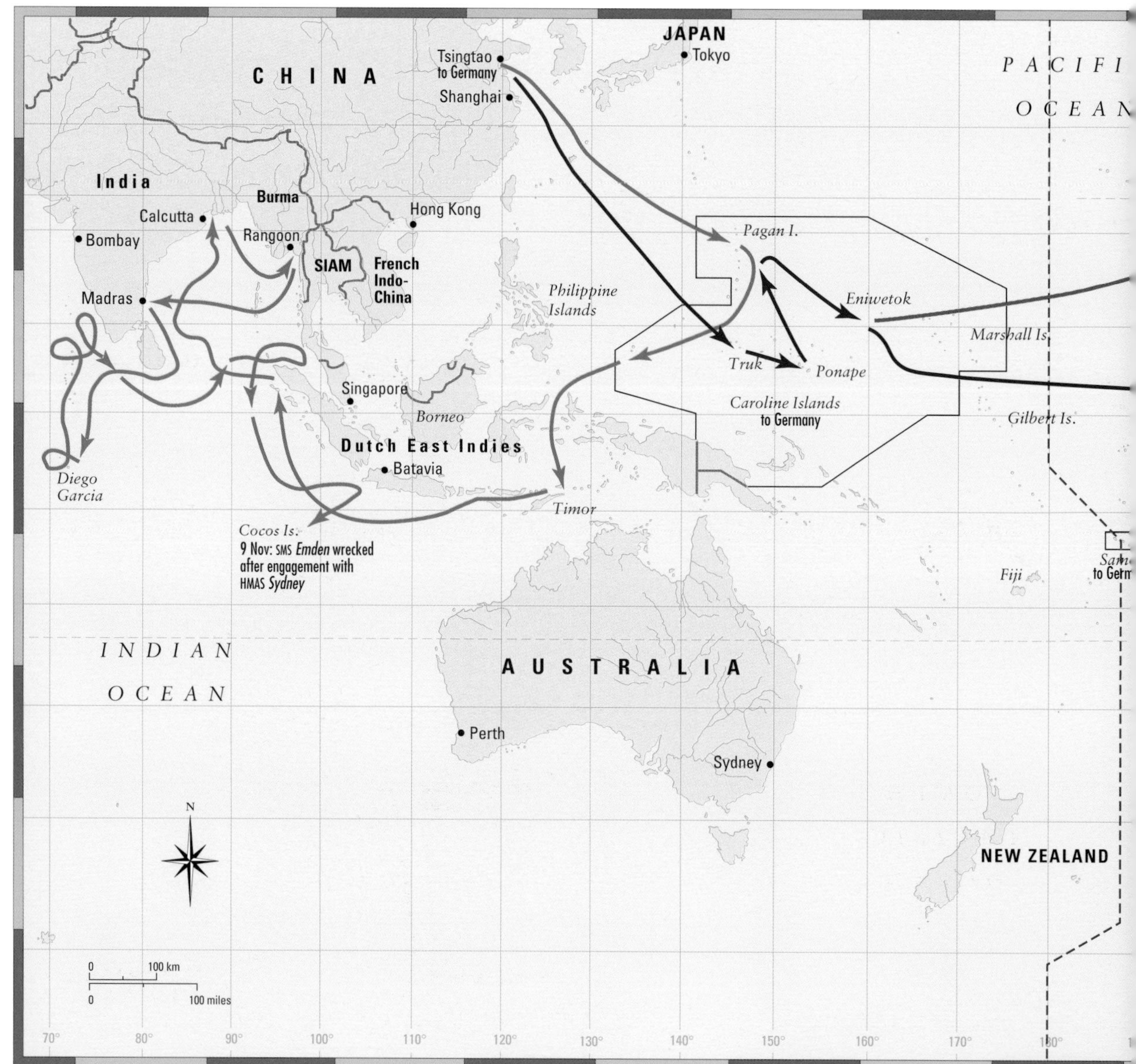

Unlike the French and Americans, the Germans had not been sidetracked into building large cruisers as commerce destroyers. Nevertheless, by 1914 they did have twenty-five modern light cruisers, with ten more under construction. Soundly designed, most were at home, attached to the High Seas Fleet. Some, however, were on foreign deployment with orders to operate against trade in the event of war.

In common with the British Admiralty, the Germans offered a modest subsidy to owners willing to incorporate good quality tonnage features, such as local strengthening, which would facilitate their conversion to auxiliary cruisers. In August 1914, when German shipping disappeared from the oceans, the British needed to take account of an estimated forty-two such ships, lying in ports both at home and abroad. From the outset the Royal Navy's cruisers were thus charged

CRUISE OF THE EAST ASIATIC SQUADRON

*Except for detaching the* Emden, *to work in the Bay of Bengal, von Spee ignored his orders to pursue cruiser warfare. After his long trek across the Pacific he defeated Cradock's scratch squadron at Coronel before doubling the Horn and being ambushed by Sturdee's battlecruisers off the Falklands.*

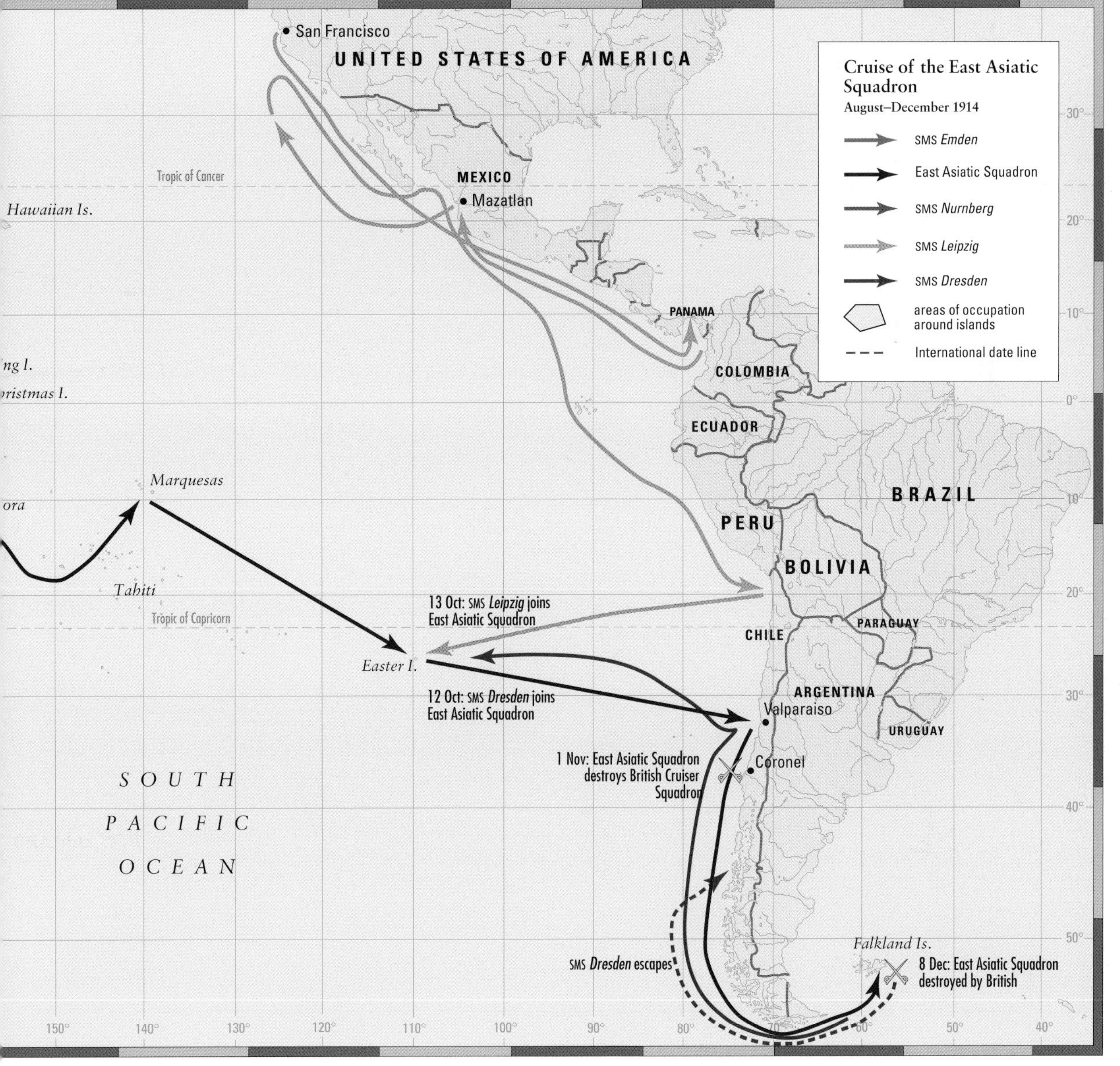

with safeguarding the trade routes against both regular and auxiliary raiders.

Germany's Chinese enclave was Tsingtao, where Vice Admiral Graf von Spee's East Asiatic Squadron was based. Its major units, all modern, were the armoured cruisers *Scharnhorst* and *Gneisenau,* and the light cruisers *Emden, Leipzig* and *Nürnberg*. Tsingtao's base facilities were minimal and should Japan, allied to Britain, declare war, the port would be indefensible. Von Spee's war orders were to operate against commerce in the Far East but, lacking proper maintenance, he knew that his ships would be rapidly wasting assets. Highly trained and efficient, their proper place was with the High Seas Fleet in the North Sea. Having detached the *Emden* to act as a raider in the Indian Ocean, he thus effectively ignored his instructions by heading eastward across the Pacific, concentrating and adding the light cruiser *Dresden* as he went. Except for appropriating a handful of ships for their coal cargoes, von Spee's subsequent brief

career had nothing to do with raider warfare, his victory over a scratch British squadron at Coronel on 1 November 1914 being followed by virtual annihilation at the Falklands on 8 December.

The lone *Emden*, however, had been most successful. Appearing suddenly off the Coromandel coast early in September 1914, she quickly took eight prizes. Two she retained for their coal; a third she released with captured crews, who arrived safely in port full of praise for the courteous manner of the *Emden's* captain, von Müller.

Hunted by British, French, Japanese and Russian warships, von Müller visited the Burmese coast, found nothing and crossed back to India. After a cheeky bombardment of oil tanks at Madras, he doubled Dondra Head and spent a month working the Indian end of the

*SMS* Scharnhorst, *Graf von Spee's flagship, pictured in East Asiatic colours during 1914. Completed seven years after the* Fürst Bismarck *(see pages 34–5) her 'family likeness' is very obvious. Note how the large patch of 150mm armour amidships cannot be pierced for scuttles.*

steamer route to Aden. Between 25 September and 19 October the *Emden* captured thirteen ships before again disappearing. Arriving with the dawn she then caught the small Russian cruiser *Zhemchug* at anchor off Penang. The Russian ship and a French destroyer were both destroyed.

Von Müller had by now caused severe disruption to trade and the vital troop convoys were heavily escorted. When, on 9 November 1914, the *Emden* landed a party in the remote Cocos Islands to destroy the important communications station, the latter's transmitted alarm was immediately answered. The Australian light cruiser *Sydney* was detached from the escort of a nearby convoy and surprised the *Emden* which, outgunned, ended her career as a gutted wreck run on to the offshore reef.

A second German cruiser, the *Königsberg*, was also loose in the Indian Ocean but her captain, Looff, was fortunately not of the calibre of von Müller. Having quickly taken a British cargo liner south of Aden, he went to ground for some weeks, not appearing again until the morning of 20 September 1914 when, off Zanzibar town, he caught the small British cruiser *Pegasus* under repair with her machinery opened up. She was quickly overwhelmed but, as if fearful of repercussions, Looff made for the ill-charted delta of the Rufiji river in what was then German East Africa. British cruisers located the *Königsberg* through papers found on an intercepted supply ship. Too deep of draught to sail up the river, the

*A contemporary popular postcard of the* Emden *as raider. The victim depicted is somewhat fanciful as all of von Müller's twenty-three captures were cargo vessels. No lives were lost through any of the sinkings and von Müller acquired a grudging respect from the British.*

British blockaded the fugitive for nine long months while an expedition was assembled and then sent out. Arriving in July 1915 this included two shallow-draught river monitors with high-trajectory howitzers. Although performing poorly in the heat, aircraft were used to locate the quarry, which was surrounded by jungle, and then to correct the monitors' fall of shot. Pounded to a wreck, the *Königsberg* was blown up and abandoned by her crew.

In August 1914 the *Karlsruhe* was in the West Indies. Quickly arming the liner *Kronprinz Wilhelm* for independent raiding, she eluded searching cruisers and disappeared. Her operating area soon turned out to be the busy shipping lanes off Brazil, where she secured sixteen prizes. Retaining some for their coal, the *Karlsruhe*'s captain, Köhler, steamed them in a line of search to facilitate sighting further victims. One he dispatched to the Canaries with numerous captured crews and, reasoning that their arrival would compromise his activities, Köhler headed northward. On 4 November 1914, when some 300 miles off Barbados, the cruiser's forward end was demolished by a sudden and unexplained explosion. The survivors, who did not include the captain, were rescued by a store ship and eventually reached Germany safely.

Including von Spee's squadron, the Imperial German Navy thus expended two armoured cruisers and six light cruisers in 'cruiser warfare'. On 1 July 1914 British shipping comprised 8,587 steamers and 653 sailing vessels, grossing some 19.25 million tons, or nearly 40 per cent of the world's merchant fleet. In support were over one hundred shipbuilding yards. Bearing in mind the relative sizes of the British fleet and the German Navy, the latter's sacrifice of a significant force of modern ships and trained crews in exchange for a few score merchantmen appears uneconomic. With certain exceptions, the auxiliary cruisers would fare little better.

*Wrecked by the* Sydney*'s heavier fire, with two-thirds of her crew dead or wounded, the* Emden *ended her career on the reef off North Keeling Island. It had been the first major action fought by an Australian warship.*

First, and least likely, was the 1897-built Norddeutscher Lloyd (NDL) ex-Blue Riband holder *Kaiser Wilhelm der Grosse*. Built for prestige rather than economy, she had an impressively conspicuous profile with four funnels spaced in distinct pairs. Quietly taking aboard six 10.5cm (4.1-1inch) guns and a naval crew, she sailed on the first day of the war and, with the British Northern Patrol not yet established, broke out into the Atlantic via the Denmark Strait.

Farcically, the first victim of this 14,350-ton raider was a 235-ton fishing trawler which, with no radio, neither knew of the outbreak of war nor was able to transmit a raider warning. Moving to the shipping focal point south of the Canaries, the *Kaiser Wilhelm* then seized four British ships on 15–16 August 1914.

*While sinkings of passenger liners tended to occupy the headlines and the attention of politicians, success or defeat for Great Britain hinged on the operation and survival of humble cargo carriers. This vessel, halted by shellfire to the bridge structure, is being despatched with a torpedo.*

Scrupulously observing International Law, her captain, Rymann, allowed the two that carried passengers to proceed; the others were sunk. They were to be the raider's last successes. Scouring the area, British cruisers picked up two of her colliers. Information from these and diplomatic sources pointed to the *Kaiser Wilhelm*, short of coal, having gone to ground on the West African coast. She was found on 26 August by the cruiser *Highflyer* and, in disregard for Spanish neutrality, was sunk where she lay.

Slipping out of Montevideo in August 1914, the new Hamburg-Sud liner *Cap Trafalgar* made for a prearranged rendezvous at the isolated Brazilian island of Trinidade. Coaling there, she also took the armament and captain of the old gunboat *Eber*. Radio traffic from searching Allied cruisers greatly affected her activities and she spent her time in evasion rather than in actively taking prizes. Returning to Trinidade empty-handed, she was surprised by the arrival of the British armed merchant cruiser (AMC) *Carmania*. To conceal her identity *Cap Trafalgar* had removed one of her funnels and painted the other two in Cunard colours. The *Carmania*, a genuine Cunarder, allowed her to close before opening fire. She destroyed the *Cap Trafalgar* but only at the cost of severe damage to herself.

At Tsingtao the NDL liner *Prinz Eitel Friedrich* was similarly armed from the

gunboats *Luchs* and *Tiger*. Spending three weeks crossing the Pacific, she took three ships before rounding the Horn early in January 1915. Her captain, Thierichsens, evaded interception by, unusually, following the sailing-ship track up the Atlantic. Only four of his eleven prizes were thus steamers and, with a mounting defect list and short of coal, he was obliged to make for Newport News where, on 11 March 1915, the ship was interned.

*Safely returned to Kiel in March 1917 following a successful four-month cruise, Korvettenkapitän Graf zu Dohna-Schlodien and the crew of the auxiliary cruiser* Möwe *pose with their numerous rescued mascots. The raider sank twenty-two independently routed steamers, all of which would have survived if convoyed.*

Originally armed by the *Karlsruhe*, the *Kronprinz Wilhelm* was more successful. She operated in the central Atlantic narrows and found adequate coal and provisions in her prizes. Of these she took fifteen before she, too, needed to seek internment. By this time, having steamed for eight months, the ship was in poor material condition and the crew sick from lack of fresh food.

Learning from experience, the Germans began to employ smaller ships with heavier armament. Thus the *Möwe*, which sailed at the end of 1915, had a concealed battery of four 15cm (5.9-inch) guns and two torpedo tubes. Some of her old reefer spaces were utilized as stowage for several hundred mines. Disguised under Swedish colours, she laid minefields in the Pentland Firth and off the Charente, the former claiming the British pre-dreadnought *King Edward VII*. Taking several ships around the Canaries, the *Möwe* then moved on to Brazilian waters. As usual, these proved productive, but the raider was damaged by the defensive fire of one of her victims. Abandoning her cruise she returned safely to Kiel following a four-month absence.

Early in 1916 the Germans sailed the *Wolf* but her foray had to be abandoned after her grounding. She was followed on 27 February by the heavily armed *Greif*. Disguised as a Norwegian, she was intercepted by the AMCs *Alcantara* and *Andes* of the Northern Patrol. As the former closed to send over a boarding party, the *Greif* let fly with guns and torpedoes. Fatally damaged, the British ship herself opened fire, engaging the raider until the *Andes* moved in to assist. The issue was settled by the arrival of the light cruiser *Comus*.

The *Möwe* sailed again in November 1916, shortly before a second raider named *Wolf*. The latter carried no less than seven 15cm guns, four torpedo tubes and, an innovation, a small reconnaissance seaplane. Under another resourceful commander, Nerger, she first laid clutches of mines off South Africa, Colombo and Bombay. Her first capture was in February 1917, employing it as an auxiliary to lay further mines near Aden. Taking the odd ship here, laying a few mines there, the *Wolf* crossed the Indian Ocean, worked her way around Australia and New Zealand, then moved on to the East Indies. Over fifty Allied warships wasted time in vain searches but, supplied from his prizes, the wily Nerger remained successfully at sea for fifteen months, arriving home in February 1918. His fourteen captures were matched by thirteen more sunk on his mines.

In May 1917 the British finally adopted a convoy system, which removed most of the 'independents' upon which the raiders preyed. As the following summary shows, the results achieved by the enemy's surface raiders were small compared with submarine sinkings. Their activities, however, were successful in the extensive disruption that they caused.

**Mercantile losses due to successful German surface raiders**

| Raider | Period of cruise | Ships sunk | Gross tonnage | Fate of raider |
|---|---|---|---|---|
| *Emden* | 13.08.14–09.11.14 | 23 | 101,810 | Sunk |
| *Kaiser Wilhelm der Grosse* | 04.08.14–26.08.14 | 2 | 10,683 | Sunk |
| *Prinz Eitel Friedrich* | 06.08.14–11.05.15 | 11 | 33,423 | Interned in USA |
| *Kronprinz Wilhelm* | 06.08.14–11.04.15 | 15 | 60,522 | Interned in USA |
| *Leipzig* | 04.08.14–08.12.14 | 4 | 15,299 | Sunk |
| *Karlsruhe* | 04.08.14–04.11.14 | 16 | 72,805 | Blown up |
| *Dresden* | 04.08.14–08.12.14 | 4 | 12,927 | Sunk |
| *Königsberg* | 04.08.14–11.07.15 | 1 | 6,601 | Sunk |
| *Möwe* (1st cruise) | 29.12.15–04.05.16 | 14 | 49,739 | Returned safely |
| *Möwe* (2nd cruise) | 23.11.16–22.05.17 | 25 | 123,265 | Returned safely |
| *Wolf* | 30.11.16–17.02.18 | 27 | 114,279 | Returned safely |
| **Total** | | **142** | **601,353** | |

Total shipping destroyed during First World War 12,850,814 grt.

Percentage loss due to surface raiders: 4.7 per cent. Percentage loss due to submarines: 86.8 per cent.

## The Grand Fleet versus the High Seas Fleet

As the pre-war British army was so much smaller than that of Germany, a superior Royal Navy posed no invasion threat. The reverse, however, was not true. British naval manoeuvres of 1913 confirmed the worst fears of the Committee for Imperial Defence (CID) when an 'enemy' fleet wrong-footed the defending naval force to successfully land an 'enemy' army. The 'enemy' commander, Vice Admiral Sir John Jellicoe, was promptly selected to head the navy's main battle force, to be known as the Grand Fleet. He hoisted his flag on 3 August 1914 .

As the Grand Fleet initially included 21 dreadnoughts, 8 pre-dreadnoughts and 4 battlecruisers against the German High Seas Fleet's 13 dreadnoughts, 16 pre-dreadnoughts and 5 battlecruisers, public and service opinion in both camps expected an immediate British quest for a decisive showdown.

Aged Admiralty diehards such as Admiral of the Fleet Sir Arthur Wilson favoured the strangulation of German trade through close blockade of its ports. Churchill and others preferred capture of a German offshore island for much the same purpose. Wise counsels pointed out that either course would whittle away British strength by mine and submarine while the Germans, safe in their bases, bided their time. The fact was that Jellicoe never needed to fight a decisive battle. A victory would certainly have been popular but would hardly have affected the outcome of the war. A British defeat, however, would have resulted either in invasion or such a threat of it that an unfavourable peace would have had to be concluded.

Jellicoe's ally was geography, for the North Sea that formed the British backyard was effectively a German prison. Exits were only by the heavily

*HM Dockyard, Rosyth in September 1916. The right hand ship in No. 1 Dock is the battleship* Warspite, *interesting in that her repair was officially completed on 20 July following heavy damage received at Jutland. HMSs* Canada *(left) and* Collingwood *(centre) were little engaged, firing only 42 and 84 main battery rounds to* Warspite*'s 259.*

Shetland Islands
Orkney Islands
Scapa Flow
Northern blockade
NORWAY
17 Oct. 1917
Cromarty Firth
North Sea
Skagerrak
Jutland 31 May – 1 June 1916
DENMARK
Rosyth
Firth of Forth
100 nautical miles
200 nautical miles
100 nautical miles
Hornsriff
Dogger Bank
16 Dec. 1914
Hartlepool
Whitby
Scarborough
German Bight
Dogger Bank 24 Jan. 1915
17 Nov. 1917
Heligoland Bight 28 Aug. 1914
Heligoland
Kiel Canal
Cuxhaven 25 Dec. 1914
Wilhelmshaven
3 Nov. 1914
24 April 1916
Gt. Yarmouth
Lowestoft
22 Sept. 1914: Aboukir, Cressy and Hogue sunk
GREAT BRITAIN
Amsterdam
NETHERLANDS
GERMANY
Rotterdam
London
patrolled mine barrier
Dover
Portsmouth
Folkestone
Calais
Ostende
Boulogne
BELGIUM
1 Jan 1915: Formidable sunk
English Channel
Cherbourg
Le Havre
LUX.
Trenches 1914–18
FRANCE
The North Sea 1914–18
major battle areas
other naval battles with date
coastal town bombardments
sinking with name and date
British mine barrier
British naval blockade
approximate extent of regular British patrols
approximate extent of regular German patrols
major British suppy route
0 100 km
0 100 miles
N

defended English Channel or by the northern gap, flanked by the Grand Fleet's base at Scapa. Here, Jellicoe was yet beyond the effective range of German submarine but could support the distant blockading forces while being able to block any enemy attempt to break out.

Although Tirpitz urged an offensive strategy, emphasizing the fleet's material superiority, the Kaiser cautioned its commander-in-chief, Admiral von Ingenohl, against risking it, seeing it as an important bargaining chip in the eventual conclusion of a satisfactory peace.

In July 1914, even before his appointment, Jellicoe had concluded in a lengthy memorandum to the First Lord that 'it is highly dangerous to consider that our ships are superior or even equal [to those of the enemy]'. Had he known that British projectiles would be liable to break up harmlessly on striking German armour, he would have been even more circumspect.

On 28 August 1914 Commodore Tyrwhitt's Harwich Force forayed against German light forces active in the Heligoland Bight. In uncertain visibility and in the face of rapid German reinforcement, the British were soon hard-pressed and Tyrwhitt called for assistance from the two battle-cruisers that comprised his deep cover. Jellicoe had not been able to inform him that he had reinforced them with three more battlecruisers under Vice Admiral Sir David Beatty. The impetuous Beatty did not hesitate to sweep in with all five capital ships. He sank three enemy cruisers but risked his big ships to mines and to uninformed friendly submarines. While the victory was due to overwhelming force rather

ABOVE: *Admiral of the Fleet Sir Reginald Yorke Tyrwhitt. He served throughout the First World War as commodore in command of the Harwich Force. A natural leader, his squadron was always in the thick of things although conflicting orders saw it uninvolved at Jutland.*

LEFT: *Admiral of the Fleet Sir John Rushworth Jellicoe. Intellectually gifted and well-respected, he commanded the Grand Fleet from the outset of the war until December 1916. He fought Jutland as he had predicted but his reputation was damaged by the intense national disappointment over the action and his subsequent pessimism over the U-boat war.*

THE NORTH SEA 1914–18

*Often termed the German Ocean by the Victorians, the North Sea became for the High Seas Fleet a German prison. The importance of the Shetlands–Norway gap is apparent as is the location of Scapa Flow at its western end.*

HELIGOLAND BIGHT
28 AUGUST 1914

*The battle of the Heligoland Bight had degenerated into a confused mêlée in which British light forces were being worsted, when Beatty took a bold gamble by intervening with battlecruisers in heavily mined waters. The resulting rout was greatly damaging to German morale.*

than good planning, it boosted British morale and caused the Kaiser to think even more defensively.

Unsuspected by the Germans, the British had obtained several of their naval codebooks. Used in conjunction with a chain of radio intercept and direction-finding stations, these proved a valuable indicator of German activity and intentions. The hub of this service was the Admiralty's later-famous 'Room 40', loosely controlled by Captain William R. ('Blinker') Hall, the Director of Naval Intelligence.

To popular disappointment, the Grand Fleet did not seek a second Trafalgar but adopted a policy of containment. The Germans responded by endeavouring to erode its superiority. By using Vice Admiral Franz von Hipper's battlecruisers to bombard English east coast towns it was hoped that Royal Navy squadrons would be goaded into pursuit, to be led into minefields or submarine traps, or into ambush by superior German forces.

Still lacking experience, Room 40 failed to warn of Hipper's first such foray when, on 3 November 1914, he shelled Great Yarmouth for twenty minutes while a cruiser mined the coastal shipping lane. In accordance with his Kaiser's

**Heligoland Bight**
28 August 1914

German ships
sunken German ships
British ships

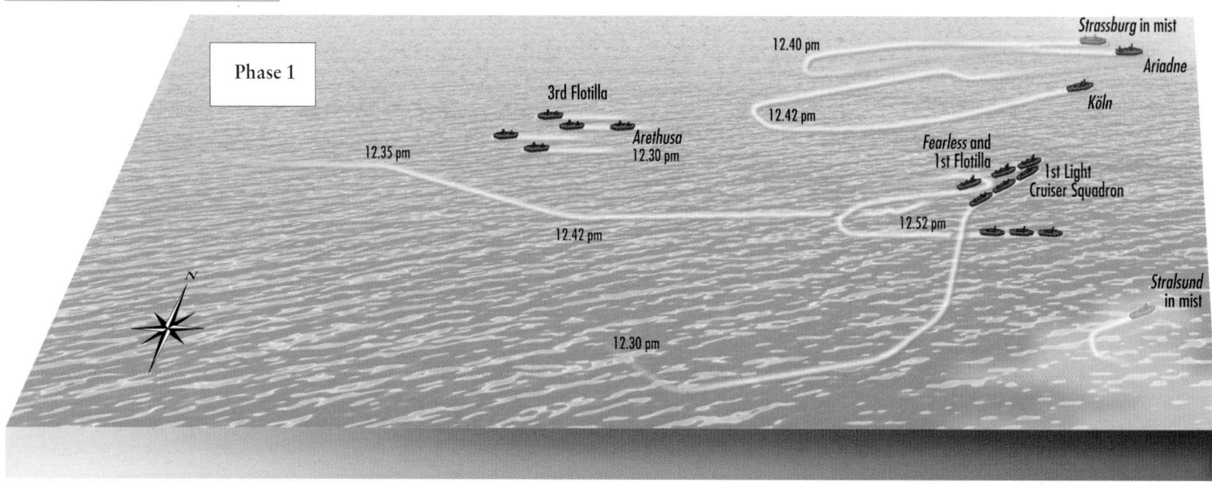


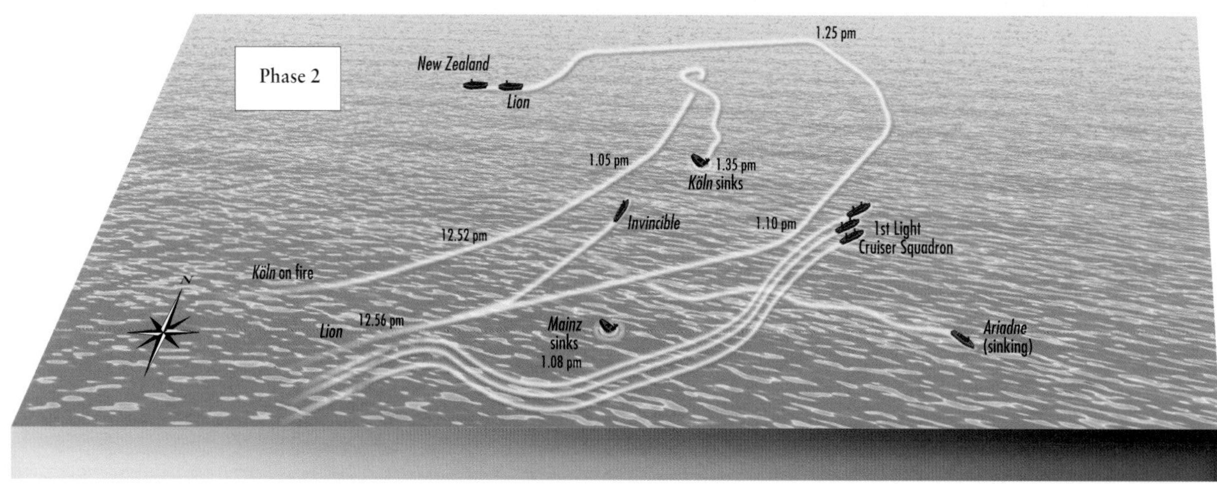

instructions, von Ingenohl brought his two supporting battle squadrons no further than the Bight.

Admiral Fisher, the First Sea Lord, predicted further such provocations and was proved correct when Room 40 discovered one due for 16 December. As Hipper's force alone was specifically identified, only Beatty's battlecruisers and one battle squadron were directed to intercept, with the Harwich Force also at sea. Von Ingenohl, too, was out in support with the battle fleet and his scouting forces clashed with those of the British in the pre-dawn darkness. Fearing that he was risking an action with the whole Grand Fleet, he broke away. Beatty, unwittingly let off the hook, and still assuming the enemy to be Hipper alone, actually pursued this enormous quarry until, at 8.54 a.m., he received word that Scarborough was being bombarded. Within half an hour, unaware of Beatty's approach or von Ingenohl's retreat, Hipper withdrew. He was contacted by British light cruisers but these lost the scent due to an ambiguous signal from Beatty.

Although the raids held no military significance, the Admiralty was stung by vehement press opinion and its own inability to guarantee intervention.

*Returning from a sweep with the Harwich Force on 11 February 1916 the light cruiser* Arethusa, *in which Tyrwhitt wore his broad pennant, struck a mine outside the port. Six men were killed and the ship, steaming at 20 knots, broke in two.*

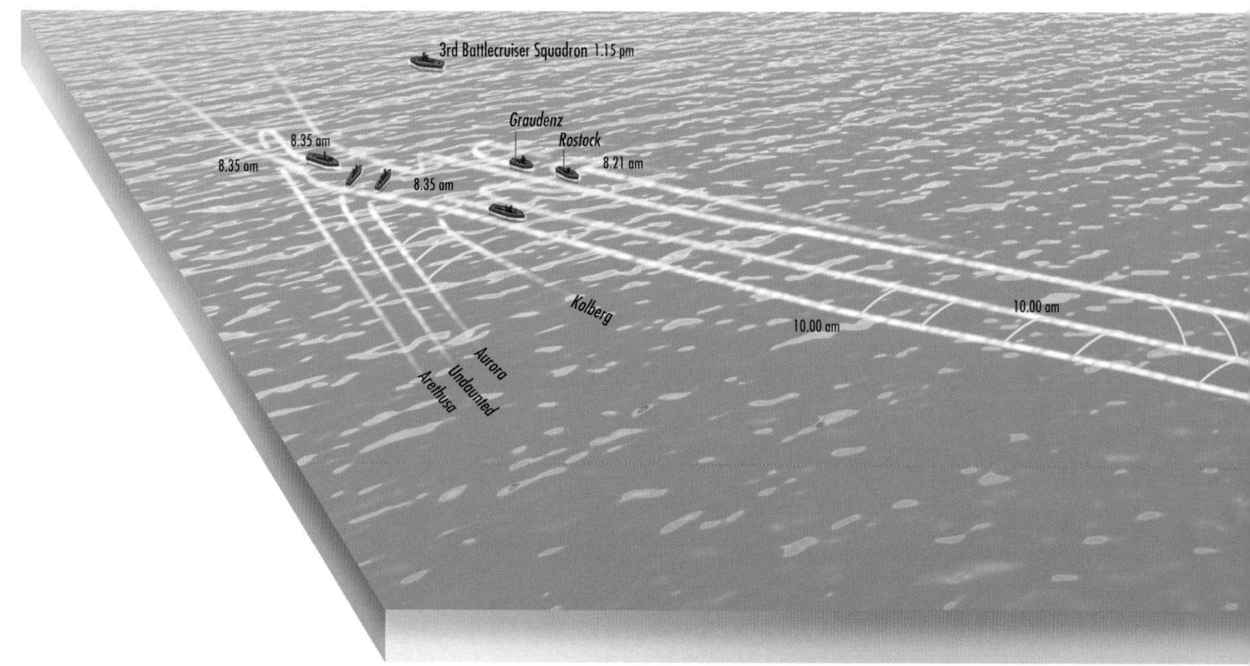
3rd Battlecruiser Squadron 1.15 pm
Graudenz
Rostock
8.35 am
8.35 am
8.21 am
8.35 am
Kolberg
10.00 am
10.00 am
Aurora
Undaunted
Arethusa

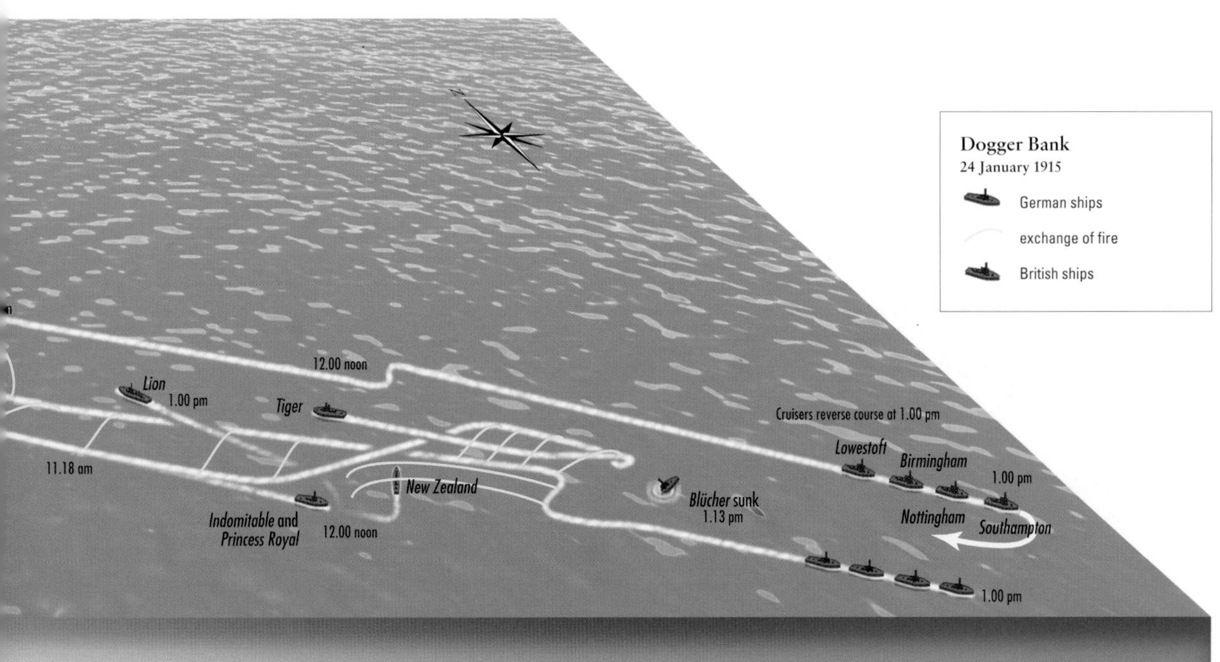


DOGGER BANK
24 JANUARY 1915

*At the battle of the Dogger Bank, Hipper's battlecruisers escaped because a misread signal from Beatty's stricken flagship caused the remainder of his force to abandon pursuit in order to finish off the already mortally injured* Blücher.

Heartened, the Germans planned a sweep against British light forces in the area of the Dogger Bank. Following a timely alert by Room 40, Beatty rendezvoused with Tyrwhitt on the superbly clear morning of 24 January 1915. Hipper was sighted almost immediately and, although outnumbered by five battlecruisers to four, was slow in attempting to escape. With the squadrons in two battle lines, Beatty's slowly overhauled Hipper's, firing commencing at extreme range. Inevitably the German tail-ender, *Blücher* and the British leader, *Lion*, took the heaviest punishment. The latter, losing all power, fell out of line. Beatty was able to make only flag signals and these were badly misread. With an amazing lack of initiative, the remaining four British ships fell on the hapless *Blücher*, allowing Hipper's remaining force to escape.

Hailed by the popular press as a victory, the battle of the Dogger Bank was a fiasco. British gunnery was outclassed, signal procedures deficient. Beatty's second-in-command was relieved. One hit on the German *Seydlitz* had burned out two turrets when fragments set off waiting charges. Only prompt magazine flooding saved the ship. The Germans learned a valuable lesson and fitted flash-proof doors to all capital ships, a measure not taken by the British. Depressed by the loss of the *Blücher*, however, the Kaiser replaced the unfortunate von Ingenohl with the more aggressive Admiral Hugo von Pohl. Yet, as the strictures remained, little changed. A gloomy Tirpitz began to support an alternative policy of unrestricted submarine warfare; and the expensive Zeppelin force, feared by the Royal Navy for its scouting potential, was largely wasted in bombing raids.

The colossal egos of Churchill, as First Lord, and Fisher made for an uneasy relationship. In May 1915 the former's incessant demands brought about Fisher's resignation. A stagnant war situation also saw the formation of a coalition

*Vice Admiral Franz Ritter von Hipper and his staff at the time of Jutland. Hipper commanded the High Seas Fleet's Scouting Forces, which included the battlecruiser squadron. Second from left appears Korvettenkapitän Erich Raeder, Hipper's Chief of Staff and destined in 1928 to head the German Navy.*

*Admiral Reinhard Scheer assumed command of the German High Seas Fleet only in January 1916 and because of the mortal illness of his predecessor von Pohl. His more aggressive policy led directly to the battle of Jutland and near catastrophe due to Jellicoe's superior fleet handling. He was succeeded by Hipper in 1918.*

government. Churchill had made too many enemies and was sidelined. The 'fiery energy' that had driven the Admiralty was replaced by a 'sound, but lethargic, administration' headed by Arthur Balfour and Admiral of the Fleet Sir Henry Jackson. At the point of Churchill's departure the Grand Fleet's numerical advantage was 25 dreadnoughts to 17, and 9 battlecruisers to 5. The lead was increasing, with 7 more dreadnoughts due to complete by the end of 1915.

Following the Dogger Bank action little happened at sea. Jellicoe chafed at the Admiralty's direction but, having failed to sting the Germans into action, he agreed with Beatty in April 1916 that the High Seas Fleet would fight only on its own terms.

During 1915 the German fleet had made five half-hearted forays and, in January 1916, the mortally sick von Pohl was replaced by Admiral Reinhard Scheer who, on 25 April, waited near Terschelling with the High Seas Fleet as Hipper shelled Lowestoft and Yarmouth. Although the Harwich Force made contact, heavy seas prevented Beatty or Jellicoe from intervention. This led directly to the Admiralty accelerating the Grand Fleet's southward move to the Firth of Forth.

At the end of May 1916 Scheer abandoned a planned bombardment of Sunderland, instead sweeping up the west coast of Jutland. The British, alerted by Room 40, were already at sea. On 31 May, as the fleets converged, each was following about 50 miles astern of its scouting battlecruisers. At about 2 p.m. these clashed, with Hipper reversing course to lure Beatty's force on to Scheer. A fierce running battle developed, with the British six-to-five advantage offset by poor fire distribution and ship design. Two battlecruisers blew up from magazine explosions.

Beatty's light cruisers sighted Scheer's main body at about 4.45 p.m. and it was the British turn to go about to entice the unsuspecting Germans on to the Grand Fleet. Knowing of the pressure on Beatty, Jellicoe had detached Hood's three battlecruisers to assist. Their intervention forced Hipper back so that he failed to sight and report Jellicoe's presence. Poorly informed by Beatty, Jellicoe deployed the Grand Fleet from cruising formation to battle line at the very last minute. Confined between the closing battle fleets, the scouting forces were heavily engaged. Several ships, including a third British battlecruiser, were destroyed. By 6.30 p.m. Jellicoe was firing on a surprised Scheer who, in a poor position to respond, reversed course, covered by a destroyer torpedo attack. Jellicoe had long made it clear in writing that, fearing a trap, he would not pursue in these circumstances. He steered instead to interpose the fleet between Scheer and his bases.

*A contemporary impression of Jutland by German artist Claus Bergen, capturing the ferocity of the encounters. On the day, over eight thousand heavy-calibre rounds were fired. Gunnery efficiency was roughly equal but that of the British was offset by poor-quality projectiles.*

With the pressure thus relieved, however, Scheer again turned about at 6.55 p.m. Coming under murderous fire from the Grand Fleet, the German admiral threw Hipper's battered force at Jellicoe as the latter once more turned away. It was 7.20 p.m., the light was deteriorating and, in accordance with his

recorded intentions, Jellicoe again did not pursue. Through the night he maintained line, hoping to resume the battle at first light. In a series of violent encounters, however, Scheer broke through the British tail. This fact, together with other signals of critical value, were not communicated to Jellicoe who, at dawn on 1 June, looked upon an empty sea.

The battle of Jutland was over. On the day the Grand Fleet had a clear advantage of 28 dreadnoughts to 16, and 9 battlecruisers to 5 yet, as the table shows, the Germans scored a *matériel* victory:

| | Tonnage committed | Tonnage lost | Personnel involved | Fatal casualties |
|---|---|---|---|---|
| British | 1,250,000 | 155,000 | 60,000 | 6,094 |
| German | 660,000 | 61,000 | 45,000 | 2,551 |

Scheer's tactical handling should have been more heavily punished. Poorly supported with signalling and individual initiative, Jellicoe erred on the side of caution. British gunnery was the equal of German, but projectiles were inferior.

Both German admirals were lauded as victors of the Skagerrak but Jellicoe was judged, by a disappointed public and service alike, to have wasted an opportunity. Despite shortcomings, Beatty emerged as the hero, which affected the previously harmonious relationship with his superior. It must be repeated, however, that Jellicoe had fought as he had said he would. His losses were far more sustainable than those of the enemy, and the enemy remained fully contained. Nothing had changed.

Convinced that the Grand Fleet would always be too powerful to defeat, Scheer firmly advocated a shift to unrestricted submarine warfare. Contrary to popular mythology, Scheer made a further foray as early as 19 August 1916. Room 40 had the Grand Fleet to sea in good time but the enemy diverted fruitlessly after the Harwich Force and no action ensued.

More caution was now evident on both sides. The Grand Fleet began to divert many of its minor warships to act as escorts for the new convoy system. The German High Seas Fleet committed submarines, previously employed in patrol lines, to the new all-out offensive. In addition it lost destroyers to assist the Flanders flotilla.

The British coalition government resigned and David Lloyd George emerged as Prime Minister. He appointed Sir Edward Carson as the navy's political head in place of Balfour, and Jellicoe for Jackson, who was worn out and without ideas on how to counter the now-critical submarine menace. Beatty succeeded to command of the Grand Fleet but, despite his legendary reputation, recognized that Jellicoe's containment policy was correct.

*Admiral Sir David Beatty, who had succeeded Jellicoe as C-in-C, Grand Fleet, greets Rear Admiral Hugh Rodman, US Navy. In a politically important gesture, the latter had brought over an American battleship division in November 1917, serving in the Grand Fleet as the Sixth Battle Squadron.*

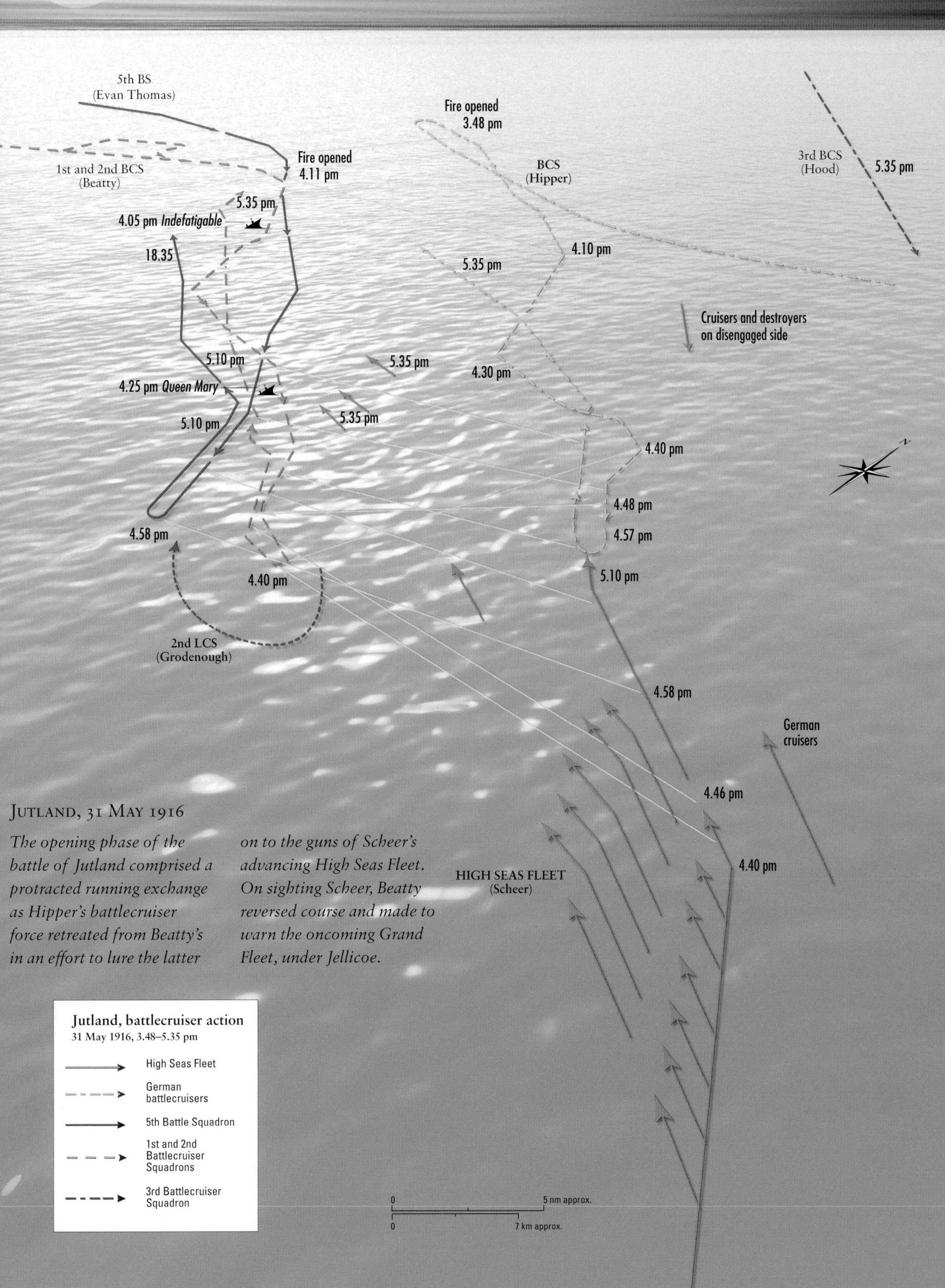


JUTLAND, 31 MAY 1916

*The opening phase of the battle of Jutland comprised a protracted running exchange as Hipper's battlecruiser force retreated from Beatty's in an effort to lure the latter on to the guns of Scheer's advancing High Seas Fleet. On sighting Scheer, Beatty reversed course and made to warn the oncoming Grand Fleet, under Jellicoe.*

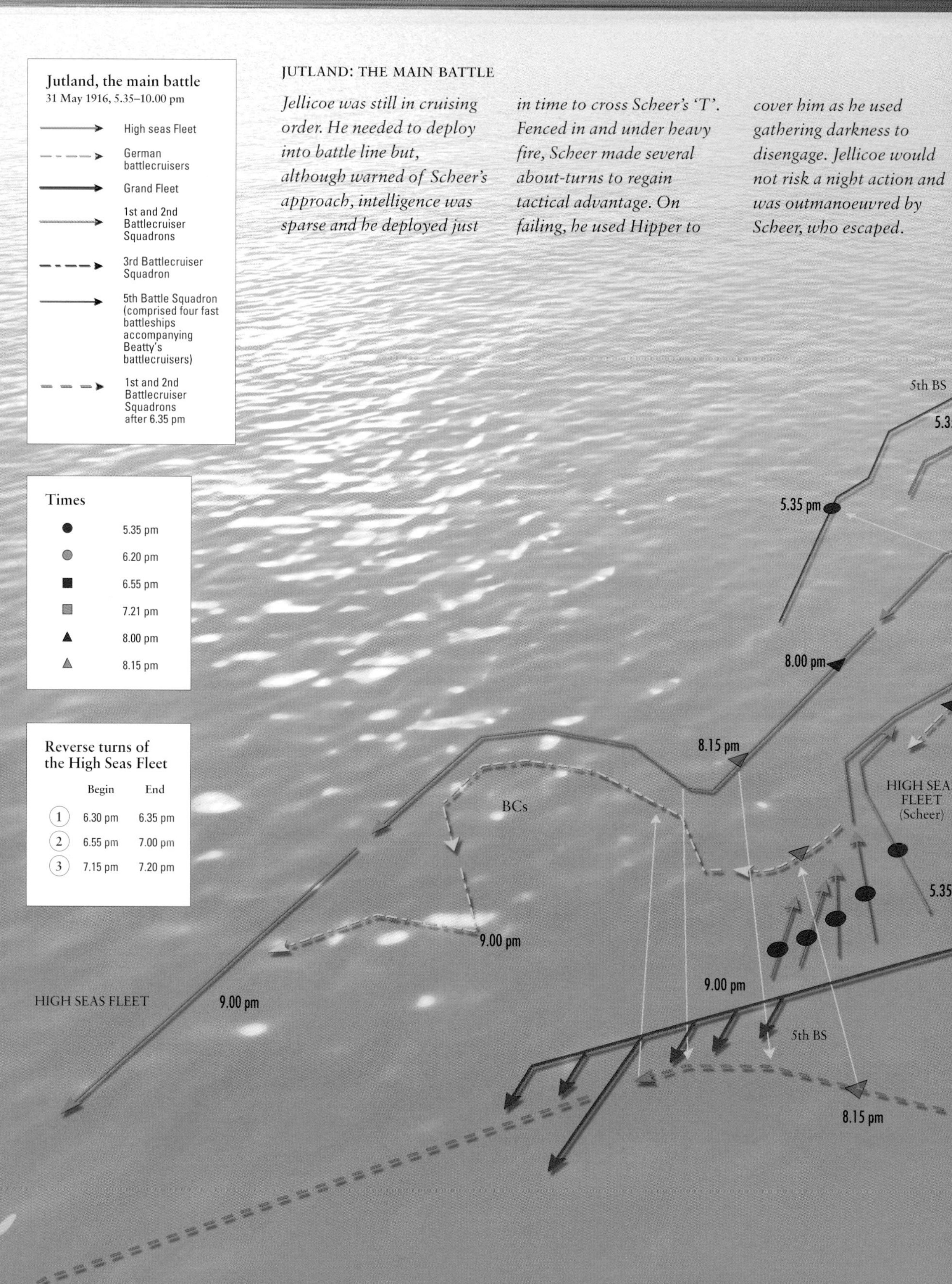


JUTLAND: THE MAIN BATTLE

*Jellicoe was still in cruising order. He needed to deploy into battle line but, although warned of Scheer's approach, intelligence was sparse and he deployed just in time to cross Scheer's 'T'. Fenced in and under heavy fire, Scheer made several about-turns to regain tactical advantage. On failing, he used Hipper to cover him as he used gathering darkness to disengage. Jellicoe would not risk a night action and was outmanoeuvred by Scheer, who escaped.*

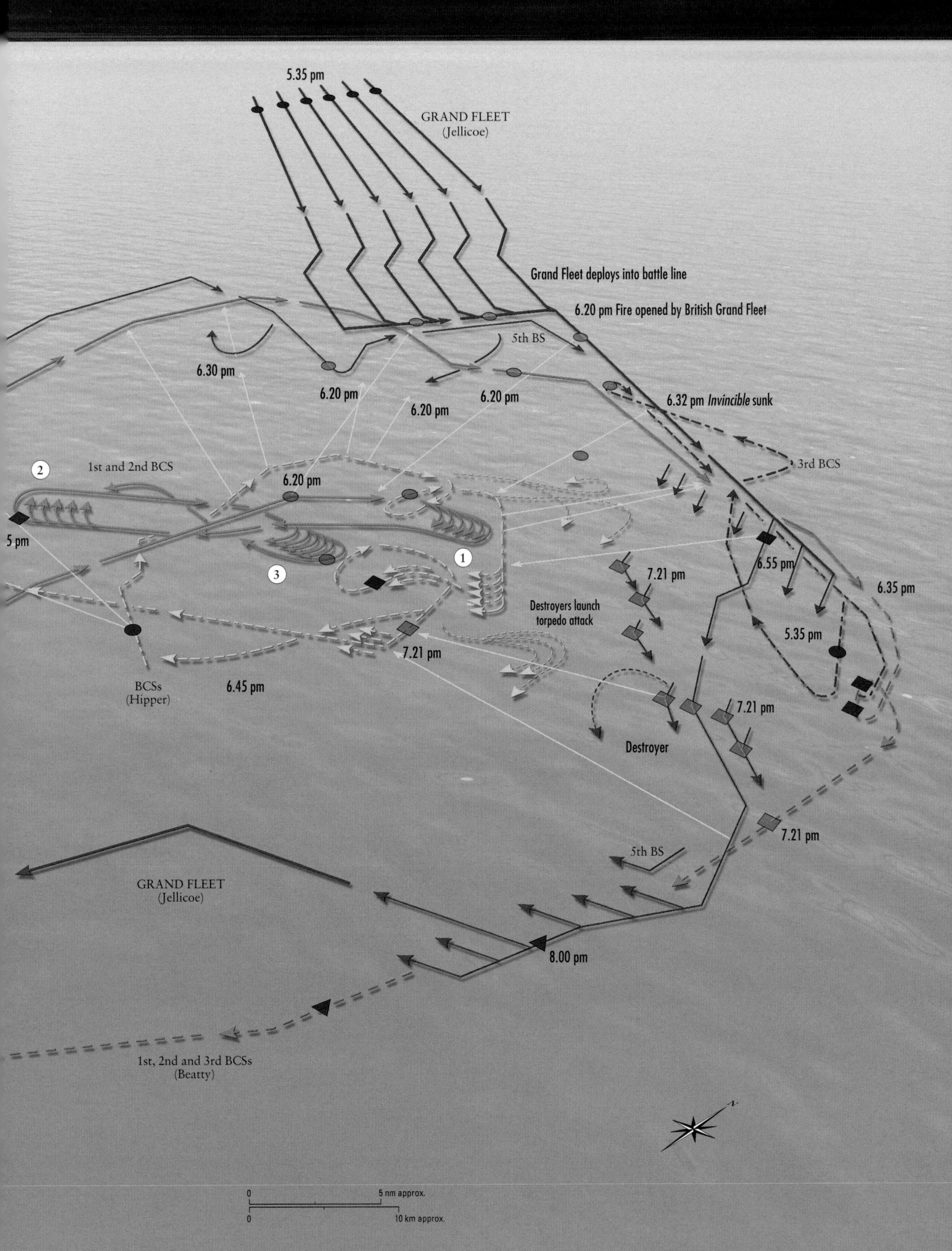
5.35 pm
GRAND FLEET
(Jellicoe)
Grand Fleet deploys into battle line
6.20 pm Fire opened by British Grand Fleet
5th BS
6.30 pm
6.20 pm
6.20 pm
6.20 pm
6.32 pm Invincible sunk
3rd BCS
2
1st and 2nd BCS
6.20 pm
5 pm
1
3
7.21 pm
6.55 pm
6.35 pm
Destroyers launch
torpedo attack
5.35 pm
7.21 pm
BCSs
(Hipper)
6.45 pm
7.21 pm
Destroyer
7.21 pm
5th BS
GRAND FLEET
(Jellicoe)
8.00 pm
1st, 2nd and 3rd BCSs
(Beatty)
0
5 nm approx.
0
10 km approx.

Again the North Sea fell quiet until, late in 1917, the Germans made a destructive raid on a Scandinavian convoy. A British riposte into the Bight was powerfully supported by six battlecruisers, now under the flag of Vice Admiral Sir William Pakenham. He operated so cautiously that all chance of an action was lost and dissatisfaction with the direction of the navy reached new heights. In December 1917 Jellicoe was summarily dismissed. In the same month, however, morale was boosted by the arrival of a squadron of American battleships to operate with the Grand Fleet.

Following the Russian revolution of October 1917 German ships were

*War-weariness and shortages at home, combined with insufficient sea-time and corrosive inactivity, defeated the High Seas Fleet from within. Hipper's appointment as C-in-C failed to halt the growing wave of disillusionment and sedition that was sweeping the service. Here, in Kiel, a week prior to the armistice, a throng of seamen listen to the government's representative, the SPD Defence Minister Gustav Noske.*

released from Baltic duties. They brought with them the contagion of revolt and the murmurings of rebellion, which, combined with war-weariness and evident disillusionment, produced growing disaffection in the fleet. Scheer dealt with it firmly, but the fleet was still under-employed. In August 1918 Hipper took over as its commander-in-chief.

October saw Germany begin peace negotiations with President Wilson. The naval leadership, none the less, saw capitulation without defeat as dishonourable. A planned final showdown, however, was scotched by the rank and file, who opted for open mutiny.

*One method of deploying high-performance fighters at sea was to fly them from specially designed lighters, towed by a destroyer at high speed. At upper left, their weight compensated by human ballast right forward, a party readies a Sopwith Camel which (right) lifts off with the lighter in a bows-up attitude. In just this manner Lieutenant S. D. Culley destroyed Zeppelin L53 on August 1918.*

## The U-boat war against commerce

Earlier wars had demonstrated the vulnerability of British commercial shipping to attack, and the resultant effects on the nation's economy and means to wage war. Where the Admiralty was still thinking largely in terms of countering surface raiders, however, the ex-First Sea Lord, Admiral Sir John Fisher, was fully alive to the potential of the submarine. In a pre-war memorandum to the Committee of Imperial Defence (CID) he foresaw a new and brutal campaign, reasoning that a submarine would not compromise invisibility, its major asset, by surfacing to attack merchantmen. Although international maritime law demanded that a merchant ship could be destroyed only if it were impossible to bring her into port, and then only after the crew had been granted every assistance, Fisher pointed out that submarines carried no spare hands to man prizes. Sinking was their sole option. The First Lord, Churchill, considered that such a course would never be considered by a civilized power. Naval opinion was that the proposition was 'impossible and unthinkable'.

Admiral von Tirpitz, the architect of the German High Seas Fleet, was single-minded in his determination to create a capital ship-based battle fleet for the

Kaiser. Once in favour of the theories of the so-called *Jeune École*, he was now actively opposed to any proposal, such as that of a *guerre de course*, which diverted resources from the true path.

Nevertheless, although the German Navy had managed to accumulate eighteen U-boats by 1910, it was only after this date that boats became truly effective with the introduction of a satisfactory diesel engine. Their major deficiency was the small capacity of eleven torpedoes (and these of only 50cm/19.7-inch diameter), making them reliant upon sinkings by gun. Together with deep-sea boats, there were built coastal (UB) and small minelaying (UC) boats.

Germany's claim to have had no pre-war plans to wage war on commerce was true in that the means simply did not exist. The early series of setbacks in the war at sea, however, enabled the arguments of such as Admiral von Pohl to carry more weight. By January 1915 U-boats had sunk several major British warships with impunity and Tirpitz, keen to divert attention from the battle fleet's lack of achievement, agreed to a submarine offensive against trade, to commence in February. The measure was justified on the legal grounds that British blockade

*Judged not worth a torpedo, a barque, hove-to for examination, is battered to destruction by a U-boat's deck gun. The strategy of wanton savagery was designed to dissuade neutral shipping from assisting in British trade.*

measures and the laying of announced minefields contravened international law. There were also grave misgivings regarding neutral, particularly American, opinion.

On 20 October 1914 the British steamer *Glitra* was the first to be sunk by a U-boat which, with no perceived threat, observed every protocol. Just six days later, however, Fisher was proved correct. The High Seas Fleet had missed a great opportunity to hit at the British Expeditionary Force during the vulnerable phase of its transport to France. The captain of the *U24* was thus very gratified to torpedo successfully what he identified as a troopship. The French ship *Amiral Ganteaume*, however, was carrying over two thousand Belgian refugees, of whom about thirty were killed. By later standards, it was a small outrage but, being a 'first', it caused considerable international disquiet.

*Although for most of the war U-boat construction outstripped U-boat losses, the margin was not overwhelming. In all, the Central Powers commissioned 419 U-boats and lost 186 of them in action. Of the remaining 233, only 196 were in a condition to be surrendered to the Allies at the armistice.*

On 4 February 1915 all waters around the British Isles were declared by Germany to be a War Zone. All ships encountered therein would be destroyed, including neutrals, whose flags were at times used by the British as a legitimate *ruse de guerre*. The safety of crew and passengers could not be guaranteed. As the safety of his boat was to be his first consideration, a U-boat commander could hardly surface to attack, making it a difficult undertaking to exclude American and Italian shipping.

Declared blockade must be enforceable to be legitimate, yet, of the 220 boats

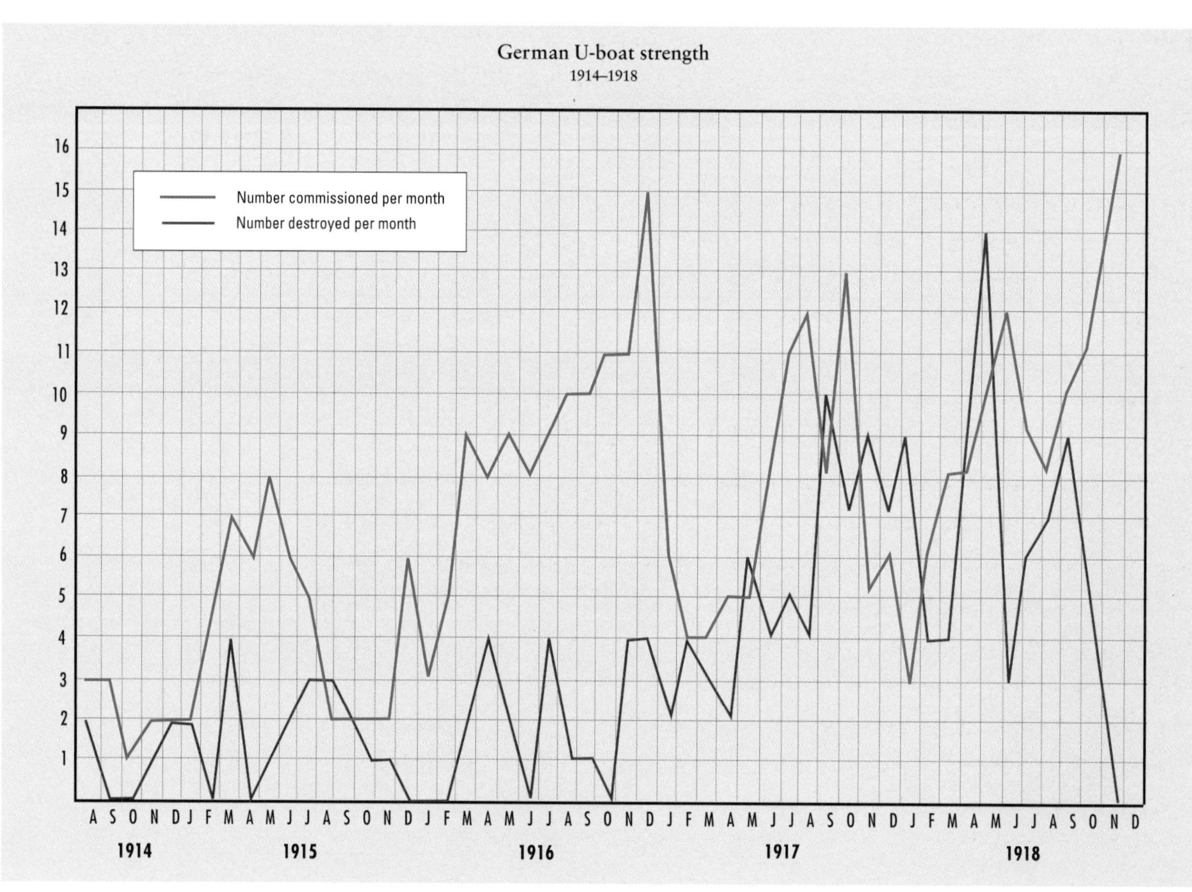

*U-boat construction required specialist techniques that limited it to comparatively few yards. Continuous ordering and strict standardization allowed for series production, with dedicated work teams moving from hull to hull. With all steel erection being done on site, however, construction was relatively slow.*

that studies indicated were needed, only twenty-nine of all types could be mustered. A lack of skilled labour precluded any rapid expansion, and numbers increased, mainly because inadequate Allied countermeasures resulted in few sinkings. Prior to the war, the British Admiralty had discounted the practicality of a submarine campaign and only in December 1914 was the nucleus of the Submarine Committee established to consider it. Work commenced on hydrophone detection early in 1915, but practical depth charges did not enter service until January 1916. Until then, destroyers relied mainly on towing explosive sweeps.

Germany's declaration of a war zone was meant to deter neutral ships, which comprised one in four movements in British ports. The United States, however, immediately warned of German accountability in the event of 'incidents'. This extracted an assurance from the German government that properly marked neutrals would be treated correctly. Because this would require submarines having to surface, it created problems for the navy, as British ships were now being defensively armed and ordered to attempt to ram any submarine seeking to attack. On the other hand, submarines carried few torpedoes and could expect to hit with less than 50 per cent of them. To accumulate a worthwhile score, therefore, a commander needed to rely on surfacing to effect destruction by gunfire or the placement of explosive charges.

As may be seen from the data chart on page 71, British shipping losses were variable but within bounds. In March 1915 the liner *Falaba* was torpedoed with the loss of over one hundred lives. Despite international denunciations of savagery not worthy of a civilized race, the German Navy persisted in declaring that it was the only effective weapon against the British.

Then, on 7 May, came the sinking of the 30,000-ton steamship, *Lusitania*. Of the 1,200 passengers who died, 128 were American. A predictable diplomatic storm swept aside German justifications and when, in August, the *Arabic* was destroyed with further high loss of life, the situation became untenable and restrictions were reimposed. In disgust, Tirpitz and the chief of the Admiralty staff tendered their resignations.

With most surface raiders neutralized, the muzzling of the U-boats caused great controversy between the naval high command and the political leadership. British shipping losses during 1915 had been more than replaced, whereas conducting operations according to the prize rules had become more hazardous for the U-boats by virtue of British decoy vessels, popularly known as 'Q-ships', that were armed with concealed guns to catch unwary submarines attacking on the surface.

Further outrages resulted in a ban on attacking all passenger liners, causing a looming revolt in the naval leadership. The new chief of Admiralty staff, Admiral Henning von Holtzendorff, was an old opponent of Tirpitz, who was still in office but with reduced powers. Both, however, agreed that a resumption of an all-out campaign was essential.

Many U-boats were switched to the Mediterranean, where targets abounded and American ships were rare. Losses to British shipping were compounded by

*A contemporary German postcard commemorating the sinking of the Cunarder* Lusitania *in May 1915. Despite protestations that the torpedoing was justified, it proved disastrous to the German government, being a major reason for the United States eventually declaring war. It is doubtful if Tirpitz would ever have approved, as here, of his name being associated with the act.*

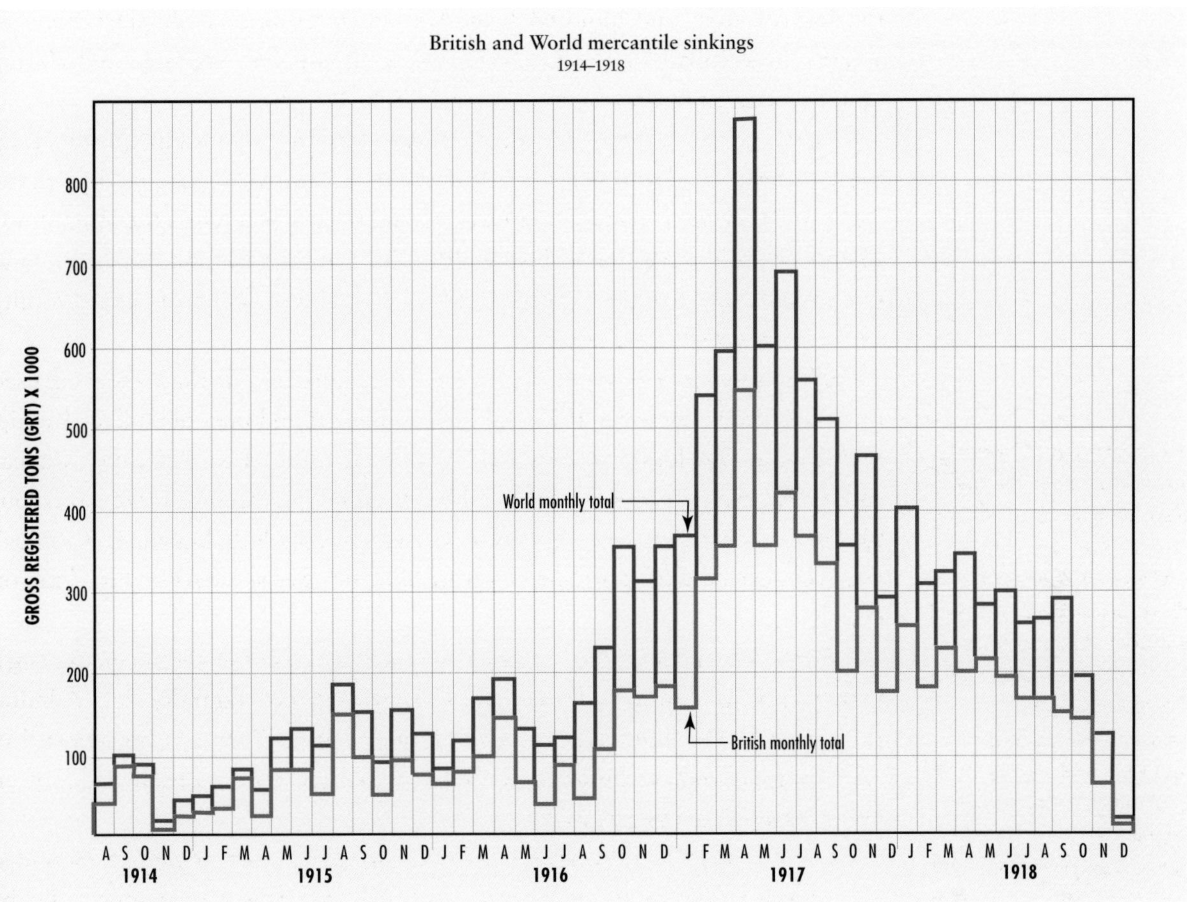


*This chart shows the catastrophic impact made by the second phase of unrestricted U-boat warfare, starting in February 1917, and, from that October, the steady decline in sinkings due to the introduction of convoys. The difference on the chart between British and World losses comprises mainly neutral tonnage.*

diversion of tonnage in support of lengthy military campaigns. The supply of captured and requisitioned shipping had all but dried up and the total available to support the population was reduced.

German theorists calculated that, with restrictions removed, each U-boat was capable of sinking an average of 4,000 gross registered tons (grt) daily. Seventy submarines should thus be able to make Britain sue for peace within six months. The United States would almost certainly declare war at such a campaign but it was felt worth gambling that Britain would be knocked out of the war before American intervention could be effective.

An embittered Tirpitz was finally squeezed out of office in March 1916 but the high command, baulking at the risks of an unrestricted campaign, agreed to 'sharpen' operations. All enemy merchantmen within the War Zone would be sunk, as would all *armed* enemy merchantmen, wherever encountered. Enemy passenger ships, armed nor not, would not be molested anywhere.

This new phase began in March 1916 but immediately ran into trouble when a U-boat torpedoed the British packet *Sussex*, resulting in American casualties. An American threat to sever diplomatic relations resulted in restrictions immediately being reapplied. Even with these and a growing rate of U-boat attrition, British losses grew alarmingly, although at only a quarter of

*In July 1916 the unarmed German cargo-carrying submarine* Deutschland *made an overt commercial voyage to the United States (note the American Chester-class scout cruiser in the background). The underlying purpose of the trip was to remind the Americans that their eastern seaboard was within submarine range.*

Holtzendorff's hoped-for 630,000 grt per month. Losses to submarine minelaying, and those in the Mediterranean, combined with port congestion and delays to generate a pending crisis. A complacent Admiralty attributed the limited losses to effective countermeasures when in reality American diplomatic protest had been the more restricting factor.

Following Jutland in May 1916, the Germans realized that only the U-boat arm, and not the battle fleet, could achieve a decisive result. The 'sharpened' campaign now employed over one hundred submarines of improved performance yet it was known that available British tonnage had still been reduced by only 6 per cent of the pre-war total. With restrictions, the campaign would thus take years to achieve the desired result. Meanwhile, the British blockade was causing shortages not suffered reciprocally by the British. In December 1916 Holtzendorff therefore submitted an updated version of his earlier argument to Hindenburg, the Chief of the General Staff. It stressed the need for ruthlessness, not least because Germany herself faced war exhaustion.

A conference decision was made to implement the proposals from 1 February 1917. Large numbers of new boats were ordered but material shortages kept their average strength to about 180. The results, immediate and brutal, saw losses, already averaging 150,000 grt monthly, doubled and even tripled.

In addition, on 29 February 1917, the American government published the text of a telegram sent by Zimmermann (the German Foreign Secretary) to Bernstorff (the German ambassador in Washington) for onward transmission to the German minister in Mexico. The telegram had been intercepted and decoded by British intelligence and passed to the Americans. In the event of war between the USA and Germany, it declared, the German minister should propose a German–Mexican alliance, which Mexico should then try to persuade Japan to join. Mexico would be rewarded by the recovery of her 'lost territories' in Texas, New Mexico and Arizona. It was in blatant disregard of the Monroe Doctrine and an indication of the depths of German hostility towards the USA. President Wilson, seeing the uselessness of further appeals to reason, persuaded Congress to declare war on 2 April 1917.

Huge pressure had to be applied by the British to keep neutrals trading but defeat was forecast by November if the haemorrhage could not be stemmed. Great effort was put into largely useless 'offensive' patrolling of shipping lanes, although intelligence was more successful in directing the precision planting of mines in U-boat access lanes.

Throughout the war, professional voices had proposed reintroducing the ancient art of convoying merchantmen for their protection. Even more professional opinion, however, had pronounced it impractical in a modern context. Commonly quoted arguments cited delays to shipping, congestion in ports, problems in close formation-keeping, lack of escorts and the vulnerability of a concentrated mass of shipping.

*The bizarre appearance of many merchantmen during the First World War inspired several marine artists, as in this* Convoy *by Herbert Everett. Popularly termed camouflage, the schemes were really disruptive painting, intended not to conceal but to confuse an observer as to the true heading of a ship.*

Regular and essential short-sea trades were maintained between Great Britain and Scandinavia, the Netherlands and France. Following German targeting and a rising loss rate, escorted convoys were tried as a local policy from February 1917. The reduction in sinkings was dramatic and, although it was argued that experience in home waters could not be extrapolated deep-sea, the awful losses of April caused the Admiralty to recommend adopting the system on the North Atlantic. The prime minister, Lloyd George, later falsely credited himself with forcing this decision upon a reluctant high command. Between June and October 1917 regular convoy cycles commenced from Canada, the United States, Gibraltar and the Mediterranean. Practical problems proved to be few and the size of convoys quickly grew to economize on escorts. 'Fast' and 'slow' convoys were also introduced. From June 1917 the trend of losses was steadily downward, assisted by a drive to employ tonnage more efficiently. Three out of four sinkings had been by submarine gunfire but convoy made this impossible. The enemy therefore probed new areas where convoys did not operate. Thus 'Independents' still accounted for 40 per cent of losses, although defensive arming doubled their chances of survival.

The loss rate had been reduced to less than one-third required for a decision and, in December 1917, the Germans belatedly created a U-boat Office to co-ordinate the campaign and to direct the efforts of up to 69,000 skilled personnel, released from the army to mass-produce submarines. It was too late.

Equally late was the Allies' so-called Great Northern Barrage. The Royal Navy had finally succeeded in almost closing the narrow and shallow Dover Strait to U-boats. Enthused, the Americans initiated a scheme to bar the deep, stormy, 250-mile wide Scotland–Norway gap by deep mining. Unconvinced of the project's practicality, the British contributed only about 20 per cent of the 70,000 mines that were laid.

## The British maritime blockade of Germany

Unquantifiable in its effect, virtually unknown to the public at large, the strangulation of her seaborne trade was one of the single most important causes of Germany's seeking a negotiated peace. A classic application of seapower, the blockade was maintained very economically by a score or so of converted merchantmen, backed by the unseen authority of the Grand Fleet.

In the days of sail the concept of blockade embraced two major areas. The first was close investment of an enemy fleet that lay a secure but latent threat in its own port. An example is the Channel Fleet's eight-year watch on Brest during the French Revolutionary War, when the 'sharp end' comprised fast-sailing frigate squadrons backed by a 74 or two. With any sign of the enemy preparing for sea, the main fleet was summoned from its anchorage in home waters. Such procedures came to an end with the development of the mine and the submarine.

The other face of blockade was the economic war waged on an enemy through the disruption of his trade. Letters of marque, in particular, authorized privateers to seize hostile vessels and their cargo, and bring them to port for condemnation by an admiralty court. The ease of enrichment, however, resulted in privateering degenerating into little better than piracy, and the practice was abolished by the 1856 Declaration of Paris.

This declaration also stated that, with the exception of contraband of war, a neutral flag protected an enemy's merchandise. Further, neutral merchandise, contraband excepted, could not be taken while under an enemy flag. British acquiescence to these clauses flew in the face of experience, for the powers of stop and search had been widely and successfully exploited during the wars with America and France. The coming American Civil War would also show the clauses to be unenforceable.

Although the searching of neutrals on the high seas had been essential to the conduct of a successful campaign, it had caused much friction, particularly with Americans, ever mindful of their freedoms. The 1856 declaration extended no protection to a belligerent's ships and cargoes, and when British war plans against Germany emphasized the need for economic blockade, it was apparent that there would be extensive scope for misunderstanding. In truth, the international law of the sea was little more than an imprecise set of rules based on centuries of experience, most of it British. The situation remained that the Americans held that private property at sea was immune to interference while the British maintained the doctrine of Right of Capture.

Further complications arose from the arbitrary classification of cargoes themselves. The Declaration of London in 1909 recognized three categories. The first, 'absolute contraband', comprised purely military goods and were liable to seizure anywhere. The next, 'conditional contraband', could be taken only if it could be shown that the goods were specifically intended for military use. Finally, the 'free list' included all commodities, particularly raw materials, inseparable from those intended for civil use. Great Britain, however, had never ratified the declaration, leaving the category of all commodities open to upgrading.

The principle of blockade had never been measured against a modern and fully industrialized society but, back in 1793, Britain had deliberately targeted French grain. An indifferent harvest made import vital, and the enforced safe passage of the resulting convoy gave Lord Howe the opportunity to inflict on the Brest fleet the sharp reverse known as the Glorious First of June. The Admiralty's war plan against Germany envisaged a blockade injuring the latter's 'interests, credit and prestige' sufficiently to provoke a response in force. History, it was hoped, would repeat itself.

With war, the control of commercial shipping in the English Channel was relatively simple. The entire width of the Dover Strait was mined except for a small-ship inshore route on the French side and a patrolled gate on the English. Eastbound deep-sea traffic was obliged to pass by this gate, thence to be escorted by the Dover Patrol into the anchorage of the Downs, where it was boarded and

*Declared and undeclared minefields were an important passive element in the economic blockade of Germany. The ex-Canadian Pacific ferry* Princess Margaret *is seen here loading mines at Grangemouth. She had a converted capacity for four hundred mines and her cruiser stern, unusual at the time, facilitated the addition of mining doors.*

examined. With no prospect of evasion, any master with ship or cargo of doubtful provenance would be attracted to using the northabout route on which, sure enough, traffic rapidly increased.

Notorious for foul weather and poor visibility, the northern approaches to the North Sea comprised primarily the 40-mile gap between the Orkneys and the Shetlands and the hundred-plus miles between the Shetlands and the Norwegian coast. The latter was fringed with islands which offered an inshore route, and it was necessary to patrol to a latitude of 62 degrees North to reach a point where traffic had to emerge into international waters.

Responsible for this considerable stretch of ocean was Rear Admiral Dudley de Chair's Tenth Cruiser Squadron (10th CS), comprising eight protected cruisers of the Edgar and Crescent classes. Until hostilities, the group had been a training squadron but was now manned mainly by reservists. All ships were at least twenty years of age and were obsolescent. Base facilities at Scapa Flow were found to be too far to the south and new arrangements were established at Lerwick and Busta Voe in the Shetlands. Diverted shipping was also sent to the Orkneys port of Kirkwall.

Still attached to Admiral Jellicoe's Grand Fleet, de Chair found his ships often diverted on Grand Fleet business, a situation eased by the early attachment of several armed merchant cruisers (AMC). Early in the blockade the navy was endlessly frustrated by apprehending neutrals with cargoes obviously bound for Germany yet being ordered to allow them to proceed. Severe criticism preceded the passing of an Order of Council applying the doctrine of 'continuous voyage', whereby any conditional contraband was liable to confiscation, wherever bound for discharge. Further amendments to the list of commodities shifted categories relentlessly so that the distinction between 'absolute' and 'conditional' contraband all but disappeared. Cargoes lost to the enemy were also to Britain's benefit through the system of compulsory purchase.

Despite anticipating blockade pre-war, the Germans greatly underestimated its likely effect. Its early sting, however, was sufficient for it to be cited as justification for unrestricted submarine warfare. Submarines were dispatched to discover the location of the patrol lines but de Chair wisely varied them. On 15 October 1914, the cruiser *Hawke* was sunk by torpedo, having just hove-to to send a boat to a consort. As the ships were regularly required to stop in the course of their normal duties, her loss highlighted their vulnerability and the need for specialist boarding vessels.

Winter rapidly exposed the limitations of the old cruisers. Weeks of slow steaming caused breakdowns. Overcrowded through carrying spare hands for boarding parties, they were wet and uncomfortable in the generally poor weather conditions. By the end of 1914, therefore, they were already being paid off in favour of further AMCs, which were planned eventually to total twenty-four. Larger and with extensive accommodation, these offered vastly increased endurance and much improved the efficiency of the patrol. Admiral de Chair, his flag in the Allan Line *Alsatian*, usually mustered sufficient ships to cover any four of seven favoured patrol lines.

Boarding from vessels without engines demanded seamanship of the highest order, for which many AMCs carried boat crews of Newfoundland reservists, all ex-fishermen and born to the life. To reduce the amount of pulling, the usual technique was for the AMC slowly to lead the ship to be boarded. Her seaboat, normally released on the lee side, was thus quickly overhauled by the other vessel. Great care had to be exercised to avoid a boat being swept beneath the overhanging counter of a ship, while the then-customary rows of protruding rivet heads were a major hazard when coming alongside.

In 1915 alone, 740 ships of 3,100 intercepted were sent in to examination. Each involved putting aboard a party of one or two officers, a signalman and armed seamen. One AMC might have a dozen such parties away at any one time. Each went supplied with its own victuals and with no idea as to how long it would be absent. Reception varied from courteous acceptance to active hostility. To reduce friction with neutrals, two of the AMCs were turned over to the French Navy, but the venture was not a success.

By March 1916, when Admiral de Chair was relieved, his squadron had already lost two ships to submarines, one to stress of weather and another to a mine. The sinking of the enemy raider *Greif* also cost the destruction of the *Alcantara*. Over the previous twelve-month period the *Alsatian* had been at sea two days out of three and had steamed 72,000 miles.

A Ministry of Blockade had been created in January 1916, the purpose of which was better to apply the utmost pressure whilst still retaining tolerable relations with neutrals. With Admiral de Chair appointed as the ministry's naval advisor, the 10th CS was taken over by Vice Admiral Reginald Tupper, whose twenty-two AMCs were now supported by a dozen distant-water trawlers. Drawn from the lists of great British companies, the ships retained the bulk of their civilian crews, drafted under T124 articles 'for hostilities only'. The Royal Navy supplied the commanding officer, commissioned gunner and bosun, and key NCOs for deck and engine room. The remaining officers were reservists, again often from the ship in question, with a sergeant and twenty to forty marines.

Ships remained at sea for thirty to forty days, anywhere between Norway and Iceland, their dreary beat earning them the wry soubriquet of the 'Muckle Flugga Hussars'. Their holds, partly converted to magazines for their aged 6-inch guns, were filled with extra bunker fuel, and void spaces with timber and sealed drums to assist buoyancy if torpedoed.

America's entry into the war in April 1917 removed perhaps the greatest obstacle to effective blockade, while the great demands of the convoy system saw 10th CS ships often diverted again for escort duties. The stranglehold was none the less maintained to the end. At the price of nine AMCs and 1,165 lives, a total of 12,979 vessels had been intercepted and boarded at sea. Because of the patrol line, a further 2,039 submitted voluntarily for examination. Only 642 ships are known to have evaded interception, representing approximately 4.1 per cent of the total.

The presence of the patrols never brought about the hoped-for fleet action as submarines proved to be the major hazard. Yet perhaps the best measure of the success of these weather-scarred ships lies in the admission of Admiral Scheer himself. 'The very surrender of our ships (i.e. the High Sea Fleet) is the best proof that we were not defeated until in the Homeland the will to continue the struggle had been so sapped by hunger and privation that the people were susceptible to the poisonous ideas spread by enemy propaganda. The fight for sea commerce was to lead to the strangling of the whole German people.'

## Enter naval aviation

When, on 14 November 1910, Eugene Ely spluttered into the air from a temporary deck aboard the USS *Birmingham*, he was making the first-ever heavier-than-air flight from a ship. Yet a mere eight years later the British commissioned the first through-deck carrier, employing the layout still in use today. War had stimulated this rapid progress in naval aviation which, frustratingly, matured just too late to make a real impact.

During this era a choice still needed to be made between 'lighter-than-air' (LTA) and 'heavier-than-air' (HTA) craft. Due primarily to the pioneering work of Graf von Zeppelin, the German Navy preferred the airship (LTA) for operations over water, while the mechanical ingenuity of the French greatly influenced the Allied camp in using winged aircraft (HTA). It was largely to give aircraft the means to tackle airships that brought about the rapid evolution of the aircraft carrier.

In 1914, aero-engines were still low-powered for their weight, and unreliable. The enormous wing areas of contemporary aircraft were necessary to create sufficient lift, but conferred the concomitant advantage of low take-off and landing speeds. The gas containments within the great envelopes of airships generated sufficient buoyancy to support little more than the machine's own weight. Neither LTA nor HTA had thus yet produced aircraft geared to an

*The commercial aspect of German airship development guaranteed a high profile and provided a valuable base for wartime expansion. Much feared by the Grand Fleet for its reconnaissance capability, the enemy's airship force was, however, largely wasted in bombing sorties over England.*

attacking role. Their greatest contribution at sea was still expected to be in reconnaissance and in spotting for the fleet's gunfire.

While wheeled aircraft could be launched from a modified ship, albeit with some difficulty, their recovery was as yet virtually impossible. Not surprisingly, therefore, the Royal Navy's interest in 1914 centred on the floatplane. Carried aboard a variety of warships, these could be set afloat and recovered by crane or boom. In practice, even a minor chop threatened their fragile construction while a flat calm would see them unable to 'unstick' from the surface, even under full throttle.

The naval wing of the Royal Flying Corps (RFC) had recently gained independence as the Royal Naval Air Service (RNAS), and the Director of Admiralty's Air Department, Captain Murray Sueter, was greatly interested in the aircraft's potential in attack. His efforts were rewarded in July 1914 when the Royal Navy followed the Italians in successfully air-dropping a torpedo. Sueter

*The Germans carefully evaluated ways in which the new technology of aviation might assist the fleet. This included naval and mercantile conversions, as in the Royal Navy. Submarines co-operated in several joint exercises, including carrying a seaplane on top of the casing, and partially submerging to float it on and off.*

*Fast and handy, several short-sea passenger vessels were converted by the Royal Navy to operate a flight of seaplanes. The 1,676-ton* Engadine *had a very active wartime career with the Harwich Force, with the distinction at Jutland of flying the first-ever reconnaissance in battle.*

immediately specified a suitable aircraft from the firm of Short Brothers, which resulted in the Short 184 seaplane. Progressively upgraded, over 650 were built, serving throughout the war as the navy's standard workhorse. To deploy the 184s, Sueter began the acquisition of cross-Channel packets. Fast and nimble, these were fitted with a hangar and cranage aft and, in some cases, a flying-off platform forward. To use the latter, the aircraft's floats were located on a wheeled trolley.

With the German battle fleet obviously prepared to give battle only on its own favourable terms, thought turned to the prospects of employing torpedo aircraft to attack it in its own bases and anchorages. Although more carriers were requested for the North Sea, the opening of the Dardanelles campaign early in 1915 meant a net loss of such ships through transfer to the Mediterranean. During August, three enemy merchantmen were hit with 14-inch aerial torpedoes, two being sunk despite the poor explosive power of small warheads. In order to

# Le Petit Journal

ADMINISTRATION
61, RUE LAFAYETTE, 61
Les manuscrits ne sont pas rendus
On s'abonne sans frais dans tous les bureaux de poste

5 CENT. SUPPLÉMENT ILLUSTRÉ 5 CENT.
26me Année Numéro 1.279
DIMANCHE 27 JUIN 1915

ABONNEMENTS

| | SIX MOIS | UN AN |
|---|---|---|
| SEINE et SEINE-ET-OISE.. | 2 fr. | 3 fr. 50 |
| DÉPARTEMENTS........ | 2 fr. | 4 fr. » |
| ÉTRANGER........ | 2 50 | 5 fr. » |

LE ZEPPELIN ABATTU

The German airship force was largely misused in pioneering the bombing of enemy targets by night. In this they proved vulnerable to poor navigation, deteriorating weather conditions and high-performance land-based fighters armed with incendiary ammunition.

damage a warship significantly, an 18-inch weapon was required but the increase in weight from 810 to 1,400 pounds pointed to the development of an entirely new type of aircraft. Attempts to use aircraft to spot for bombarding warships at the Dardanelles were bedevilled by the bulk and weight of contemporary radio equipment. For the moment kite balloons, lofted from modified merchantmen, were more satisfactory.

The Short 184 could carry 500 pounds of bombs and a Lewis gun, and attacking Turkish positions was part of every naval pilot's routine. Naval aircraft also repeatedly bombed the Turkish battlecruiser *Yavuz*, recently transferred from the German Navy

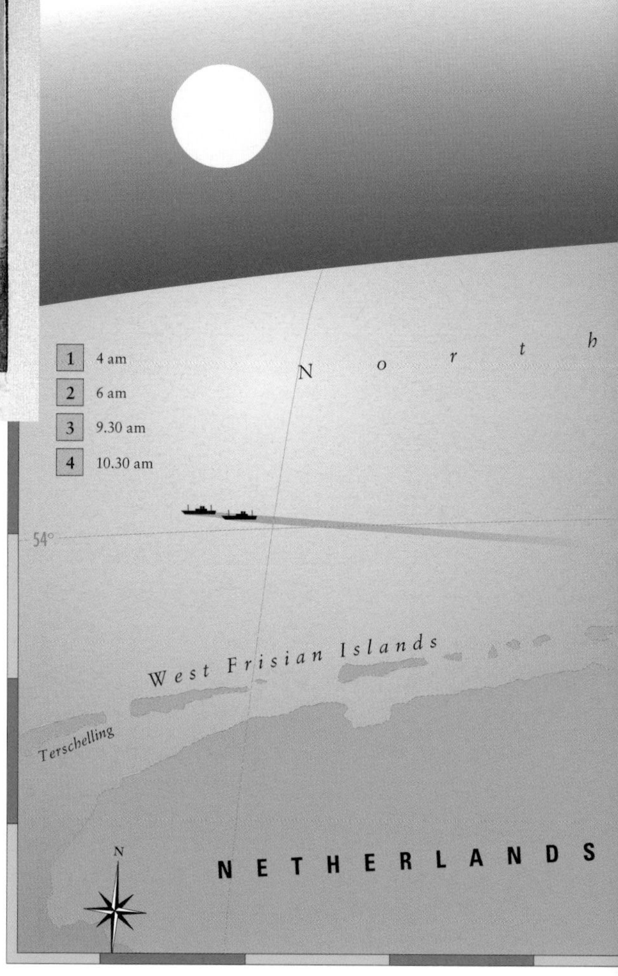

and grounded in the Dardanelles. Their small bombs, however, were defeated by her horizontal protection.

Admiral von Tirpitz viewed the Zeppelin, like the submarine, as a distraction from his primary task of creating a battle fleet. Although the craft were already operated by the German Army and making commercial flights, it was the autumn of 1912 before the Naval Airship Division and its first airship materialized. Facilities became established along the Frisian and Schleswig coasts and, with hostilities, the very few craft began to prove their worth in reconnaissance.

Unaware that Zeppelins could rarely operate on more than one day in four, the Royal Navy rapidly acquired the jitters. 'Zeppelinitis' convinced all personnel that the fleet's every move was being watched and reported. Laden with fuel rather than with bombs, the hated gas-bag could hover around all day just beyond gun range. Fast seaplanes, such as the Sopwith Schneider, were deployed by the British but, by dumping ballast, the Zeppelins outclimbed them with ease. High-performance land fighters were required, and several ingenious solutions were attempted for their deployment.

CUXHAVEN RAID 1914

*Christmas Day 1914 saw the Harwich Force penetrate deep into enemy waters, with three seaplane carriers, to attack the Zeppelin base near Cuxhaven. No damage was caused by the seven aircraft involved and, in another 'first', the ships were bombed by enemy airships and seaplanes.*

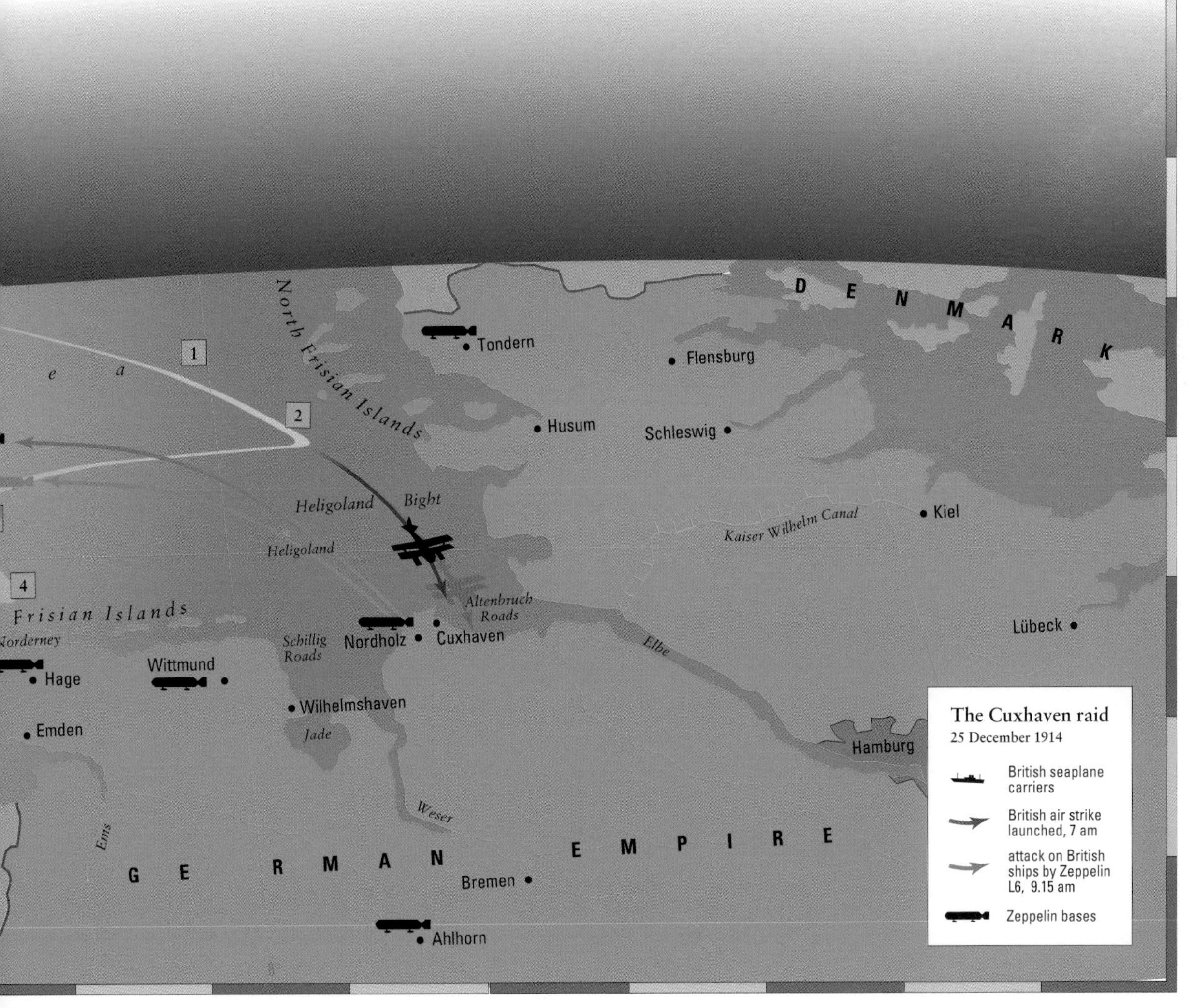

It was every admiral's dream to possess the means whereby an opponent's situation could be reliably reconnoitred and, in its Airship Division, the German Navy possessed something approaching an ideal. Inexplicably, however, its high command enthusiastically co-operated with the army-led campaign to direct the joint airship force towards high-profile bombing raids on England. The situation thus arose whereby the main strength of the Naval Airship Force was dissipated for little return over English soil, while most of the RNAS aircraft operated not at sea but in supporting the RFC in the defence of London and over the Western Front.

In contrast with the Royal Navy's first essay into rigid airships, where the prototype suffered structural failure before its first flight, German craft continued to haunt British naval movements. The fleet had addressed the problem from the outset and as early as Christmas Day 1914 the Harwich Force had escorted three seaplane carriers deep into the Heligoland Bight. The seven aircraft launched failed to find the enemy airship sheds that were their targets, but it would not be the last attempt to strike the Zeppelin's bases.

It was a succession of compact and sturdy fighters from Sopwith that eventually enabled the navy to take interceptors to sea. If taking-off was precarious for the pilots of the Pups and Camels, recovery was impossible except by fitting the aircraft with flotation bags and, following 'ditching' alongside a friendly ship, hoping for retrieval by crane or derrick. Being able to rise in a relative wind speed of 40 knots or less, fighters were to be seen on platforms at the forward end of light cruisers, from June 1917, and, increasingly, on the top of

*Tough, well-armed and capable of remaining airborne for over nine hours, when carrying extra fuel, the Felixstowe F.2A was the successful marriage of a Porte-designed hull with wings and tail assembly by Curtiss. In flying AS patrols over the North Sea the aircraft frequently had to engage enemy fighters and airships.*

*One of the RNAS's twenty-seven 'C', or Coastal, airships, C26 watches over a convoy. The type served from the end of 1915, the crew in the open gondola being on duty for up to an eye-watering twenty-four hours.*

turrets of capital ships. A stranger expedient, which successfully claimed a Zeppelin in August 1918, was to loft a Camel from a specially configured lighter towed at high speed by a destroyer.

While the neutral US Navy put much effort into catapaults, the Royal Navy found them to be an unnecessary complication for early aircraft, although independent development and sea trials were continuously progressed.

A major contribution to the war at sea was made by flying boats which, using their hulls for flotation, were more robust than floatplanes. Credit for their early development is due to the American Glenn Curtiss, but the refinement of his H.4 and H.12 ('Small and Large Americas') into the ubiquitous Felixstowe F.2A was the work of his British collaborator, Squadron Commander John Porte. Well armed for their day, long-legged and surprisingly manoeuvrable, they operated from a string of east coast stations to cover the southern North Sea in a 'spider's web' patrol pattern. Surfaced U-boats were their primary quarry, against which they carried 230-pound bombs. On several occasions they managed to surprise unwary Zeppelins, and scraps with enemy aircraft were not uncommon.

From 1916 the RNAS took delivery of small, non-rigid airships ('blimps') which began to fly convoy escort in the following year, together with the flying boats. Like the Zeppelins, blimps had long endurance and could hover or fly at

*The veteran express liner* Campania *in her second reconfiguration. The forward funnel has been split to allow the maximum length of sloping flying-off platform to be built over the bows. She carried a useful dozen aircraft, both fighters and seaplanes, but was sunk by collision just a week before the armistice.*

low speeds. Although never credited with the outright sinking of a submarine, their presence overhead worried attacking U-boat commanders, contributing greatly to the reduction in sinkings.

With the conversion of the aged *Campania* the Grand Fleet possessed from April 1916 a ship that could maintain fleet speed and carry seven Short 184s for reconnaissance, and up to four interceptors. Her lack of subdivision, however, made her vulnerable and a better solution was sought. The war was expected to be over too quickly to warrant the design and procurement of a new building but, in September 1916 (shortly after the *Campania*'s disappointing non-attendance at Jutland and the *Engadine*'s consequent flying of the first reconnaissance mission in battle), the Admiralty approved the reworking of an incomplete liner hull by Beardmore and promised for the end of 1917.

A conversion was performed in parallel on the large, 31-knot cruiser *Furious*. At 228 feet, her new forward flying-off deck was about 17 feet shorter than that of the *Campania* but below it was situated accommodation for six reconnaissance and four fighter aircraft. She commissioned in this guise in July 1917. It was daringly demonstrated in August that a Pup could be sideslipped around the superstructure to land on the foredeck, although a later attempt proved fatal. The feat influenced a decision to add a 184-foot flying-on deck aft, connected by elevator to an aircraft hangar below. In this second state, the *Furious* recommissioned in March 1918.

In June 1917 deliveries were begun of the Sopwith Cuckoo. Designed to carry of an 18-inch torpedo, the aircraft was to be built in hundreds for mass attack on the enemy fleet.

The after-deck concept aboard the *Furious* proved to be totally unworkable due to the violent eddying downstream of her superstructure. For this reason, the fleet impatiently awaited the Beardmore conversion. To be named *Argus*, this featured a near full-length flush flight deck, unencumbered by top-hamper. Her delivery was badly delayed but the Admiralty approved a second full flight deck conversion, using an incomplete battleship hull for what would eventually

*HMS* Argus *was converted from the hull of a passenger liner to become the world's first through-deck carrier, but commissioned just too late to see war service. Island superstructures were believed to be a danger to aircraft and to cause stability problems.*

*HMS* Furious *in her second configuration, with separate forward (flying off) and after (flying-on) decks. The latter has a barrier to prevent aircraft from flying into the superstructure. A small SSZ blimp of the RNAS is secured.*

become HMS *Eagle*. Embodying the same principles but designed to task, HMS *Hermes* was laid down in January 1918 as the first true carrier.

Despite her deficiencies, the *Furious* gave a promise of things to come when, in July 1918, she dispatched a specially trained force of Camels against the Zeppelin base at Tondern. Carrying two 50-pound bombs apiece, seven aircraft carried out history's first successful carrier air strike, destroying two enemy airships in their shed. To the huge disappointment of the service, the *Argus* was not delivered until September 1918. As she was still working up when the armistice was agreed two months later, the planned aerial torpedo attack on the High Seas Fleet never materialized.

*One reason for the success of the German auxiliary cruiser* Wolf *was her use of a small Friedrichshafen FF.33e floatplane. Careful maintenance allowed it to make over fifty flights, which widened the ship's horizon and threatened its merchantmen into submission.*

Although the British were responsible for most of the essential HTA developments during the period under consideration, others also operated aircraft at sea and in maritime support. The German Navy converted merchantmen to carriers of floatplanes but made no significant use of them. One exception was the little aircraft carried by the auxiliary cruiser *Wolf*, which made over fifty flights in support of the ship's commerce-raiding activities during 1917. Shore-based German floatplanes nevertheless proved a nuisance on occasion. A surfaced submarine off Harwich was surprised by a flight and peppered by machine-gun fire almost to destruction. The same medium accounted for a whole

flotilla of six British coastal motor boats (CMB) in August 1918. Several aerial torpedoings of merchantmen occurred off the Thames Estuary during 1917.

While a Turkish torpedo boat was the largest warship to be destroyed by bombing during the war, a few submarines were sunk. These included the British *B10*, sunk by Austro-Hungarian aircraft at Venice Arsenal in 1916, and the British *D3*, sunk in error by a French airship in 1918. During 1916 the French *Foucault* was detected submerged in clear water and sunk by Austrian aircraft.

## The Dardanelles and Mesopotamian campaigns

Two campaigns which commenced early in the war serve to illustrate not only the traditional naval role in supporting the army but also that operations, simply embarked upon, may well degenerate into inextricable quagmires.

To impress wavering Balkan states, to relieve military pressure on the Russians and to lift the threat of attack on the Suez canal, the British decided to move quickly against Turkey, largely through the enthusiasm of the First Lord of the Admiralty, Winston Churchill. An Anglo-French fleet would force the Dardanelles, appear off the capital, Constantinople and, by threat of bombardment, force Turkey out of the war.

The Germans, however, had concluded a Treaty of Alliance with the Turks and were acting as military advisors through the very able Lieutenant General

*The looming presence of the* Goeben *and her consort,* Breslau, *at Istanbul tied down disproportionately large Allied naval forces. However, their first sally from the safety of the Dardanelles went disastrously wrong.*

Liman von Sanders. The German Vice Admiral Wilhelm Souchon, effectively head of the Turkish fleet, echoed much senior opinion in the Royal Navy by doubting that an Allied squadron could operate beyond the Dardanelles due to problems of supply. The French also had reservations but participated because they regarded the Levant as a French sphere of interest. Their objections to the choice of Senior Naval Officer (SNO) were also overridden. Rear Admiral Sir Sackville Carden was due for retirement, had little command experience and even less initiative. In Rear Admiral Sir John de Robeck, however, he had an able deputy.

Together with the Sea of Marmara and the Bosphorus, the 40-mile Dardanelles waterway provides the only link between the Black Sea and the Mediterranean. Generally 2 to 4 miles in width, it closes to only three-quarters of a mile at the Chanak Narrows, some 13 miles from the Mediterranean entrance. Studding both shores, fortifications both ancient and modern housed over 200

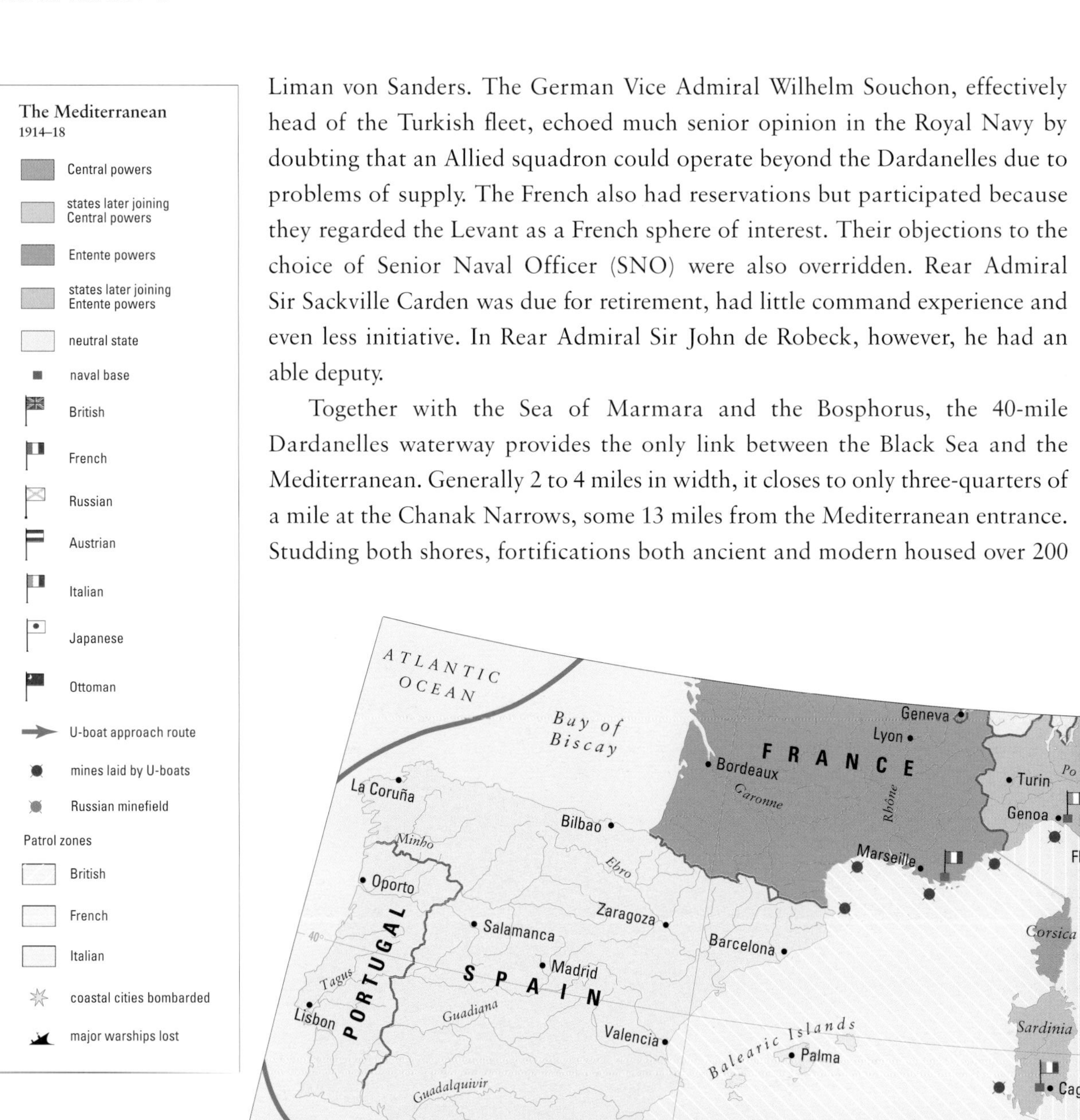

guns. Ten rows of mines, some 375 in all, were quickly established over the 5 miles below Chanak.

Battleships could not force the strait until the mines were swept, but the minefields were commanded at close range by many fixed and mobile gun batteries, supported by searchlights. Minesweepers could operate only if the batteries were suppressed. Many officials, including the First Sea Lord, Admiral Sir John Fisher, believed it essential that military forces would need to clear either shore as the fleet advanced. For the moment, it suited Fisher's purposes to go along with the plan.

At Mudros, on the Greek island of Lemnos, a substantial fleet was soon assembled, headed by the British battlecruiser *Inflexible* and sixteen pre-dreadnoughts, four of which were French. Much to Fisher's unease, the new battleship *Queen Elizabeth* was also under orders to join.

Carden planned to overcome the defences in three stages. First to be targeted

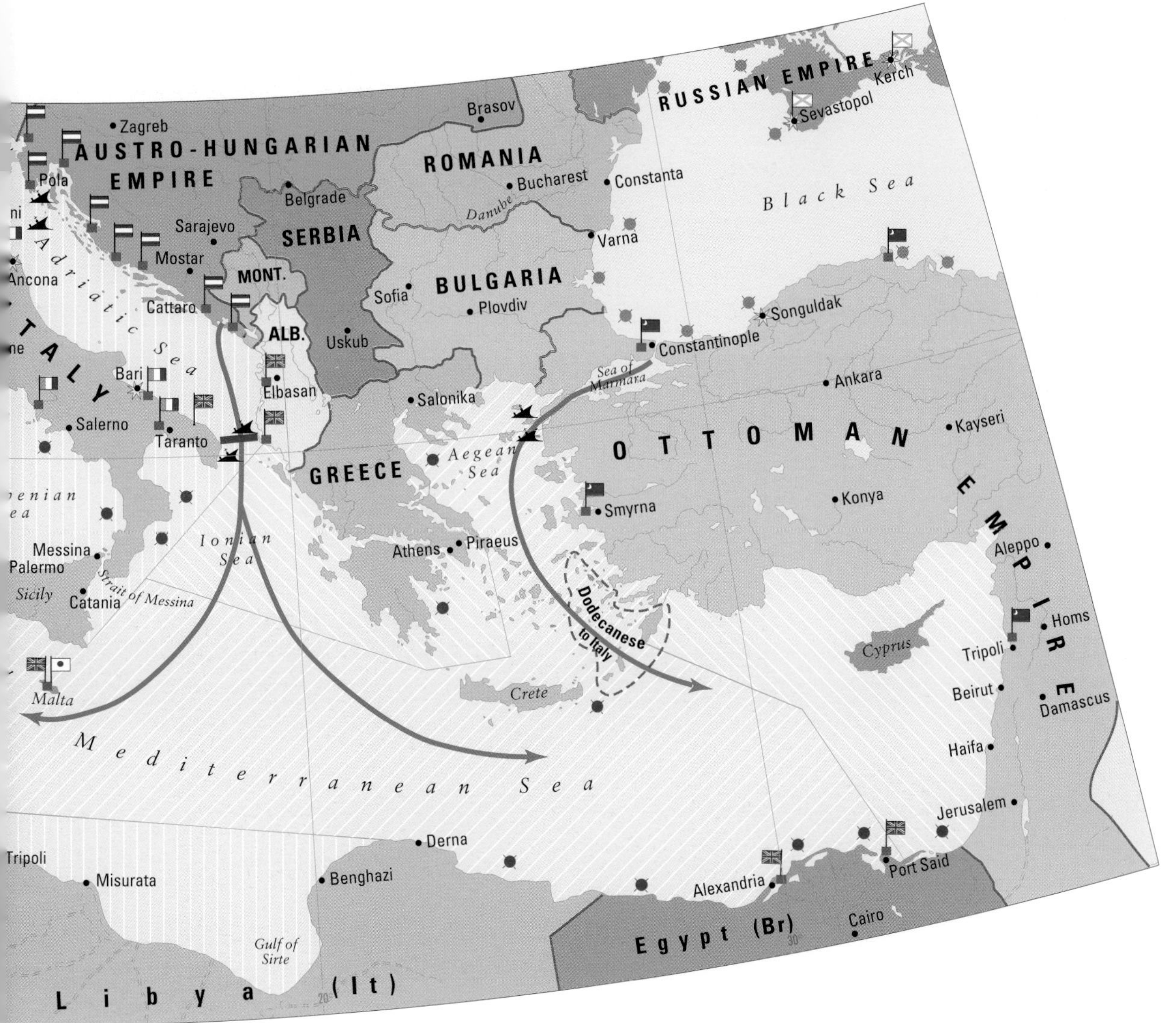


## THE MEDITERRANEAN 1914–18

*A glance at a map of the Mediterranean is sufficient to show the strategic importance of the British bases at Gibraltar and Malta and in Italy, which permitted the Allies to patrol the Strait of Otranto, and the Aegean, which reduced the options to enemy naval forces.*

were the forts covering the entrance, confirmed by aerial reconnaissance to mount twenty-seven guns of up to 11-inch calibre. Then would follow the wider intermediate section, the more scattered strongpoints of which housed about one hundred guns of up to 8.2-inch calibre. Finally the Narrows, with racing currents and covered closely by eighty-eight guns, including six 14-inch weapons. Von Sanders had enjoyed adequate time to organize the defences, which supported fixed positions with mobile batteries, including howitzers for high-angle indirect fire.

In February 1915, with the question of military support still under debate, Carden initiated the first phase of his plan. In foul weather the *Inflexible*, supported by six British and French pre-dreadnoughts, opened up on the outer forts at long range that was progressively reduced. Heavy-calibre return fire kept ships on the move, reducing accuracy when naval ammunition was already in short supply. Royal Marine parties thus led very exciting lives as they were landed to complete the task with demolition charges.

The Australian and New Zealand Army Corps (ANZAC) began to be transferred from Egypt to Lemnos, joined later by the British 29th and a French

division. Carden had already moved against the intermediate defences but used his ships piecemeal. Restricted in manoeuvre, they were harassed by mobile batteries; unable to anchor, their fire was inaccurate. Spotting by aircraft was ineffective due to still-primitive equipment.

Under pressure, but with the intermediate defences virtually unscathed, Carden ordered an attempt to reduce the first mine barriers. On the night of 10/11 March 1915, seven civilian-manned minesweeping trawlers moved up, supported by warships. The latter proved wholly unable to suppress either searchlights or guns and the attempt was quickly abandoned. Two further attempts, one British, one French, also failed, even with the use of naval crews. On 16 March Carden resigned and was replaced by de Robeck.

Two days later de Robeck launched a major attack. As the four modern British capital ships advanced slowly in line abreast, laying long-range fire on the Narrows defences, flanking squadrons of older British and French ships engaged the attentions of the intermediate defences. As the force neared the mine barriers, the sweepers again went forward, and again attracted unendurable fire. Withdrawing, the heavy ships then ran into a new line of just twenty mines, laid

*The main naval assault on the Dardanelles outer and intermediate defences, made on 18 March 1915, involved fourteen old battleships and two dreadnoughts. Mobile Turkish batteries kept the ships on the move, reducing their accuracy in bombardment, and a minefield sank three old battleships.*

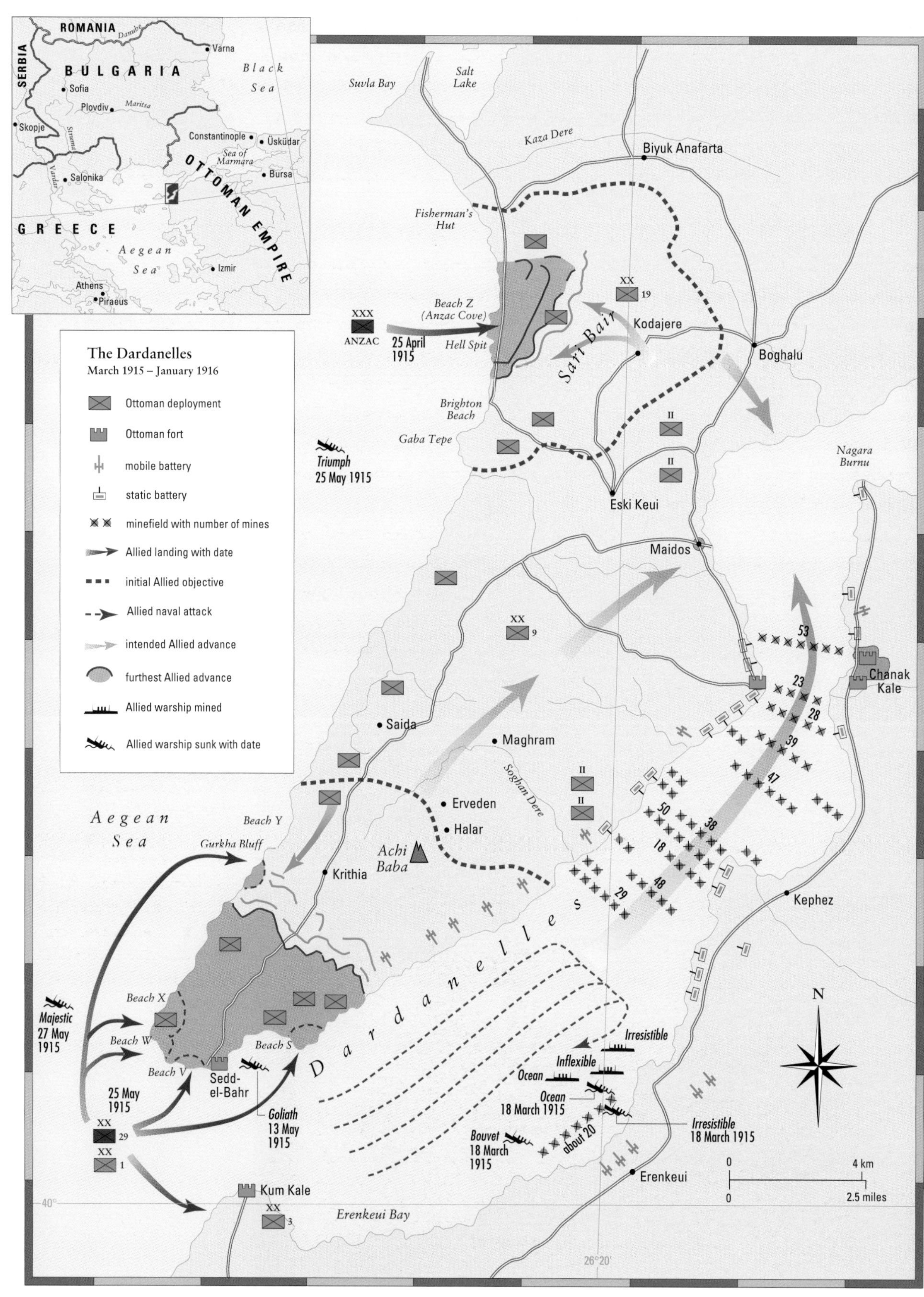
The Dardanelles
March 1915 – January 1916
Ottoman deployment
Ottoman fort
mobile battery
static battery
minefield with number of mines
Allied landing with date
initial Allied objective
Allied naval attack
intended Allied advance
furthest Allied advance
Allied warship mined
Allied warship sunk with date
ROMANIA
Danube
SERBIA
BULGARIA
Sofia
Plovdiv
Maritsa
Varna
Black Sea
Skopje
Constantinople
Üsküdar
Sea of Marmara
Bursa
OTTOMAN EMPIRE
Salonika
Vardar
GREECE
Aegean Sea
Izmir
Athens
Piraeus
Suvla Bay
Salt Lake
Kaza Dere
Biyuk Anafarta
Fisherman's Hut
Beach Z (Anzac Cove)
ANZAC
25 April 1915
Hell Spit
Sari Bair
Kodajere
Boghalu
Brighton Beach
Gaba Tepe
Triumph 25 May 1915
Eski Keui
Nagara Burnu
Maidos
Chanak Kale
Saida
Maghram
Soghan Dere
Erveden
Halar
Achi Baba
Krithia
Aegean Sea
Beach Y
Gurkha Bluff
Dardanelles
Kephez
Majestic 27 May 1915
Beach X
Beach W
Beach V
Beach S
Sedd-el-Bahr
25 May 1915
Goliath 13 May 1915
Irresistible
Inflexible
Ocean
Ocean 18 March 1915
Irresistible 18 March 1915
Bouvet 18 March 1915
about 20
Erenkeui
Kum Kale
Erenkeui Bay
N
0 4 km
0 2.5 miles
40°
26°20'

at night by a Turkish auxiliary. The French *Bouvet* was lost with nearly all hands. The *Inflexible* and *Irresistible* both struck mines, the latter slowly foundering. In attempting to assist, the *Ocean* suffered a similar fate. For the loss of three battleships and three more heavily damaged, de Robeck's big effort had reduced neither minefield nor defences. Viewing old capital ships as expendable, Churchill dispatched four more, while the French sent one. Destroyers were modified for high-speed minesweeping.

De Robeck now suddenly echoed the opinion of General Ian Hamilton, the senior military officer on Lemnos, that a combined operation was necessary to protect the navy's line of communication. Churchill disagreed furiously, but had to bow to the unanimity of Fisher and the Sea Lords, together with the commanders on the spot. None the less, an offensive was necessary to encourage the reluctant alliance of Italy, to offset the growing stalemate of the Western Front, and to relieve continuing Turkish pressure on the Russians. On 25 April 1915 Anzac and British troops were landed on the Gallipoli peninsula, with French forces on the Asiatic shore. From this point, naval operations assumed a supporting role.

Germany, unsure of Turkish ability to withstand further naval assault, decided to dispatch U-boats to the scene, although these would take time to arrive. On the night of 12/13 May a single enemy destroyer slipped down the strait and torpedoed the anchored battleship *Goliath*, sinking her with great loss of life. Knowing U-boats were also *en route*, Fisher was fearful for the *Queen Elizabeth* and successfully demanded her return. Churchill's response was a

THE DARDANELLES MARCH 1915 – JANUARY 1916

*The Dardanelles were impregnable to orthodox naval attack. Minefields barred capital ships from breaking through. Fixed and mobile batteries prevented clearance by minesweepers. A military campaign was thus essential, but was appallingly misdirected.*

*In the course of the main naval attack the British pre-dreadnought* Irresistible *was disabled by heavy artillery, thence drifting on to a moored mine. Under withering fire the destroyer* Wear *took off about 600 of her crew but, in assisting, the* Ocean *too was mined. Both veteran battleships foundered.*

demand for yet more pre-dreadnoughts and monitors. Exasperated, Fisher resigned. His going coincided with a political storm at home that resulted in the forming of a coalition government which banished the unpopular Churchill from its ranks. Its twin driving forces gone, the pace of Admiralty slowed markedly.

Warned by the Admiralty's Room 40 of the *U21*'s imminent arrival, de Robeck ordered all except direct support vessels to remain at Mudros, with trawlers being used to ferry troops and stores to Gallipoli. Bombardment ships anchored within their crinolines of torpedo nets but the inability of these to defeat modern weapons was demonstrated by the *U21* sinking the *Triumph* and *Majestic* in the space of two days. Smaller U-boats also harassed lines of communication sinking, among others, one transport with the loss of over one thousand lives. Mines and torpedoes had brought to a close the long era of blockade.

Undeveloped land communications likewise increased the enemy's dependence upon sea transport. From April 1915 German traffic between

*No organized pre-landing bombardment, no close air support, no spearhead assault with amphibious armoured vehicles. To modern eyes the landings on Gallipoli appear hopelessly amateur. The courage of the individual squaddie was squandered by incompetence at high level.*

*Supposedly secure in her crinoline of torpedo nets, the pre-dreadnought HMS* Duncan *uses her 6-inch secondary armament in support of the army ashore. On 27 May 1915, similarly protected, the battleship* Majestic *was sunk by two torpedoes from the U21. Nets were then removed from all heavy ships.*

Constantinople and the peninsula was disrupted by Australian, British and French submarines. Braving roaring currents, mines and nets they sank eight warships, sank or wrote-off thirty-five transports and destroyed countless cargo-carrying sailing craft for the loss of eight of their own number.

Considerable military reinforcement failed to break the Gallipoli stalemate and, when Bulgaria joined the Central Powers, a new Allied intervention was required to aid Serbia. In October 1915 General Hamilton was replaced and his successor recommended evacuation. Considerable casualties had attended the initial landings but, as a result of careful planning that had been absent through much of the campaign, the force was evacuated by the navy at the end of the year virtually without loss.

MESOPOTAMIA

*Commitment by the Royal Navy to oil-firing meant that sources of oil had to be safeguarded. War with Turkey thus led to the Mesopotamian campaign, whose initial objectives were simply those necessary to cover the Ahwaz-Basra-Abadan region. Military necessities, however, added further complication in difficult terrain.*

Having decided in 1912 that the Royal Navy would move to oil-firing in all ships, the British government acquired a controlling interest in the Anglo-Persian Oil Company. Its refinery stood at Abadan, where the Shatt-al-Arab waterway entered the head of the Persian Gulf. The Shatt emptied the combined flow of the Mesopotamian (now Iraqi) Tigris and Euphrates, and the Persian (now Iranian) Karun. Long and vulnerable, the pipeline roughly followed the course of the Karun, north-eastward to Ahwaz. The vast expanse across which these rivers flowed was devoid of major feature and seasonally inundated to form a waist-deep wilderness of mud and reed. Small islands then abounded but the only continuous communication was by way of the rivers and their embankments, thickly fringed with groves of date palms.

This hostile land, where the Ottoman Empire met Persia, was peopled by nomadic Arab tribes with scant allegiance to any authority. The British had

*Braving the hazards of mines and powerful currents in the Dardanelles, Allied submarines enjoyed considerable success beyond, in the Sea of Marmara. Lt. Cdr. Martin Nasmith earned a Victoria Cross in the E.11 sinking, among other vessels, the old Turkish battleship* Barbaros Hayreddin, *once the* Kurfürst Friedrich Wilhelm.

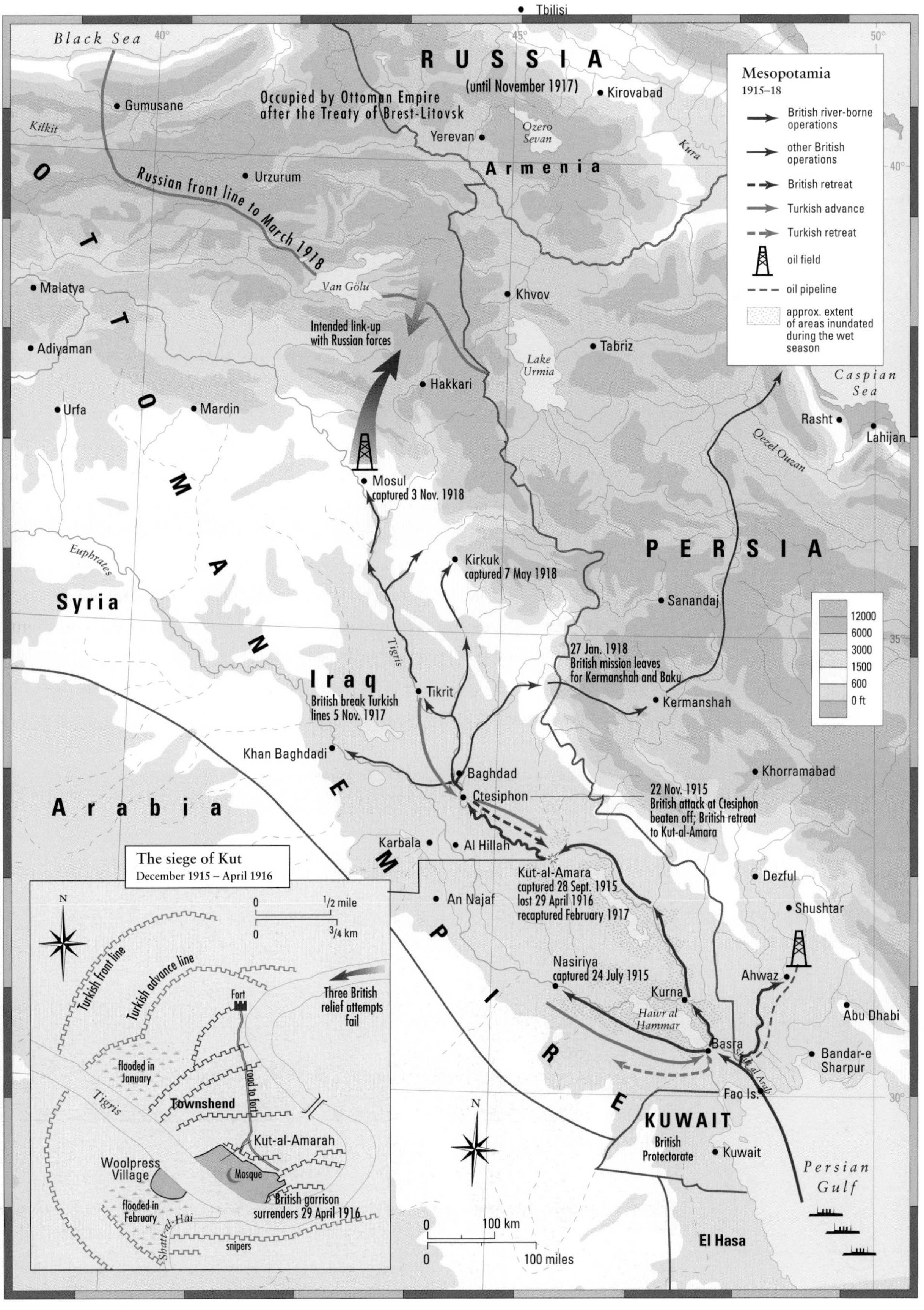
Mesopotamia
1915–18
British river-borne operations
other British operations
British retreat
Turkish advance
Turkish retreat
oil field
oil pipeline
approx. extent of areas inundated during the wet season
12000
6000
3000
1500
600
0 ft
Black Sea
RUSSIA
(until November 1917)
Occupied by Ottoman Empire after the Treaty of Brest-Litovsk
Russian front line to March 1918
OTTOMAN EMPIRE
Armenia
PERSIA
Syria
Iraq
Arabia
KUWAIT
British Protectorate
El Hasa
Caspian Sea
Persian Gulf
Tbilisi
Gumusane
Kirovabad
Yerevan
Ozero Sevan
Kura
Kilkit
Urzurum
Malatya
Van Gölu
Khvov
Intended link-up with Russian forces
Adiyaman
Tabriz
Lake Urmia
Hakkari
Urfa
Mardin
Rasht
Lahijan
Qezel Ouzan
Mosul
captured 3 Nov. 1918
Euphrates
Kirkuk
captured 7 May 1918
Sanandaj
Tigris
27 Jan. 1918
British mission leaves for Kermanshah and Baku
British break Turkish lines 5 Nov. 1917
Tikrit
Kermanshah
Khan Baghdadi
Baghdad
Khorramabad
Ctesiphon
22 Nov. 1915
British attack at Ctesiphon beaten off; British retreat to Kut-al-Amara
Karbala
Al Hillah
Kut-al-Amara
captured 28 Sept. 1915
lost 29 April 1916
recaptured February 1917
Dezful
An Najaf
Shushtar
Nasiriya
captured 24 July 1915
Ahwaz
Kurna
Hawr al Hammar
Abu Dhabi
Basra
Bandar-e Sharpur
Shatt al Arab
Fao Is.
Kuwait
0
100 km
0
100 miles
The siege of Kut
December 1915 – April 1916
N
0
1/2 mile
0
3/4 km
Turkish front line
Turkish advance line
Fort
Three British relief attempts fail
flooded in January
road to fort
Townshend
Tigris
Kut-al-Amarah
Woolpress Village
Mosque
British garrison surrenders 29 April 1916
flooded in February
Shatt-al-Hai
snipers

commercial interests on the waterways, where all the major centres of habitation lay. Their relaxed earlier relations with the Turkish authorities had deteriorated since the rise to power of the German-influenced 'Young Turks'. There was British concern that, in the event of war, Turkey would be encouraged into calling a general *jihad*, the effect of which would cross all frontiers and unite disaffected tribes in Afghanistan and north-west India.

With Turkey on the verge of declaring hostilities, and with warnings that crews of stranded German merchant ships were planning to scuttle them in the vital Shatt, Britain unobtrusively moved an Indian army brigade to Bahrain. Its transports were escorted by the old battleship *Ocean*, which rendezvoused in the Gulf with the sloops *Espiègle* and *Odin*, and the Indian Marine armed transport *Dalhousie*. On 6 November 1914, the day after Turkey's declaration, the *Espiègle* silenced the enemy battery at Fao, allowing the force to enter the Shatt and to disembark a little above the refinery. A second brigade arrived on the 14th.

The deep-draught *Ocean* was unable to cross the bar but her captain, Arthur Hayes-Sadler, armed tugs and launches for upriver service and embarked in the *Espiègle* as Senior Naval Officer (SNO). Thus began a strange, one-dimensional naval operation, where there was rarely water under the keel and ships were piled with sandbags and steel plate to soak up rifle bullets that spat randomly from thick cover on the river banks. The sloops' lofty masts offered the highest vantage point for miles. Violent sandstorms would suddenly halt operations with nil visibility and winds strong enough to swamp requisitioned native craft.

A brisk military action at Sahil began a Turkish withdrawal, allowing the navy to enter the Karun and retrieve a group of shallow-draught river steamers. It was the time of seasonal low water and any attempt at a defensive stand could be outflanked across the desert. The abandoned town of Basra was thus quickly occupied and the navy reconnoitred up to Qurna (Kurnah), about 110 river miles from the sea and the point at which the Tigris and Euphrates unite to form the Shatt-al-Arab.

The *Odin*, with her 12-foot draught, damaged her rudder on a submerged obstruction and an ad hoc flotilla went forward to land a military force some 10 miles below the town. A maze of thicketed side creeks had to be cleared by infantry before Qurna could be attacked. On 9 December, as the navy occupied the attention of the Turks from the front, the town was taken by an encircling movement from the rear. With the length of the Shatt-al-Arab secure, Hayes-Sadler returned to the *Ocean*, leaving Commander Wilfred Nunn of the *Espiègle* as SNO.

As the British consolidated their exposed situation at Qurna, the Turks made two thrusts across country. One probed the British front towards Ahwaz, at the head of the pipeline. The other headed south-eastward to Basra, threatening the rear of the Qurna force. Seasonal inundation had by now converted the wastes into a vast shallow lake, and troops by now of corps strength and commanded by General Sir John Nixon, employed large numbers of native *bellums* in turning

*Here seen at Basra, the ubiquitous Short 184 was the RNAS's workhorse. Note the huge wing area to compensate for the limited, 275 hp of the engine. Taking-off could be difficult in conditions of great heat and the radiator, set in the centre of the upper wing, could be given to boiling.*

back these thrusts. Also very effective as mobile artillery were four naval 4.7s mounted on Suez canal horseboats.

The threats had emanated from Nasiriya on the Euphrates and Amara on the Tigris. Assisted in reconnaissance and mapping by a new agency – aircraft – and reinforced by the newly arrived sloop *Clio*, a column under Major General Charles Townshend took Amara on 3 June, the surrender being effected to two armed tugs, an armed paddle yacht and two horseboats, all precariously far ahead of the main body. A second column then moved against Nasiriya but due to heat, sickness and the barrier of the huge, shallow Lake of Hammar, the town did not fall until 25 July.

Commanders on the spot had overcome immense difficulties, Nunn describing the land as having 'too much water for the army, not enough for the navy'. From the London perspective, however, objectives had been achieved comfortably and the decision was made to press on for the politically desirable prize of Baghdad itself. Still on poor defensive ground, the Turks fell back to Kut-al-Amara. Due to seasonal low water only the smaller naval craft could now navigate but these again occupied the front as the army entered from the side, taking the town at bayonet point. Baghdad lay just 110 miles distant overland, perhaps double that on the meandering river. Twenty miles short of the capital the ancient city of Ctesiphon was situated on good defensive ground, and here the Turks made their stand in depth.

The navy now began to receive what it had always needed: Fly-class gunboats, shipped to Abadan in sections for local reassembly. Drawing less than 3 feet of water, they carried three medium calibre and five automatic weapons. During the battle for Ctesiphon the gunboats attacked a heavy redoubt on the enemy's flank. The river's deep embankment protected the hulls of craft to an extent but also hindered their fire. Townshend's attempt to roll up the Turkish line failed on fierce resistance and, having suffered 30 per cent casualties, he had insufficient strength to renew the attack. It was now the British turn to retreat, covered by the navy as rearguard. Hit by artillery and disabled, the new gunboat *Firefly* had to be abandoned. By early December 1915 the British had withdrawn to a point well south of Kut, where Townshend and a full division had been left to annoy the enemy's rear pending relief, anticipated in a few weeks. Determined Turkish resistance made that relief impossible and, by April 1916, conditions in Kut were critical. Two Victoria Crosses were won in a desperate and unsuccessful attempt to resupply the garrison with a river steamer and, on 29 April, Townshend was obliged to surrender.

*Shipped out in sections for assembly at Abadan, the 'small China gunboats' of the Fly class proved indispensable on the rivers, drawing less than 3 feet of water. They packed a 4-inch gun, one 12- and one 6-pounder, a pom-pom and four Maxims. Note the large areas of protective screen.*

Even before this disaster the campaign, well beyond the capacity of the Royal Indian Marine to administer, had become the responsibility of the War Office. A naval yard was established at Basra, and a logistic build-up included specialist river steamers and cargo lighters. There were even some stretches of railway. The little Fly-class gunboats were supplemented with the larger Insect type. In July 1916, after preparations of Roman thoroughness, the Mesopotamia

Expeditionary Force was placed under the command of Lieutenant General Sir Stanley Maude, who moved forward in greatly superior force in December 1916. Resistance was dogged but, on the night of 24 February 1917, Nunn's flottila, again well ahead, had the satisfaction of raising the flag over the ruins of Kut. As retreat assumed disorder, the Turks found the navy moving up as cavalry, overtaking their rearguard. The fleeing enemy armed flotilla was overhauled and routed, the *Firefly* again assuming the White Ensign. This naval action, fought nearly 600 river miles from the sea and some twenty-eight months since the original flotilla had entered the Shatt-al-Arab, marked the end of the navy's armed involvement, for Baghdad fell on 11 March 1917.

## The Baltic

Shallow, constricted and largely ice-bound in winter, the Baltic imposes its own complications on naval warfare. Admiral Sir John Fisher favoured a plan to seize its exits and pass in a fleet that would oversee the landing of a Russian army on the Pomeranian coast, less than 100 miles from Berlin. Such high-risk strategy found support neither with the Admiralty nor with the service, and the proposal died with his resignation in 1915.

The sea thus remained a backwater, bounded to the west by neutral Scandinavian states and to the east by Germany and Russia, mutually at war. For Germany the North Sea carried priority, with its ever-present threat from the British Grand Fleet. In emergency the Kiel canal enabled powerful forces to be transferred quickly to the Baltic, which was normally secured by older squadrons and much used for training and working-up.

Germany, in any case, had little reason to fear the Tsar's battle fleet. Its main function was the protection of the Russian capital, St Petersburg, shortly to be renamed Petrograd. This lay at the eastern end of the Gulf of Finland, a 250-mile-long cul-de-sac. The fleet was based at Kronstadt, on Kotlin island, close to the capital. The bulk of its strength remained behind the two patrolled mine barriers that blocked the gulf at its mid point and western end.

The eastern shore of the Baltic bounded the Russian-dominated Baltic States and, from the military point of view, formed Germany's far left flank. The area was of low strategic importance and offensives were useful mainly in tying down Russian divisions. Because of the reluctance to commit major fighting ships and the shallowness of the waters, the naval war centred mainly on skirmishing between cruiser–destroyer groups, and widespread mine-laying.

An early German initiative led to a disaster that was the greater for going apparently unremarked. On 26 August 1914 the cruiser *Magdeburg* grounded at Odensholm, her wreck being taken by the Russians before it could be thoroughly destroyed. Naval codebooks retrieved from her were copied to the British. These, together with a couple of more invaluable sources, formed the basis upon which the Admiralty's highly effective intelligence branch was established in Room 40 just two months later.

The British Admiralty refused Russian requests for assistance with surface ships but in October 1914 sent three E-class submarines. Although all under competent commanders, they could achieve little before the onset of winter except to make the Germans excessively cautious. More E-boats joined during 1915 but shallow water and variable salinity made operations very difficult. None the less, useful targets were to be found on the iron-ore route between Sweden and Germany. Also during 1915 the Germans made several powerful incursions in the Gulf of Riga. Although their immediate purpose was that of large-scale

*Holed by a shell from a Bolshevik destroyer, the British submarine L55 sank quickly with the loss of all hands. Between 1928 and 1931 the Soviet Navy salvaged her and, repaired, added her to their fleet. The boat is here seen docked at Kronstadt.*

mine-laying, the operations were covered by front-line units from the High Seas Fleet. Any hopes of enticing the Tsar's capital ships into action, however, were stillborn.

By the 1916 season German manpower shortages were already requiring the decommissioning of labour-intensive pre-dreadnoughts in order to crew more important escorts as merchant shipping began to be organized in convoys. In June one such convoy of about ten ships, escorted by only three armed auxiliaries, was the subject of an attack by a Russian cruiser–destroyer force.

Although beginning their attack efficiently enough, the latter disengaged in the face of a resolute defence.

As British submarine commanders chafed at the restrictive orders placed on them by the Russians, the Germans probed the Gulf of Finland with a flotilla of modern destroyers. This ran into one of the infestation of minefields, with a disastrous loss of seven ships. From March 1917 both the Russian Army and Navy became infected with the nation's deepening revolutionary fervour. In October, Germany took advantage of this situation by moving eleven capital ships from the North Sea and landing 25,000 troops to take the islands of Ösel, Moon and Dagö. Occupation of these would bottle up Russian naval forces in the Gulf of Riga and free the German army's flank from their attentions. In the heaviest naval exchanges of the war the Russians lost the battleship *Slava,* while the Germans suffered a dozen minor warships sunk and, lacking sufficient minesweepers, mine damage to three capital ships.

By December, the Bolsheviks had seized Petrograd and agreed an armistice with the Germans, the latter forcing a full peace agreement in March 1918. Under certain conditions, the Russians were permitted to withdraw their fighting ships to Kronstadt where the British, still at war with Germany, needed to prevent the latter from appropriating them. Seven British submarines, based in the port, had to be destroyed.

*Anchored in company with an Invincible-class battlecruiser, HMS* Vindictive *shows off her new conversion from the cruiser* Cavendish. *Taking her name from the old cruiser famous for the Zeebrugge raid, she usefully reinforced Cowan's Baltic force with fighters and seaplanes.*

*Admiral Sir Walter Cowan, late captain of the battlecruiser* Princess Royal, *commanded the Royal Navy's forces during the difficult Baltic intervention. A strict disciplinarian, he craved action, seeing it in the Sudan, the Boer War, Jutland, Heligoland and finally, at the age of 70, in Libya and the Adriatic.*

The states of Finland, Latvia and Estonia declared independence but, with German military units experiencing mutiny and demands for repatriation, the new régime in Petrograd was confidently speaking of the Baltic becoming a 'Soviet sea'. Allied military forces were already safeguarding the northern supply ports and the new independents appealed directly to Britain for support. The Foreign Office could not approve the sending of troops but agreed to dispatch a naval force with arms and equipment.

On 22 November 1918, therefore, a cruiser–destroyer force, accompanied by minesweepers and auxiliaries sailed for Latvia and Estonia. Britain was not at war with the Bolshevik ('Red') régime but the SNO, Rear Admiral Alexander-Sinclair, was instructed to assume that any warship encountered off the coasts of the independents was there with hostile intent and was to be 'treated accordingly'. Even before the force reached Estonia it lost the cruiser *Cassandra* to a mine. On Boxing Day 1918, however, it captured two destroyers attempting to bombard Reval (Tallinn) and then went on to the offensive by giving fire support to the seaward flank of Estonian 'White' forces resisting the westward advance of the Reds.

In Latvia, with loyalties divided, conditions were wretched. The British had to instruct volunteers in the use of supplied weapons and remind the considerable remaining German forces that, under the terms of the general armistice, their priority was not repatriation but to maintain order for as long as the Allies considered necessary.

Riga, the capital, fell to the Reds on 3 January 1919 and British ships evacuated refugees until increasing ice obliged their withdrawal to Copenhagen. In a complex situation, Britain had guaranteed protection of the independents from the Bolsheviks, with whom she was not at war. In support of this policy, she used German troops with whom no peace treaty had yet been signed. The German commander, General Graf von der Goltz, was actively seeking to create a new, pro-German Baltic superstate, also using sympathetic Russian forces. In a final inconsistency, the armistice terms required the British to maintain the blockade of Germany, although von der Goltz's forces had to be transported and supported by sea.

Early in 1919, Sinclair was relieved by the fire-eating Rear Admiral Walter Cowan, whose official remit was equally vague. Considering Reval to be too remote, however, Cowan established a forward base at Biorko Sound, on the

Finnish coast only 30 miles from Kronstadt. From here he deployed torpedo-armed coastal motor boats (CMB) against the bombarding Red warships, sinking the cruiser *Oleg* on the night of 16/17 June 1919. Reinforcements to Cowan included the cruiser–carrier *Vindictive* and, on the night of 17/18 August 1919, her aircraft made a diversionary attack on Kronstadt to cover a penetration by CMBs. Their torpedoes put two battleships and a depot ship on the bottom in shallow water.

In September, although the new Soviet government offered to end the hostilities and to recognize the independence of the Baltic states, von der Goltz had other ideas and, through his loyal Russian subordinates, he made a strong bid to take Riga. In mid October – in one of their final actions, therefore – Cowan's ships blasted the rebels from fortifications commanding the port. Following similarly direct action at Libau, the Germans departed. By the end of November, all was quiet.

*A Royal Navy 55-foot Coastal Motor Boat (CMB), forerunner of the Motor Torpedo Boat (MTB). Based in Finnish waters and using the* Vindictive *as depot ship, CMBs sank the Russian cruiser* Oleg *and successfully penetrated the Russian fortified fleet base of Kronstadt.*

The apparent end of 'the war that was not a war', together with the onset of another Baltic winter, now exacerbated grievances in the force. 'Hostilities only' personnel were being retained when those at home had been demobilized. Leave was haphazard and inadequate, gratuities unfairly apportioned. Pay and allowances, needless to say, remained abysmal. Following widespread disaffection both in regular warships and auxiliaries, Cowan returned to London in January 1920 to argue a drastic reduction of British naval presence in the Baltic. Despite the obviously improving stability of the theatre, the withdrawal was phased over a year.

Of the Allied navies, the British was the only one to be engaged on a war footing. It supplied 238 of the 280 ships involved. Of these, 1 cruiser, 2 destroyers, 2 minesweepers, 1 submarine, 8 CMBs and 3 auxiliaries were lost, together with 37 aircraft. The Royal Navy suffered 123 personnel killed, the nascent Royal Air Force, 5. Many wondered for what purpose.

CHAPTER THREE

# A Time of Treaties 1918–39

*The British carrier* Furious *following her final remodelling in 1925. In place of an island, she had retractable control positions, flanking the forward run-down of the flight deck. Note that fighter aircraft may be flown directly from the hangar, across the forecastle.*

# A TIME OF TREATIES

SOMETIMES KNOWN AS the Twenty-Year Truce, this period was dominated by the relentless progress of totalitarianism in Germany, Italy and Japan, and the not wholly ineffective struggle by the western democracies to rein back the international trend to naval growth.

Although at local level the Royal Navy and US Navy enjoyed harmonious relations during 1917–18, the American Chief of Naval Operations (CNO), Rear Admiral William S. Benson, had no patience with the British policy of economic blockade and pressed for a more offensive strategy.

As early as 1915 the pacifist President Wilson had espoused a policy of 'preparedness' and, against a possible future threat from a powerful European victor, proposed to create 'incomparably' the world's greatest navy. The largely anti-British senior naval establishment took up the theme of a 'navy second to none'. The outcome was a 1916 programme incorporating 10 battleships, 6 battlecruisers and 140 lesser vessels. Once realized, this would have resulted in a fleet qualitatively superior to the Royal Navy. On their entering the war, however, the desperate need proved to be escorts and merchant ships; capital ships were not only superfluous but would take too long to build to be of use.

President Wilson deferred the 1916 programme but told the British that their post-war naval supremacy would not be tolerated, it being the instrument of

*As long as the High Seas Fleet lay rusting at Scapa following its surrender, its final disposal caused dissent among the late Allies. Its scuttling solved the problem neatly. The battleship* Baden, *whose great 38cm guns dominate the foreground, was raised and finally expended as a Royal Navy gunnery target.*

'global dictatorship'. Britain's impartial economic blockade had caused considerable friction with still-neutral American operators. Americans, in turn, appeared oblivious to the fact that Britain was being impoverished by the war, and greatly resented American commercial manoeuvrings for post-war markets.

As a condition of the armistice of November 1918, the Germans had to surrender all of their U-boats and the bulk of the High Seas Fleet for ultimate disposal by the victors.

For seven months the fleet rusted at Scapa Flow as allies argued. The French and Italians wished to acquire as much as possible, a solution that the British and Americans sought to avoid. The British wanted it destroyed to obviate any chance of the Germans re-acquiring it. Some Americans also wanted it scrapped, convinced that the British would engineer a tonnage share-out in proportion to wartime losses, which would yield the British the overwhelmingly greater part. American moderates proposed avoiding the over-humiliation of a beaten foe by the return of a substantial tonnage.

The impasse was resolved by the Germans themselves. On 21 June 1919, having learned the details of the imminent Versailles peace treaty, they took advantage of the temporary absence of the British guard squadron and scuttled the greater part of the fleet. Allied indignation was quickly replaced by relief. In recompense, commercial tonnage was seized and remaining modern light units taken for distribution between the French and Italian navies.

The peace treaty signed on 28 June 1919 defined, *inter alia*, the size of future

*The 28,500-ton battleship* Baden *was put ashore by the Royal Navy, settling in only shallow water. As may be apparent, restoring buoyancy in a ship of this size, weight and complexity is no easy task. She was raised in July 1919 after only one month in a flooded condition.*

German warships. Armoured ships would not exceed 10,000 tons, cruisers 6,000 tons, destroyers and torpedo boats 800 and 200 tons respectively. Submarines and aircraft were excluded and manpower limited to 15,000 volunteers. A British proposal to ban the submarine internationally as a weapon of war failed in the face of American reluctance and French hostility.

At the Peace Conference Britain accepted all of President Wilson's 'Fourteen Points' except that of absolute freedom of the seas in peace and war. Wilson's necessary acknowledgement earned an American observation that British naval supremacy was no better than 'Prussian militarism'. The President reaffirmed the '1916 programme' but hinted that it might again be deferred if his ambition of a League of Nations be realized. An unsympathetic American press accused him of 'spreadeaglism' and the British of 'diehard commitment to supremacy for no good strategic reason'.

*Designed before Jutland, the battlecruiser HMS* Hood *had a further 5,000 tons of protection worked in as a result of lessons learned at the action. Although reducing her designed speed by two knots, it was still deficient in the horizontal plane. Constantly in service as a flagship, she never received a planned further upgrade.*

None the less, Britain had already scrapped nearly four hundred warships, including forty capital ships. In August 1919 the government adopted the notorious Ten-Year Rule, whereby the continuing assumption that Britain would not be involved in a major war during the ensuing decade enabled the Treasury to eviscerate defence budgets.

Diminished by war, Britain certainly did not seek a further naval race, particularly one that she could not win. Much American antagonism was, in reality, directed at Japan, with whom Britain was in alliance. Japan's newly acquired mandate over Germany's western Pacific island groups threatened American interests. She was in an expansionist mood and building up her fleet which, in conjunction with British support, would outnumber any planned American Pacific fleet.

Britain's only post-Jutland capital ship was the battlecruiser *Hood*. Launched in August 1918, and the only one of a planned quartet to be completed, she attracted approbation in a confidential report to Admiral Benson, the American CNO. Her 'perfect balance' of hitting power, speed and protection combined, it said, the best features of battleship and battlecruiser. As casually as if specifying a new family car, the report proposed responding to the lone *Hood*'s main parameters (41,200 tons, 30.5 knots, eight 15-inch guns) with ships of 45,000 tons, 32.5 knots and eight 16-inch guns. Both would have only 12-inch belt armour. Japan had introduced the 16-inch gun in the two Nagato*s* and the United States were already responding with the four 32,500-ton Maryland*s*. These, too, carried eight 16-inch weapons but could manage only 21 knots.

The readiness to build contrasted with the American calls for armament reductions in the League of Nations. Adverse criticism, however, was countered not by citing Japanese precedent but by pointing out that the Royal Navy now

*Second of the three 'pocket battleships', the* Admiral Scheer *is commissioned in Wilhelmshaven in 1934. Commandant Marschall is reading a congratulatory telegram from the new president, Adolf Hitler, to the assembled crew. In the background is the old battleship* Hessen*, shortly to be converted to a target ship.*

faced no opposition worthy of the name, that the British historically went to war eventually with every serious commercial rival, and that they had always come out on top.

The Anglophobe CNO, Benson, thus drove the 1916 programme hard. Six 43,200-ton South Dakota-class battleships and six 43,500-ton Lexington-class battlecruisers were commenced during 1920–21. Simultaneously, Japan began her 'Eight/Eight' programme of 38,500-ton battleships and 40,000-ton battlecruisers.

*Between the wars the British Mediterranean Fleet was an important stabilizing influence in the region. Lying in Malta's Grand Harbour are, at the head of the line, two Queen Elizabeth class battleships, with an R-class beyond. Two County-class heavy cruisers complete the line. The unconverted QE in the floating dock suggests a date of about 1930.*

By 1925 the British knew that their battle fleet would be totally outclassed. With the now-One Power Standard and national prestige at stake, four 46,000-ton battlecruisers were ordered. A lack of finance held up the go-ahead for four 48,500-ton battleships with 18-inch guns.

During 1921 the new Harding administration in the United States rallied opposition against the hawks, whose policies were damaging international relationships and proving ruinously expensive. The five major naval powers were invited to a 'conference on the limitation of armament', to be convened in Washington in November 1921. Throughout the proceedings the Americans were always one step ahead by virtue of their secret service monitoring every communication between delegations and their governments. By offering to abandon their building programmes both they and the Japanese were able to make large paper sacrifices. Britain, as yet with no real programme, could match these only by further cutting the existing fleet. Already worn and outdated, this would become more so during the construction 'holiday' now proposed.

The Washington Treaty, signed in February 1922, was to influence major

*The extraordinary size and speed of the US Navy's first-generation fleet carriers (*Lexington *and* Saratoga*) taught it very early the advantages of large air groups and smooth flight-deck organization. The precise role of the carrier was still being defined, as evidenced by the armament of 8-inch guns.*

warship parameters until 1936. Britain, the United States and, reluctantly, Japan agreed a 5:5:3 ratio in capital ships, with aggregate tonnages of 525,000: 525,000: 315,000 respectively. France and Italy accepted limitation to 175,000 tons each. Individual replacements would be limited to 35,000 tons and 16-inch guns. Aircraft carriers would be subject to the same ratio as capital ships, with the two largest fleets being allowed 135,000 tons. Existing carriers would be classed 'experimental' and could be replaced at any time. New carriers would be limited to 27,000 tons each, except where specifically allowed by treaty. Other warships should not exceed 10,000 tons nor carry guns of greater than 8-inch calibre. This clause was to have the unintended result of encouraging signatories to build up to a new and powerful type, generally termed a 'treaty cruiser'. Signatories were also prohibited from further fortifying Pacific territories and insular possessions.

Dating from 1902, the Anglo-Japanese alliance was due for a second renewal. Militarily, it obliged each to aid the other if attacked by more than one aggressor. Japan's increasingly strident attitude worried British and Americans alike and the latter judged it a major diplomatic coup to render the alliance almost worthless by converting it at Washington into a four-power pact, including themselves and France. Japan left Washington feeling slighted, snubbed by Britain and unable to gain the 10:10:7 ratio that she felt her naval status warranted.

Two capital ship hulls which would otherwise have been scrapped were permitted by the treaty to be converted to aircraft carriers by each signatory. Neither should exceed 33,000 tons. Both the United States and Japan thus acquired two large carriers apiece, thereby learning at an early date the advantages of large air groups. Already having sufficient tonnage, Britain waited before converting the smaller *Courageous* and *Glorious*.

Post-Washington, the United States scrapped 15 capital ships, Japan 10. Britain destroyed 20 but, because of the war-worn state of the remainder, was allowed to build 2 new ships, the Nelsons, whereupon 4 more older hulls had to be deleted.

With the formation of the unified Royal Air Force (RAF) in April 1918 the Royal Navy not only transferred 1,500 aircraft and 55,000 personnel, it handed over with them its fund of experience, enthusiasm and innovative talent. In the abolition of the post of Fifth Sea Lord, it also lost its top-level aviation voice.

At Japanese request, a British mission assisted in the creation of the Imperial Navy's air arm. Both the Japanese and United States navies retained control of

*The Washington Treaty had the unintentional result of promoting a competition among its signatories, with the objective of producing the best 8-inch cruiser on a limiting displacement of 10,000 tons. Although the Japanese designed some particularly fine ships, they cheated on tonnage. This is the* Ashigara, *launched in 1928.*

their aviation, the early British lead being eroded and lost. Aircraft were specified by the navy but supplied by the air force. Because of space restrictions aboard carriers, multi-purpose types proliferated, with consequent lower performances.

Although the RAF in 1923 created the Fleet Air Arm (FAA) as part of its Coastal Area, it was more concerned with developing its own operational strategies and the Navy's particular requirements were not well addressed. The insidious damage sustained by British naval aviation between the wars severely affected its performance in the Second World War.

In the United States, the War and Navy Departments retained separate control over their aviation elements, although this did not prevent the ambitious

Brigadier General William ('Billy') Mitchell promoting strategic bombing as an unaided war winner. Anxious to assess the effect of large bombs on warships, the US Navy ran a series of trials from 1921. Targets, including ex-enemy ships, would be at anchor and, between each bombing run, would be boarded to record damage. Invited to participate, Mitchell had his own agenda; to prove that army bombers could sink battleships. Ignoring all agreed procedures, his fliers easily disposed of the battleship *Ostfriesland* with 2,000-pounders. In the circumstances it proved nothing but gave Mitchell all the publicity he sought.

Successive commanders-in-chief of the German Navy systematically circumvented the restrictions imposed by the Versailles Treaty. Guns, recorded as destroyed, were in storage. Optics and mining equipment were lodged with caretaker firms in the Netherlands and Denmark. Equipment sales generated funds for 'black' projects, among which was a Dutch-based bureau employing the wartime U-boat design team. Working for the German Admiralty through a Berlin front company the bureau gained, on advantageous terms, contracts to design and oversee construction of submarines for Finland, Spain and Turkey. By this means and by conducting protracted trials for their clients, the Germans developed designs later to be put into series production for their own service.

Within five years of the Washington Conference Britain had twelve, and the

*In 1921, the US Navy's planned bombing trials on ex-German warships were hijacked by 'Billy' Mitchell's army air force. Although the results were thus largely invalidated, Mitchell demonstrated very publicly that battleships, here the* Ostfriesland*, could be sunk by heavy bomb alone.*

Japanese ten of the new 8-inch 'heavy' cruisers complete or under construction. What Britain really needed, however, was a good number of 'light' cruisers for trade protection. The United States sought to extend the Washington limitations to smaller classes and called a conference for 1927 in Geneva. Italy and France declined to attend and the conference collapsed when Britain and the United States refused to compromise on their cruiser requirements. Versailles left Germany with a small, primarily pre-1914 fleet fit only for training. Rapacious demands by France and Belgium for war reparations left the German economy in ruins, and fleet renewal was necessarily slow. In 1925 the training cruiser *Emden* marked a new start. She was followed by a short series of light cruisers which, being severely displacement limited, incorporated much of the new technique of welding to save weight.

Versailles allowed German designers 10,000-ton 'armoured ships' with no limit on gun calibre. As ever, the governing parameters were protection, speed and armament, leading to three favoured options for a new ship:

1. 30.5cm (12-inch) guns; 200mm belt armour; 21 knots
2. 30.5cm guns; 280mm belt armour; 18 knots, or
3. 28cm (11-inch) guns, 100mm belt armour; 26 knots.

The third option was selected and commenced in 1928. With six 28cm and eight 15cm (5.9-inch) guns she could outfight any treaty cruiser. Her speed enabled her to decline action with any ship that could outgun her, with the exception of the three remaining British battlecruisers. Diesel propulsion provided an endurance of 21,000 sea miles at 19 knots and the potential for

*A red letter day for the new Kriegsmarine, 19 May 1931 saw the launch of the first heavy unit, the pocket battleship* Deutschland. *Her name was, however, so prestigious that, on outbreak of war, she was renamed* Lützow. *Following an undistinguished active career, she was destroyed by the RAF with 12,000-pound bombs in April 1945.*

*Versailles rules limited German 'armoured ships' to 10,000 tons displacement. As gun calibres were not capped the Germans designed the* Panzerschiff, *popularly called the 'pocket battleship', with six 28cm (11-inch) guns and eight of 15cm (5.9-inch). Diesel propulsion conferred a speed of 26 knots and a large endurance. The* Graf Spee *was 23 per cent over stated displacement.*

commerce raiding was obvious. Three of these armoured ships, popularly dubbed 'pocket battleships', were built by 1934.

Trying once more to regulate smaller classes of warship, the five Washington signatories met in 1930 in London. Japan said that she would not be bound by the Washington 5:5:3 ratio. She already had twelve heavy cruisers built or building, their actual displacements being up to 15 per cent greater than that declared. Settling to about the same aggregate figure of 335,000 tons, the Americans and British finally agreed on cruisers. The former would build eighteen heavies and an unspecified number of lights, the latter fifteen and thirty-five respectively. General agreement was reached on destroyers not exceeding 1,850 tons nor mounting guns of greater than 13cm (5.1-inch) calibre. Only 16 per cent of each destroyer fleet should, however, exceed 1,500 tons. Submarines should not exceed 2,000 tons surfaced nor have guns larger than 130mm. In this class Japan was allowed full parity.

With France and Italy locked in impasse, the conference agreed the following totals, expressed in imperial tons:

| | Great Britain | United States | Japan |
|---|---|---|---|
| Heavy cruisers | 146,800 | 180,000 | 108,400 |
| Light cruisers | 192,200 | 143,500 | 100,450 |
| Destroyers | 150,000 | 150,000 | 105,500 |
| Submarines | 52,700 | 52,700 | 52,700 |

The capital ship building holiday was confirmed until 1936 while Britain, the United States and Japan agreed to scrap four, three and one respectively of their

older capital ships. Japan continued to cheat. One of each of the above could be retained in a demilitarized state but Japan's (the *Hiei*) was maintained in a condition whereby she was later modernized and rearmed. By adopting common barbette diameters for triple 6-inch and twin 8-inch turrets, Japan was able simply to upgrade cruisers from 'light' to 'heavy'. Various types of warship and auxiliary were designed with hulls that could later be converted to aircraft carriers.

Although Britain was not happy at having to accept a figure of fifty cruisers, rather than the seventy required, the conference marked a thawing in Anglo-American naval relations. Between 1922 and 1930, as both argued about superiority, they were outbuilt by the remainder. In crude terms of numbers of warships, built or building: United States 11; Britain 74; Italy 82; France 119; Japan 125.

As Japan expanded and her armies laid China waste, the US Hoover administration responded to deepening financial crisis by slowing naval construction, reducing specifications and discharging half the Naval Academy's graduates.

A further General Disarmament Conference, held at Geneva in 1932, failed through each delegation pursuing its nation's interests. Britain sought to reinstate her claim for seventy cruisers, but impose global tonnage limits. The United States wished to limit numbers of hulls; the British wanted to abolish submarines; the French demanded larger ones. The conference was notable, too, for the return of Germany. Still in a state of political turmoil, her delegation insisted on an 'equality of rights'.

In Italy, Mussolini had removed the last powers from the monarchy. Germany was intent on rearming. The League of Nations was an ineffective deterrent and Geneva a dead letter. Both Britain and the United States began to look at the state of their forces.

*Of 6 million cubic feet capacity, the US Navy's dirigible* Akron *was commissioned in October 1931. She was wrecked during a storm in April 1933, when seventy-three were killed, including the Chief of the Bureau of Aeronautics, Rear Admiral W. A. Moffett, a pioneer of American naval aviation. The tender is the modified oiler* Patoka *(AV.6).*

The British government's search for economies had resulted in service pay cuts, the inequality of which resulted in the Invergordon Mutiny. The 1931 building programme had been abandoned. Although the iniquitous Ten-Year Rule was quietly dropped, Britain began a building programme of cruisers with six or eight 6-inch guns where foreign equivalents were mounting up to fifteen. Franklin D. Roosevelt, on taking over in 1932, actually sought to reduce the size of the active American fleet, until Congress approved the National Industrial Recovery Act. This allowed funds to be devoted to new construction in the guise of aid to the industry.

Adolf Hitler was democratically appointed Chancellor of Germany in January 1933. With the death of Hindenburg in August 1934, he assumed the presidency and through it the title of Supreme Commander of the Wehrmacht. Germany pulled out of the General Disarmament Conference and joined Japan in leaving also the League of Nations. Japan announced that she considered herself no longer bound by the 1930 London agreement. With the German Navy already breaching Versailles by embarking on a three-stage 're-organization plan', Britain and France recognized realities and, early in 1935, signalled their willingness to relax its conditions. Hitler's response was illegally to reintroduce conscription.

Naval rearmament was already a reality. France, alarmed by the 'pocket battleships', replaced over-age tonnage with the two Dunkerques. Commenced in 1932, these 30-knotters were of 26,500 tons and mounted eight 33cm (13-inch) guns. Mussolini responded in 1934 by commencing the two 35,000-ton (actually over 41,000-ton) Vittorio Venetos, also of 30 knots but carrying nine 38cm (15-inch) weapons; and with an intended second trio of 'pocket battleships' effectively trumped by the French, the Germans secretly began work in 1935 on the two 31,850-ton Scharnhorsts.

Supporting both economy and Navy, President Roosevelt engineered the Vinson-Trammell Act in 1934. The United States had consistently underbuilt and the act provided both for replacement and expansion to legal limits. Involving about one hundred ships, it was, however, widely interpreted as rearming against Japan.

Her own fleet run down and largely outdated and facing growing threats in the Far East and Mediterranean, Britain now sought to reach a naval accommodation with Germany. In a bilateral agreement, indicative of Britain's weak position, Germany would be 'permitted' to build to 35 per cent of the Royal Navy's tonnage in each category. It was an open secret that Germany was again building U-boats, but in view of recent history it was nothing short of pusillanimity to exempt submarines from it. Not only was 45 per cent agreed but also 100 per cent if 'in Germany's opinion', it was deemed necessary. In return, both parties agreed the so-called 'London Protocol', that submarines should be bound by international law and not sink merchant ships without warning.

Believing that even 35 per cent would tax German resources to the limit, the British were shocked when the Germans tabled their intention to build, by 1942, six capital ships, 44,000 tons of carriers, eighteen cruisers, 37,500 tons of destroyers and 17,500 tons of submarines.

France signed a worthless treaty of mutual assistance with the Soviet Union and announced her intention to match Mussolini's two 35,000-tonners with her own. These were commenced in 1935–6 as the *Richelieu* and *Jean Bart*.

Mussolini's campaign in Abyssinia in 1935 drew heavy condemnation from the League of Nations but only ineffectual sanctions. Unable to risk a shooting war, Britain embarked on a policy of non-alienation which served only to earn the Italian dictator's contempt. Abyssinia was duly annexed in 1936 and an emboldened Hitler remilitarized the Rhineland. Four months later, the

*No fleet, including the Royal Navy, ever had enough destroyers which, consequently, frequently worked in mixed groups. Here, the older-style destroyer* Fury *leads three of the new and more heavily-gunned vessels, two Tribals and a J-type. The 20mm Oerlikons in the* Fury's *bridge wings, and lack of mainmasts, show this to be a wartime picture.*

Spanish Civil War erupted, with both Germany and Italy supporting the fascist insurrection.

Seeing Europe squandering the peace that they felt that they had gifted, the Americans began to move into isolationism. Although Congress passed the first Neutrality Act in August 1935, it still sent a delegation to the scheduled London Disarmament Conference in December. Portents were not good, with the Italians refusing to accept any new strictures. The Japanese walked out, their government already making preparation in unprecedented secrecy for constructing the monster Yamato-class battleships, 65,000-tonners with guns exceeding 18-inch calibre.

In such an atmosphere it appears in retrospect strange that the remaining powers should seek to limit themselves further. Britain's proposal for future capital ships of only 25,000 tons and 12-inch guns was totally unrealistic, and 35,000 with 14-inch was adopted. This carried the important proviso that Italy and Japan also had to agree it by 1 April 1937, failing which 16-inch weapons would be acceptable.

Britain's rearmament had been so scandalously delayed that it was not possible to await the deadline and the new King George V-class battleships were thus armed with 14-inch guns. More remote from the crisis, the Americans wisely held out for 16-inch.

The new *Ark Royal* demonstrated that an adequate carrier could be built on only 23,000 tons, which figure was adopted. The threat from bombing, however, was soon better appreciated and the addition of horizontal protection in succeeding ships limited to the same displacement greatly reduced aircraft capacity.

Cruisers were now limited to only 8,000 tons apiece but not in numbers. Having built the expensive 9,400-ton Towns in response to large foreign 6-inch cruisers, the Admiralty now tried to pack the same offensive power into the 8,000-ton Colonies, with cramped results.

Following the Anglo-German agreement, Admiral Raeder, as commander-in-chief, oversaw the conception of what was to be a balanced fleet by 1946–8, only to be told by his Führer that war with the British Empire was possible after 1938. The battleships *Bismarck* and *Tirpitz*, laid down in 1936, exceeded their official displacement by over 10,000 tons and went on to prove that in action cheating not only paid off but paid off handsomely.

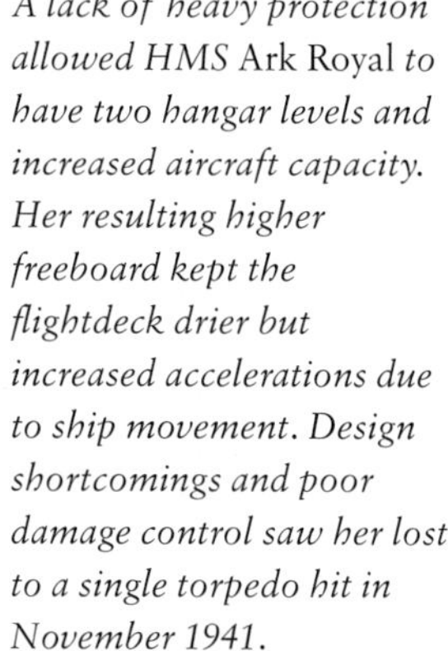

*A lack of heavy protection allowed HMS* Ark Royal *to have two hangar levels and increased aircraft capacity. Her resulting higher freeboard kept the flightdeck drier but increased accelerations due to ship movement. Design shortcomings and poor damage control saw her lost to a single torpedo hit in November 1941.*

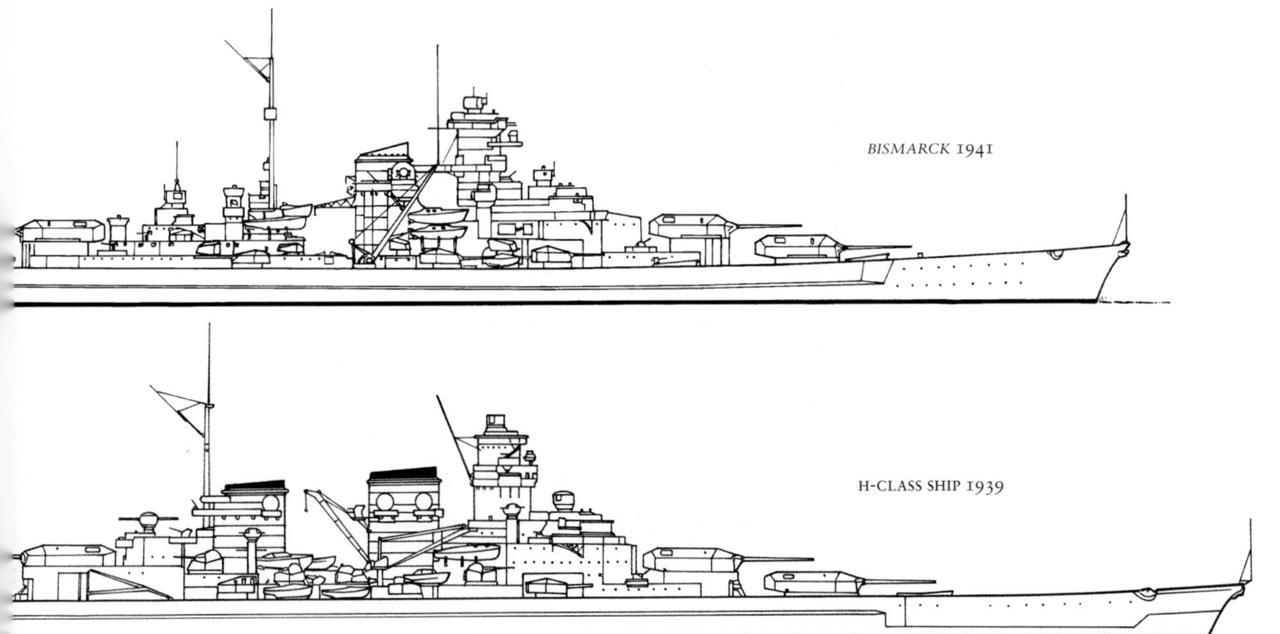


**Ships of the Z-plan**

*Admiral Raeder's ambitious Z-plan included the two 46,000-ton Bismarcks (upper profile) as 'smaller battleships'. They were to be followed by six 56,000-ton H-class battleships (lower profile) with diesel propulsion and 40.6cm (16-inch) guns. Two were actually laid down late in 1939 but were subsequently discontinued and dismantled on the ways.*

Short-circuited by Hitler's chaotic policies, Raeder's so-called 'Z-plan' would have created a formidable fleet, but the procedure would certainly have elicited massive response abroad. As it was, Germany annexed Bohemia and Moravia in March 1939 and, in the following month, renounced the London agreement. Hostilities were now only a matter of time.

In September 1939, the effective strength of the combatant fleets were as follows:

| | British Empire | France | Germany | Italy |
|---|---|---|---|---|
| Capital ships | 15 | 7 | 2 | 4 |
| Aircraft carriers | 6 | 1 | – | – |
| Pocket battleships | – | – | 3 | – |
| Heavy cruisers | 15 | 7 | 2 | 7 |
| Light cruisers | 49 | 12 | 6 | 15 |
| Destroyers/TBs | 183 | 72 | 34 | 133 |
| Submarines | 57 | 78 | 57 | 102 |

For comparison, the effective strengths of the fleets of the United States and Japan in December 1941 were:

| | United States | Japan |
|---|---|---|
| Capital ships | 17 | 10 |
| Aircraft carriers | 8 | 10 |
| Heavy cruisers | 18 | 18 |
| Light cruisers | 19 | 20 |
| Destroyers | 165 | 102 |
| Submarines | 106 | 64 |

CHAPTER FOUR

# Second World War 1939–45

*Epitomizing the 'new order' in the US Navy, carriers lead a line of battleships and cruisers. Nearest the camera is a CVL, converted from a cruiser hull and with funnels characteristically cranked out to starboard. Next in line is an Essex-class CV. The large aircraft 'deck-parks' were typical of American ships.*

# SECOND WORLD WAR

## THE WAR AGAINST COMMERCE

As war approached in 1939, the recent experience of the First World War suggested that, once again, British commercial shipping would be especially targeted. The industry was not in good shape, its health undermined during the 1930s by the collapse of the coal trade, increasing foreign protectionism and a major recession. Operating companies had ceased to trade or had diversified; so too had shipbuilders and component manufacturers. Whereas the United Kingdom in 1914 had owned nearly 19 million grt of shipping, representing about 44 per cent of the world total, this had declined by 1937 to 17.5 million and 28 per

*September 1940. London's East End and docks blaze following the Luftwaffe's opening daylight raid. Sustained bombing of ports was an element in the enemy's overall strategy to destroy Britain's economy. Levelling the adjacent areas, where the associated workforce lived, was of questionable legality but practised by both sides.*

cent respectively. Yards that had produced over 2 million grt annually before 1914 now built less than half that total.

During hostilities, shipping needs not only to fulfil its conventional role in supporting the population but also to transport huge quantities of materials necessary to prosecute a major war, while supplying tonnage for military needs. Particularly in the last role ships could 'disappear' for months as they waited for discharge or acted as floating warehouses. Hire of neutral tonnage was expensive and could not be relied upon.

The enemy's ability to bomb ports had added a new uncertainty. Ports tended to specialize and could not necessarily assume sudden responsibility for unusual quantities of unfamiliar cargo. Although there was an obvious requirement for a powerful central body to control shipping, ports and associated areas, it was not until May 1941 that the Ministry of War Transport was created. Admiralty planning assumed that commerce would be assaulted by four main elements, namely surface raiders, submarines, aircraft and mines. In this it was correct, but was fortunate in that Germany herself was ill-prepared.

In November 1936 Germany had also been a signatory to the London Protocol, denouncing submarine attack on merchant shipping and when Hitler's chaotic policies precipitated war in 1939, the navy was deficient in all classes of warship. None the less, Operational Order No. 1 of the High Command of the Wehrmacht, dated 31 August 1939, defined the navy's primary task as 'the waging of war on enemy commerce, concentrating largely against Britain'. For this, Commodore Karl Dönitz, Head of U-boats, had only fifty-seven of the three hundred boats that he had stipulated. Many were too small for ocean

*Most of a U-boat's time was spent surfaced – in transit, searching or re-charging. The boat's wake here tells of constant rudder changes to hold course in an uncomfortable quartering sea. Visible are a 3.7cm deck gun and a twin 20mm, suggesting that the boat is a Type IXD, the picture dating from 1944 or later.*

work and initially only nine could be expected in their operational areas at any one time. Dönitz argued successfully that he could not produce decisive results unless submarine construction enjoyed priority at the expense of other warships.

Until the U-boat arm was up to strength, surface raiders would have a greater significance. In the previous war, regular warship raiders had tended to be light cruisers, which enjoyed a brief existence living on their wits. The new generation would be heavy cruisers, the so-called 'pocket battleships' and capital ships. Inherently more robust and reliable, these would be supported by pre-positioned supply ships.

The adoption of convoys had proved Britain's salvation twenty years before but, in the new era of air attack, the principle was again hotly debated. The Naval Staff held it to be still valid and argued that properly armed escorts would reduce both the air and submarine threat to 'manageable proportions'. They thought also, in light of his earlier experience, that the enemy would not risk alienating neutral opinion by unrestricted warfare. The Air Staff considered that to group ships in convoy would 'positively invite' mass air attack. This theory paralleled earlier arguments but in practice convoys remained difficult to find while the Germans, at least initially, possessed few specialist maritime strike aircraft. Moreover, all too few of the Admiralty's 'properly armed' escorts were available. With respect to neutral opinion and international law the enemy, while observing some initial niceties, stated that 'it ... goes without saying that effective ... fighting methods will never fail to be employed merely because some international regulations ... are opposed to them'.

The defensive arming of merchantmen had earlier greatly increased their chance of survival when attacked by a surfaced submarine. A huge effort was,

*A situation dreaded by the anti-convoy lobby. The route to northern Russia was flanked by Luftwaffe bases in Norway and, in September 1942, convoy PQ.18 was attacked by about forty torpedo aircraft which approached in line abreast 'like a huge flight of nightmare locusts'. Only one ship survived from the two starboard wing columns – eight ships in exchange for five aircraft.*

therefore, made to arm some three thousand British deep-sea ships and about fifteen hundred coasters, and to train personnel in gunnery.

The English south and east coasts defined inshore routes that teemed with shipping, not only the vital coasters and colliers but also deep-sea vessels in transit between convoy assembly and dispersal points and their ports of destination. Frequent and regular convoys ran between the Thames Estuary and the Firth of Forth. The east coast channels, constricted by offshore shoals, caused convoys to become dangerously attenuated and difficult for the escorts to protect adequately. Although Fighter Command airfields in their sector could provide cover, it was very difficult to prevent hit-and-run attacks by single or small groups of aircraft. Torpedo attacks by enemy S-boats became a major nuisance with the enemy's occupation of Dutch and Channel ports in 1940.

*At the height of the magnetic mine campaign in 1940, shallow British east coast channels were studded with forlorn, half-submerged wrecks. The Union Castle liner* Dunbar Castle *was an early casualty, being sunk off the North Foreland on 9 January 1940.*

Short distances enabled the enemy to make nocturnal minelaying forays by destroyers, S-boats and aircraft, with further contributions by submarine. Some mines were moored, others were ground-laid influence types. Careless laying of the latter varieties permitted specimens to be recovered and for antidotes to be produced, but the melancholy spectacle of masts and funnels protruding from shallow waters was all too common. Mines were to cause 6.5 per cent of Allied mercantile losses by tonnage overall, while causing immense disruption and the expenditure of major resources in their clearance.

Initial lack of escorts saw ocean convoys covered only to the meridians of Iceland and Newfoundland, or the latitude of the Morbihan. Beyond, convoys proceeded in unescorted, gradually dispersing groups. This was the heyday of the enemy's surface raiders. As in the earlier war, the initial emphasis was towards regular warships, with heavily armed auxiliary cruisers later assuming the role.

The new-generation regular warship raiders had the speed and firepower to enable them to dispose of the escort before savaging the convoy. In this they enjoyed some success, although the strategy exposed them to being themselves hunted down. The *Admiral Graf Spee, Bismarck* and *Scharnhorst* were all thus expended, representing together perhaps 40 per cent of Germany's small force of capital ships. Due to their economical diesel propulsion the 'pocket battleships' proved superior to more conventional ships, which relied more heavily on the network of supply ships, specifically targeted by British cruisers.

Early Atlantic convoys, often of considerable size, enjoyed pitifully inadequate escort. The thirty-seven ship HX.84, for instance, eastbound from Halifax NS, was covered by the single armed merchant cruiser (AMC) *Jervis Bay* when it encountered the pocket battleship *Admiral Scheer* on 5 November 1940.

*Operating in remote waters and cut off from proper dockyard facilities, raiders often had short working lives. Once damaged at the battle of the River Plate, the pocket battleship* Admiral Graf Spee *had little prospect of reaching Germany, 6,000 miles distant, and was blown up by her crew in December 1939.*

Selling her life dearly, the armed liner gained sufficient time for her convoy to scatter, limiting losses to six ships.

The Admiralty's response to these formidable raiders was to accompany ocean convoys where possible with old battleships or cruisers. Far from repair facilities, a raider dare not incur damage and almost invariably refrained from attack. An aggressive light escort could also be a deterrent, as instanced by that of convoy JW.51B. Fourteen ships bound for North Russia were intercepted off North Cape on 31 December 1942 by the pocket battleship *Lützow*, heavy cruiser *Admiral Hipper* and six destroyers. The fighting escort comprising six smaller destroyers held off the enemy in appalling weather until the arrival of two light cruisers caused the attackers to withdraw. No merchant ships were lost.

In distant waters beyond the regular convoy network, there were still many independently routed ships. It was on these that the powerfully armed, but innocently disguised, auxiliary cruisers preyed. Nine of these made successful and highly disruptive cruises, one of their tactics being to lay small clutches of mines at shipping focal points. Surface raiders are credited with the destruction of 237 merchantmen, aggregating 1.33 million grt, or about 6.1 per cent of total tonnage lost.

Aircraft accounted for as many losses as raiders and mine warfare combined. Many ships were safely convoyed only to be destroyed in ports, the bombing of which was integral to the disruption of the British commerical network. Warehouses could contain huge quantities of high-value merchandise, and the likes of London and Leith, Hull and Swansea were regularly and profitably targeted.

Bigger ships were usually fast and tended to be independently routed and the

*The British heavy cruiser* Suffolk *in the grip of a northern winter. To smaller ships overloaded with extra crew, equipment and armament, and merchantmen heavily laden with bulk deck cargo, ice accumulation was a real menace that slowly reduced stability range.*

largest casualty was the 42,350-ton Canadian Pacific liner *Empress of Britain*, bombed in the Western Approaches in October 1942. Another particularly grievous loss was that of the 16,250-ton Cunarder *Lancastria,* bombed and sunk off St Nazaire in June 1940. Evacuating troops from France, she went down with over three thousand personnel.

Long-range maritime aircraft, particularly the FW200 Kondor, were an important element in Dönitz's campaign although, fortunately for Britain, the Luftwaffe was not very co-operative in their availability. Covering large areas of ocean, their task was to find and orbit convoys, homing-in attacking submarines and disposing of stragglers on opportunity.

Submarines accounted for about 68 per cent of all tonnage destroyed. Dönitz, himself an ex-submariner, fully comprehended that Britain could be defeated through the destruction of her merchant fleet and he pursued this objective remorselessly. During the 1930s he developed the theory of 'wolf-pack' tactics to defeat the convoy system. Operating in groups, U-boats would proceed on a line of search. When one of these, or perhaps an aircraft, sighted a convoy its duty was to maintain contact at all costs, homing-in the remainder. Only when the whole group was in contact would a simultaneous attack be launched, overwhelming the efforts of the escort. It was to dispose of the 'snooping' Kondor

*Krupp's Germaniawerft facility at Kiel had a total of eight slips for U-boat construction. As with other facilities, it suffered little direct damage by bombing before April 1945, disruption to production being caused indirectly by damage to railways and inland waterways.*

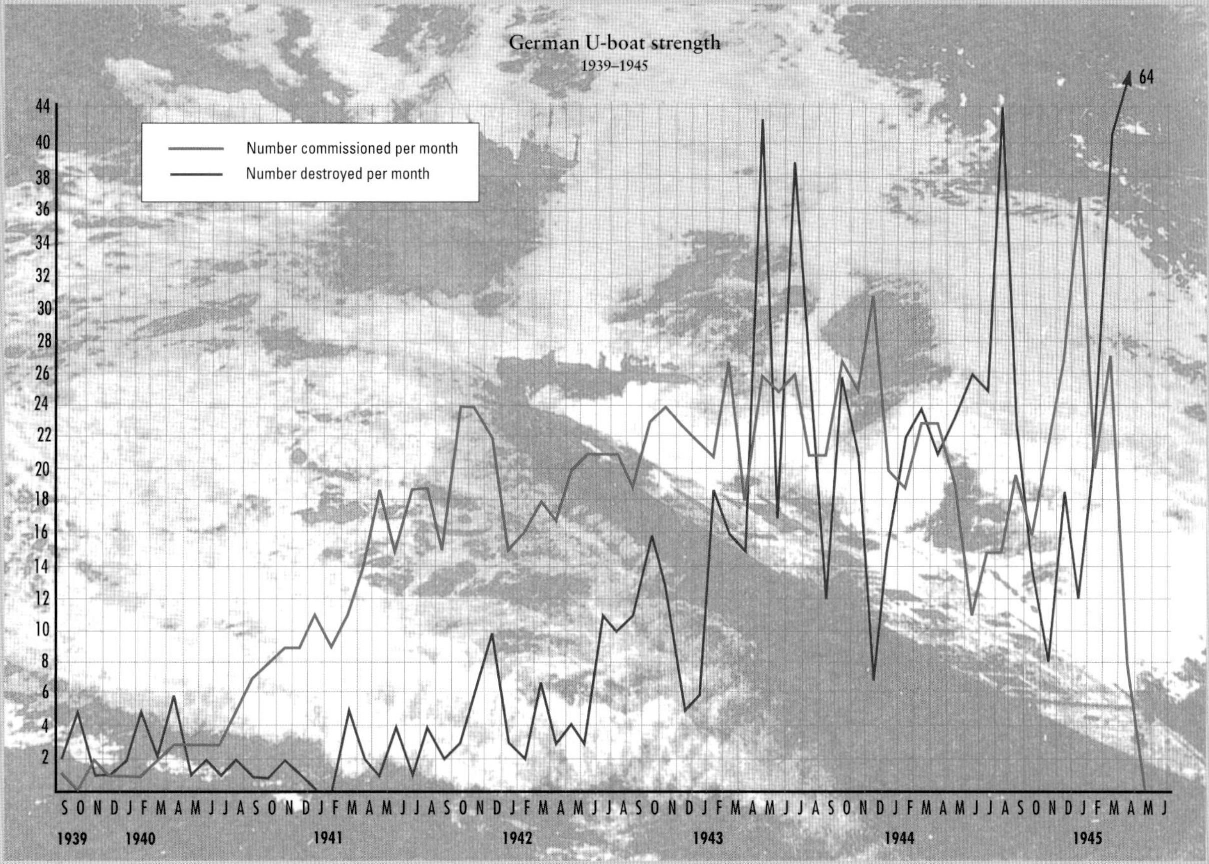

**German U-boat strength**
1939–1945

Number commissioned per month
Number destroyed per month

*Comparison of this chart with that on page 68 shows a not dissimilar pattern. Although in both wars the rate of sinkings of U-boats increased with time, so did the rate of construction which comfortably outstripped it. The essential parameter was that U-boat effectiveness diminished with time.*

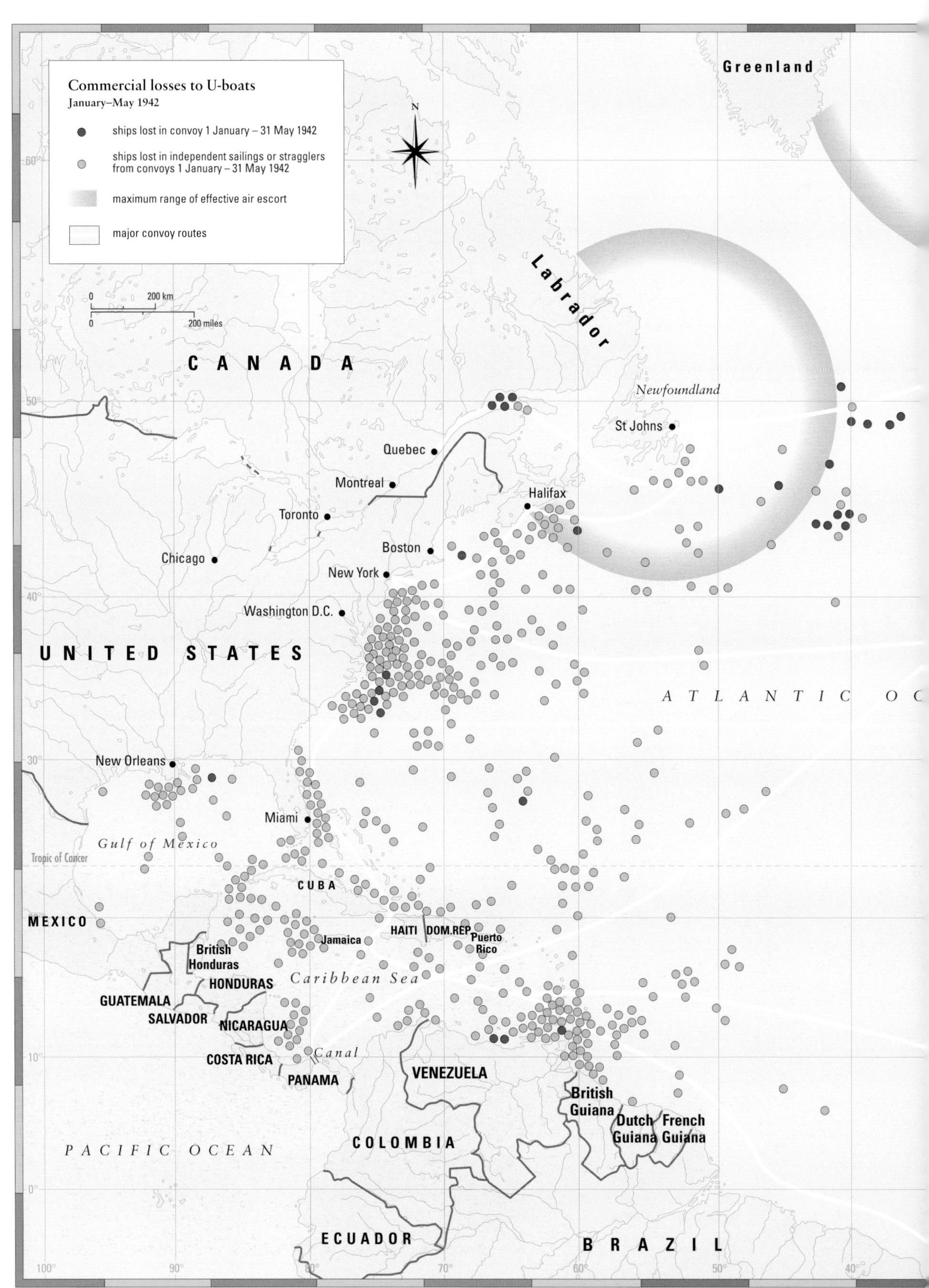
Commercial losses to U-boats
January–May 1942
ships lost in convoy 1 January – 31 May 1942
ships lost in independent sailings or stragglers from convoys 1 January – 31 May 1942
maximum range of effective air escort
major convoy routes
0 200 km
0 200 miles
N
Greenland
Labrador
CANADA
Newfoundland
St Johns
Quebec
Montreal
Toronto
Halifax
Chicago
Boston
New York
Washington D.C.
UNITED STATES
ATLANTIC OC
New Orleans
Miami
Gulf of Mexico
Tropic of Cancer
CUBA
MEXICO
HAITI
DOM.REP.
Puerto Rico
Jamaica
British Honduras
HONDURAS
Caribbean Sea
GUATEMALA
SALVADOR
NICARAGUA
COSTA RICA
Canal
PANAMA
VENEZUELA
British Guiana
Dutch Guiana
French Guiana
PACIFIC OCEAN
COLOMBIA
ECUADOR
BRAZIL
60°
50°
40°
30°
10°
0°
100°
90°
80°
70°
60°
50°
40°

Glasgow
UNITED KINGDOM
IRELAND
Liverpool
NETH.
London
Southampton
BEL.
Brest
Lorient
St Nazaire
FRANCE
PORTUGAL
SPAIN
Azores
Gibraltar
N
Madeira
Casablanca
Morocco
Algeria
Canary Islands
Rio de Oro
French West Africa
Cape Verde Islands
Dakar
Gambia
Port. Guinea
Freetown
Sierra Leone
Liberia
Gold Coast
Takoradi
20°
10°
0°

COMMERCIAL LOSSES TO U-BOATS JANUARY–MAY 1942

*The price of unpreparedness. Despite Europe having been at war for over two years, the United States had taken virtually no precautions in their own waters. For the first half of 1942 a small number of U-boats was thus able to extract a disproportionately high price. Sinkings are concentrated around Nova Scotia and New York down to the Chesapeake (many of the ships already convoyed across the Atlantic), around the Gulf ports and Venezuela's Lake Maracaibo, and the approaches to the Panama canal. Note the activity of one boat inside the St Lawrence estuary.*

*Peas from a pod. A line of Liberty ships fitting out at one of the specialist American facilities. In crude terms the key to defeating Dönitz's submarine campaign lay in building ships faster than they could be sunk. Of Liberties alone, over 2,700 were built, representing nearly 19.5 million grt.*

*Oil was one of the most valuable of war materials and loaded tankers were prized targets. Gutted and broken, this tanker is typical in being still very resistant to sinking, due to her many tanks forming an efficient system of subdivision.*

that the escort carrier evolved. Overrating (as indeed did the British) the efficiency of Asdic (later termed Sonar), Dönitz ordered his boats to attack on the surface by night. This tactic was very successful until the escorts were fitted with radar. The occupation of France and Norway gave an enormous boost to Dönitz's efforts, enabling him to base U-boats much closer to their areas of operation.

U-boats had no opportunity to economize on torpedoes by using deck guns against ships in convoy. As the average boat carried only fourteen torpedoes, which often needed to be expended in salvoes, they could be kept on patrol only through resupply by the specially designed Mark XIV submarines. These, too, were especially targeted by Allied forces.

Damaged merchantmen awaiting repair soon began to choke yards that could otherwise have produced new tonnage. With losses exceeding replacements it was vital to acquire more ships. Considerable numbers of over-age American vessels had been laid up and were available for purchase but the British were slow to bid. Most were snapped up by neutral owners for later charter at high rates.

During the First World War, British and American yards had built standard ships, simplified for speedy construction. In September 1940 a British mission went to the United States to arrange a new programme. The specification that they took was that of a workhorse capable of transporting 10,000 deadweight tons at a modest 11 knots. A prototype, the *Empire Liberty*, was already being built in the United Kingdom. Although they considered the design too basic, the Americans took it on, modified it to suit their building methods and, as the Liberty ship, it went to 2,710 units. Specialist yards, some in Canada, produced other standards – Victory, T2 tankers, Oceans, Forts, Parks and others. There came the point in 1943 where this avalanche of new construction exceeded that being destroyed. From that moment, Dönitz's attritional campaign was defeated.



20-Ship Convoy

This, however, is to anticipate for, early in 1942, the United States, catapulted into the conflict, suddenly faced a U-boat onslaught of her own. Dönitz, equally surprised by the Japanese action, could divert only a few boats across the Atlantic, but these unleashed veritable slaughter. The Americans observed initially few or no precautions; there were few escorts, few patrols, no convoys. Between January and mid-August 1942 a force, rarely exceeding a dozen U-boats, recorded 285 attacks, mostly fatal, in American and Canadian waters. Many were vital tankers, others had already been safely convoyed across the Atlantic. This 'Happy Time' ended as defences became organized and forced the U-boats eastward and southward. Just seven of their number had been sunk.

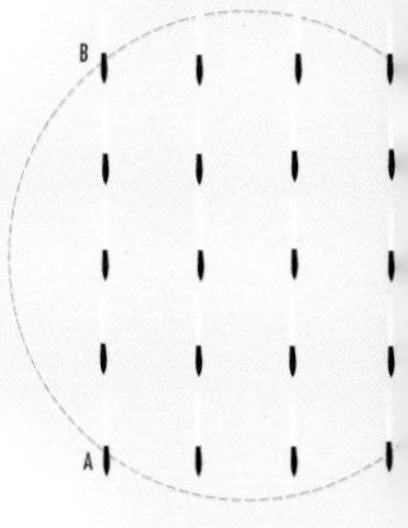

In the early stages, inexperienced and inadequate escorts were occasionally overwhelmed by Dönitz's tactics, and their convoys underwent a harrowing

CONVOY FORMATIONS

*The original arguments governing the number of escorts necessary were based on the false premise that it was directly proportional to the number of ships in convoy. Operational analysis showed that it should be based on that proportion of the convoy's perimeter that a single escort could efficiently cover. Extending this argument to the diagrams it can be shown by measurement that, if the diameter of the circle enclosing the 20-ship convoy is called unity, then that around the 40-ship convoy will be of diameter 1.45 and that around the 60-ship convoy 1.85. As the length of the perimeter of the circle is directly proportional to its diameter, it follows that doubling the size of a convoy will require less than half as many escorts again, while tripling it will still require fewer than twice as many. In practice, convoys were wider and shallower in plan, but the same principle holds.*

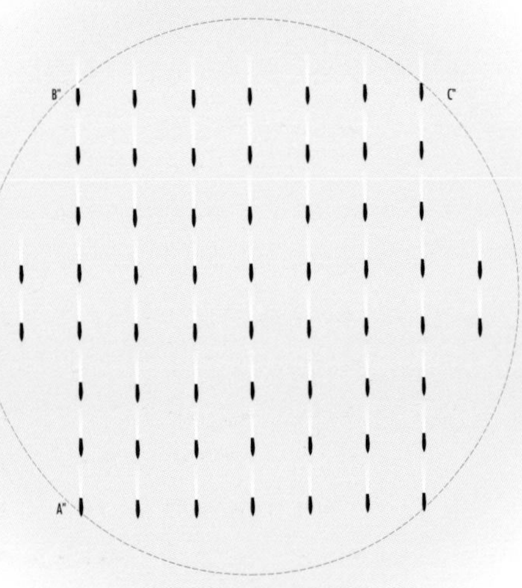

60-Ship Convoy

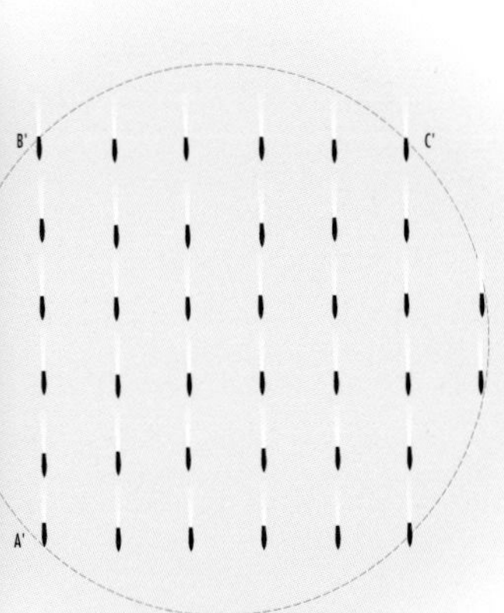

40-Ship Convoy

time. Powerful images of blazing tankers and pitiful groups of frozen, oil-soaked survivors tend to conceal the fact, however, that the huge majority of convoyed ships arrived safely. As the early U-boat 'ace' commanders were eliminated they were replaced by others less skilful. Facing larger and better defences, their sinkings per patrol decreased, offset by the greater number of operational boats.

The climax came suddenly. In March 1943 the adjacent Atlantic convoys SC.122 and HX.229 were faced by up to 40 U-boats in several groups. For sixteen days the escorts countered the attacks but succeeded in sinking only one U-boat in exchange for 21 merchantmen of 141,000 grt. Then, during May, no fewer than 41 submarines were sunk. Five were lost for no result when the 38-ship SC.130 was assaulted by four hunting groups.

Figures so vast inevitably vary, but reliable statistics indicate that 5,150 Allied merchant ships were lost to enemy action during the Second World War, a total of over 21.5 million grt. This wanton destruction claimed the lives of nearly 27,000 British seamen alone.

The experience was not repeated in the Pacific. From the western seaboard the lines of communication to the areas of Nimitz's and MacArthur's campaigns were very long, and vulnerable to submarine attack. Rigid Japanese doctrine, however, prescribed that laurels were to be won only in sinking warships. Destroying merchantmen was virtually an unworthy action. It was fortunate that the Japanese lacked a Dönitz.

*Compared with the equivalent chart for the First World War (see page 71) this shows that mercantile sinkings were more severe and from an earlier point in the war. One reason for the higher tonnages was that individual ships had on average about doubled in size.*

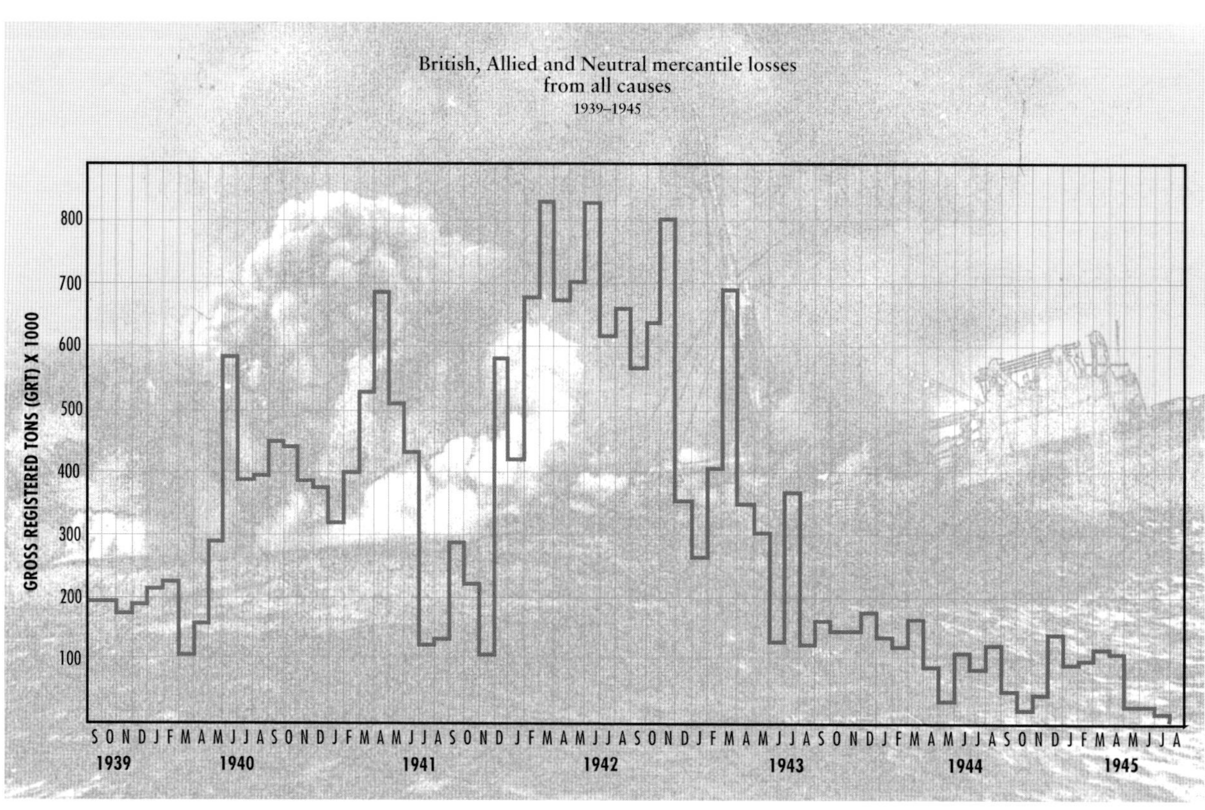

*The highly experienced depth charge team of HMS* Starling *in action. The sloop was commanded by Captain F. J. Walker, who pioneered the 'creeping' attack whereby one sloop 'fixed' a submerged target, guiding an unsuspected second sloop to attack. The* Starling *was here zeroed-in by the* Wild Goose.

## THE WAR AGAINST THE U-BOAT

Before the adoption of convoy in the First World War, anti-submarine (AS) vessels wasted much of their time in fruitless hunting. Convoys not only made merchantmen more difficult to find and to attack but also obliged submarines to approach the escorts. With the German Navy so far below its planned strength in the late 1930s, another U-boat-led onslaught against the British mercantile marine could be confidently predicted, and the Admiralty initiated a basic convoy system at the outbreak of hostilities. Escorts and aircraft to protect the convoys, however, were deficient in terms of both numbers and quality.

Successive classes of sloop had produced the fine but expensive Black Swans. Their excellent qualities saw them employed in hunting groups rather than as escorts. Light destroyers of the Hunt classes likewise had powerful armaments that saw them used mainly in the Mediterranean and on the English east coast. For the Atlantic, the scene of the major struggle against the U-boat, the ring was held largely by a mix of elderly fleet destroyers and corvettes. Destroyers were manifestly unsuitable for convoy duty. They were very wet, recorded high fuel consumption at continuous low speed, and had space and weight margins for too few depth charges.

Corvettes, the famous Flowers, were designed originally to escort coastal convoys. Costing a quarter that of a Black Swan or a Hunt, and requiring just one-sixth of the crew, a Flower was small enough to be built in scores of little-known yards around the United Kingdom and Canada. Magnificently seaworthy, yet desperately uncomfortable in the open ocean, Flowers were also far too slow. They were, however, what could most quickly be made available. Design of a larger type of escort, for which the generic term 'frigate' was revived, was soon put in hand, but it would be the spring of 1942 before the first of the new 'Rivers', was commissioned.

Most escorts had been fitted with Asdic, for which unrealistically high expectations can only have resulted from insufficient pre-war trials testing. It was indispensable, though swamped by water noise at high speed or in a seaway, and almost useless in the vicinity of a convoy with its high levels of radiated noise. Early Asdics had a fixed angle of declination so that, when running in for an attack, an escort lost contact with a submerged target at about one thousand

*Small ship in a large ocean. The Flower-class corvettes were distantly related to pre-war whale catchers. Designed originally to escort coastal convoys, they spent their lives in the deep ocean. Although superb sea boats, their motion was such as to reduce crew effectiveness through sheer fatigue.*

yards. As depth charges were released aft from rails and from the quarters by throwers, and at a point over the target, there was significant 'dead time' from the moment contact had been lost. This was not helped by the time that a drum-shaped depth charge took to sink to even the 600-foot limit of earlier U-boats. Patterns of four charges were quickly increased to ten or fourteen, but an astute submarine commander had time to get beyond their lethal range.

What was required was an ahead-throwing weapon that could reach a target while its position was still firmly defined by the Asdic. The answer was the spigot mortar, known as 'Hedgehog', which went operational at the end of 1941.

The Coastal Command of the RAF existed to service the particular

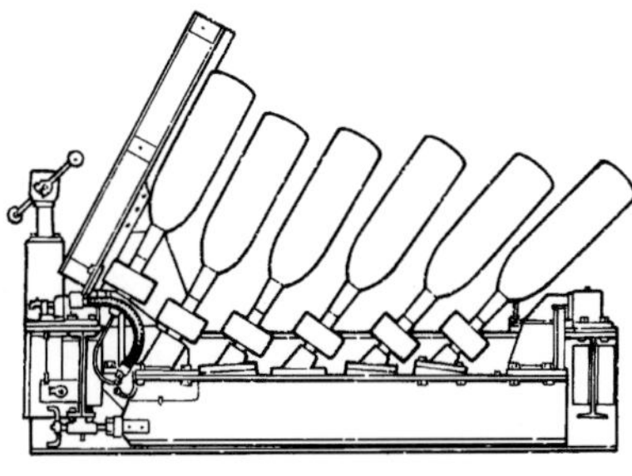

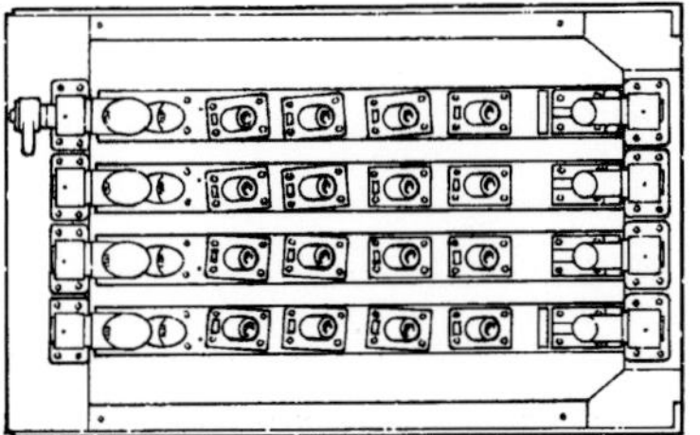

HEDGEHOG THROWER

HEDGEHOG SPIGOT MORTAR

*Ahead-firing weapons allowed an escort to attack a submerged target while it was still firmly fixed by the Asdic (Sonar). The first effective type was the Hedgehog spigot mortar, here shown aboard an American ship (below) and in diagram (left and right). The frame held twenty-four contact-fused projectiles, mounted in groups of four and angled so as to spread the pattern in ellipse of 140 x 120 feet. To reduce the stress on the ship's deck, the salvo was ripple-fired in rapid sequence.*

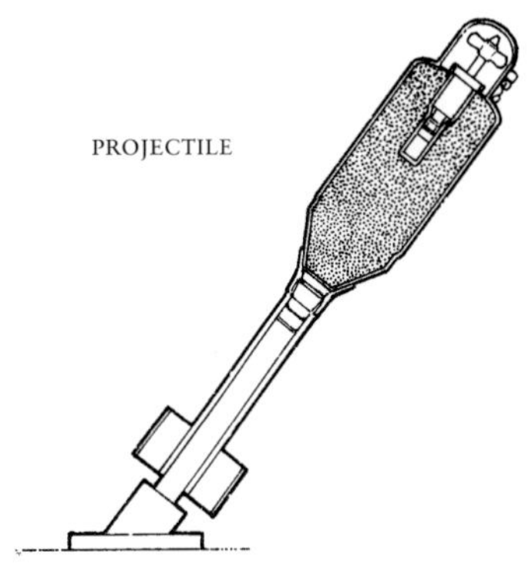

PROJECTILE

requirements of the navy yet, and not entirely the fault of the RAF, pilots had received no specific training in AS operations. Nor for the most part did they fly appropriate aircraft. In September 1939 there were just two squadrons equipped with the new and robust Sunderland flying boat, with a third working-up with the American-designed Hudson.

Standard AS bombs were found to explode on contact, endangering the dropping aircraft, so 450-pound naval depth charges were fitted with discarding aerodynamic fairings. As most contacts were on the surface, new ultra-shallow hydrostatic fuses had to be developed.

Admiral Dönitz's control over his widely scattered U-boats depended upon considerable two-way radio traffic. As in the earlier war, British intelligence capitalized on this by ringing the North Atlantic with direction-finding (DF) stations, which could plot the positions of transmitting submarines with surprising accuracy. The messages themselves were enciphered in what was known as Naval Enigma. Early French, Polish and British groundwork, however, enabled the last-named to read much of what the enemy considered unreadable. From April 1940 the Royal Navy assisted in this highly secret enterprise by a series of captures of encoding machines and codebooks, mainly from mortally damaged U-boats or specifically targeted weather reporting ships. Although occasionally suspecting it, Dönitz never learned for certain that Naval Enigma had been compromised.

By collecting and correlating every scrap of intelligence the British director of the Atlantic battle, Admiral Sir Max Horton, could maintain a reasonably accurate and continuously updated plot of U-boat dispositions. Many losses were thus avoided by routing convoys evasively.

High frequency direction finding ('Huff-Duff') was used to deadly effect at

tactical level. French, American and British research led to the production of a shipboard unit, whose birdcage antenna at the masthead became a familiar sight from 1942. It enabled escorts to pinpoint and suppress any U-boat transmitting in the vicinity of a convoy.

With its poor submerged performance, a U-boat operated on the surface whenever possible. The sudden appearance of any aircraft would necessitate an urgent dive. By early 1940 crude prototype radars had been sufficiently refined to allow to be put into production the first airborne set, known as the ASV Mark II (i.e. Air to Surface Vessel, as opposed to Air to Air). Hard on its heels came the important development of the cavity magnetron, permitting the transmission of high powers at high frequencies. Small rotating antennae were now possible.

As U-boats surfaced at night to refresh and recharge, radar was particularly valuable. Like Asdic, however, it unavoidably blanked-out at close range, with the aircraft at the point of attack. The solution to this was the Leigh Light, a standard naval searchlight in a trainable mounting that fitted into an aircraft's ventral turret ring.

*Dönitz pioneered the tactic of U-boats attacking on the surface by night. Relying on their small silhouette and much higher speed, bold U-boat commanders could penetrate a convoy and fan a full salvo from bow and stern torpedoe tubes before escaping in the ensuing confusion.*

A huge effort by the British and Canadian navies saw escort coverage gradually extended to the whole Atlantic crossing, corvettes taking fuel and replacement depth charges from tankers. U-boat commanders, accustomed to attacking on the surface by night, were now frustrated by escorts fitted with radar, powerful illuminants and reliable inter-ship communications.

Air cover was essential to keeping submarines submerged, where they could do limited harm. Twin-engined Wellingtons and Whitleys had been transferred from Bomber Command but could not operate beyond 500 miles. Early American-built Catalinas could work out to about 800, the Sunderlands somewhat less. Even the commissioning of airfields in occupied Iceland left a mid-Atlantic gap where the U-boats concentrated, untroubled by air patrols.

The large, four-engined B-24 Liberator proved to be the ideal but, needed for high-priority strategic bombing, these were available in very limited numbers. To operate against both submarines and the marauding enemy Kondors, on-the-spot carrier-borne aircraft were required.

*Originating with a 1933 design, the Consolidated PBY Catalina ran to about 3,500 units and served throughout the war in reconnaissance, AS patrols and air-sea rescue. An amphibian, equipped with both wheels and floats, it could range nearly 2,600 miles and carry a 4,000-pound pay load.*

*Once completed, German U-boat pens proved virtually impervious to bombing, as were these at St Nazaire. The pens are in the conspicuous rectangular structure, opening on to the basin. Leading from the river obliquely, almost hidden by smoke and dust, is the great graving dock immobilized in the British commando raid in March 1942.*

As fleet carriers were too few and too valuable, stopgaps were introduced in the shape of catapult-armed merchantmen (CAM) and merchant aircraft carriers (MAC). The latter were working tankers and bulk carriers with a flight deck topside. These lacked all facilities but pointed the way to the first auxiliary, or escort, carrier HMS *Audacity*, completed in June 1941. Her career was short and hectic but her half-dozen fighters had proved invaluable. A mainly American programme was initiated, ultimately producing over one hundred escort carriers based on standard mercantile hulls. Among their many applications some were used in roving escort groups, which could quickly reinforce threatened convoys or exploit good intelligence to target independently the enemy's supply submarines.

Along the Biscay coast, from Brest to Bordeaux, five major U-boat facilities had been established, based on monolithic, multi-cell pens covered in thicknesses of reinforced concrete that made them all but impervious to the bombing that progressively levelled the towns around them. But en route to their operational areas U-boats had to transit the Bay of Biscay, where the pressing attentions of the

*HMS* Audacity *was the first British escort carrier, being converted from a German prize and commissioned in July 1941. As there was no hangar her six aircraft (six Martlet fighters or four fighters and two Swordfish AS aircraft) had to remain on deck. As a prototype, she was invaluable.*

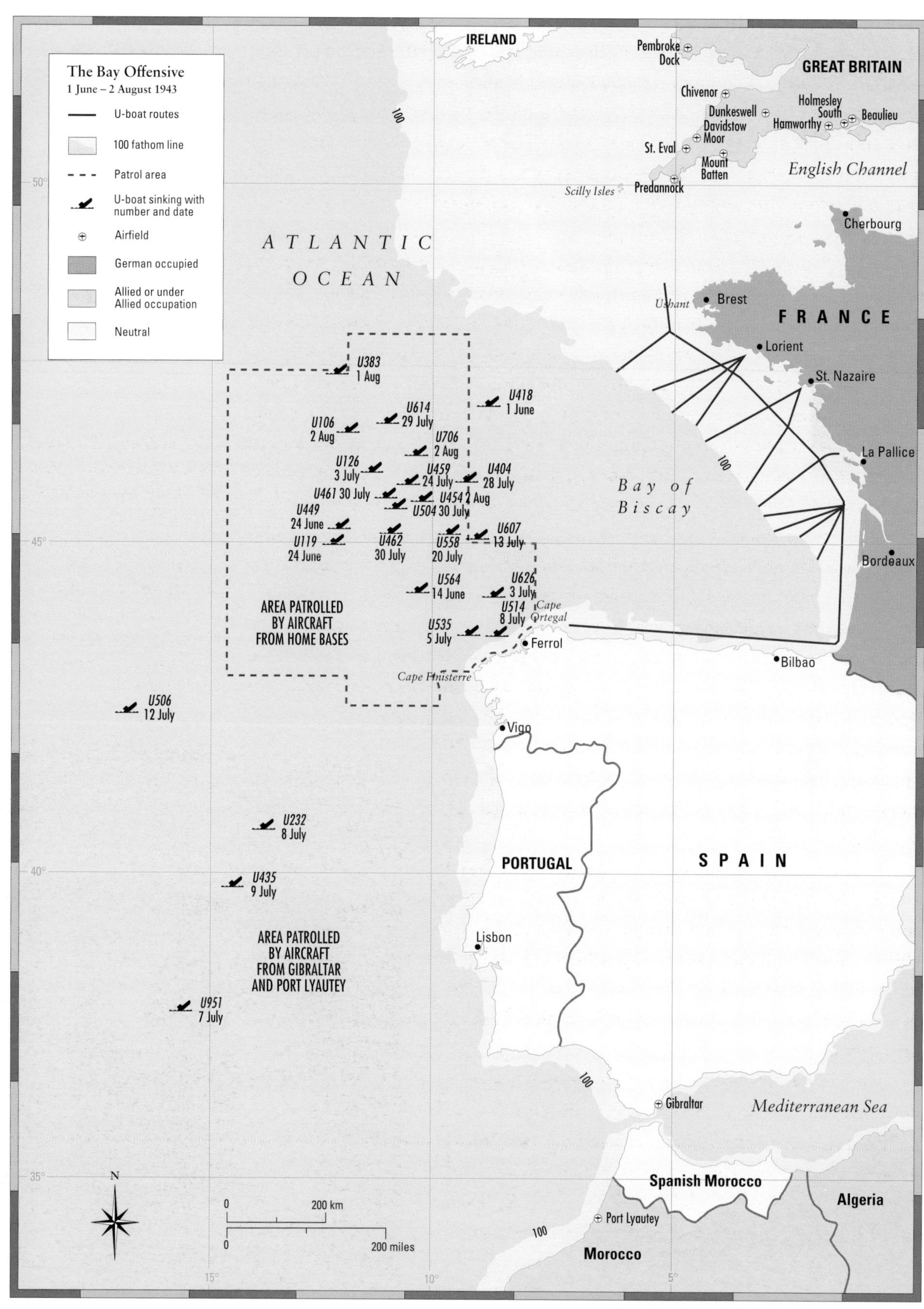
The Bay Offensive
1 June – 2 August 1943
U-boat routes
100 fathom line
Patrol area
U-boat sinking with number and date
Airfield
German occupied
Allied or under Allied occupation
Neutral
IRELAND
GREAT BRITAIN
Pembroke Dock
Chivenor
Dunkeswell
Davidstow Moor
St. Eval
Mount Batten
Predannock
Holmesley South
Hamworthy
Beaulieu
Scilly Isles
English Channel
Cherbourg
ATLANTIC OCEAN
Ushant
Brest
FRANCE
Lorient
St. Nazaire
La Pallice
Bordeaux
Bay of Biscay
Bilbao
Cape Ortegal
Ferrol
Cape Finisterre
Vigo
U383 1 Aug
U418 1 June
U614 29 July
U106 2 Aug
U706 2 Aug
U126 3 July
U459 24 July
U404 28 July
U461 30 July
U454 2 Aug
U504 30 July
U449 24 June
U119 24 June
U462 30 July
U558 20 July
U607 13 July
U564 14 June
U626 3 July
U514 8 July
U535 5 July
AREA PATROLLED BY AIRCRAFT FROM HOME BASES
U506 12 July
U232 8 July
U435 9 July
AREA PATROLLED BY AIRCRAFT FROM GIBRALTAR AND PORT LYAUTEY
U951 7 July
PORTUGAL
SPAIN
Lisbon
Gibraltar
Mediterranean Sea
Spanish Morocco
Algeria
Port Lyautey
Morocco
100
50°
45°
40°
35°
15°
10°
5°
N
0
200 km
200 miles

RAF triggered a leap-frog technological contest between attackers and attacked. In July 1942, after Leigh Light Wellingtons had inflicted some unpleasant surprises out of total darkness, Dönitz ordered boats to surface by day. This was very risky but, by courtesy of an ASV set from a crashed aircraft, his scientists were able to produce a radar detector ('Metox') of the correct wavelength. Thus, from September 1942, boats so fitted could again surface by night. The Luftwaffe also mounted patrols over the Bay but the RAF countered by escorting their AS aircraft with Beaufighters and Mosquitoes.

THE BAY OFFENSIVE

*The five large U-boat facilities established on the French Atlantic coast greatly decreased transit times to and from the submarine's operational areas. Their passage across the Bay of Biscay was, however, long and successfully disputed by aircraft operating from southern England.*

As the British worked to neutralize Metox with a centimetric ASV Mark III, the Americans followed a different path. A low-flying aircraft could detect a submerged submarine through its ferrous mass distorting the natural terrestrial magnetic field. The effect was only transient and, to isolate its position, the disposable 'sonobuoy' was developed. Dropped in a pattern, these transmitted machinery and propeller noise to the aircraft. As the origin could be only approximately deduced, depth charge attack was impractical, and an air-dropped acoustically homed torpedo was substituted. The combination was coming into service by early 1943 and scored some kills, but was not made really effective until after the war, with later improvements in electronics. By 1943, too, experts such as Captain Frederick Walker were perfecting AS tactics. Larger frigates were entering service, with early problems on Hedgehog being resolved.

As escorts could no longer be simply evaded the Germans, likewise, employed electric acoustic torpedoes, tuned to home on to a frigate's propellers. Escorts countered by towing the unloved 'Foxer' noise generator. Sonars gained a 'Q-attachment', essentially a second set configured to measure target depth. The U-boats tried to baffle Sonar operators by launching fixed or mobile decoys, and having hulls clad with rubber-based, sound-absorbing (anechoic) coatings.

Metox-equipped U-boats then suddenly began to be attacked at night without warning. Convinced that radar could not operate on wavelengths sufficiently short, Dönitz's scientists persuaded him that Metox must itself be radiating detectable energy. The equipment was banned pending a replacement ('Tunis') which did not go operational until May 1944.

The U-boat's temporarily reduced protection was doubly serious for, as well as having to admit defeat in the Atlantic in mid 1943, they had suffered a depressing number of losses in the Bay. Here Allied aircraft had mounted a major effort against U-boats, many fitted with extra anti-aircraft weapons and armour plate, and moving in groups.

By late 1944, Hedgehog was proving a greater killer

*Captain Frederick 'Johnny' Walker comes ashore from a ship of his Second Escort Group. The Royal Navy's most consistently successful U-boat hunter, he was directly involved in the sinking of at least fourteen. On 9 July 1944, aged 48, he died of a stroke, probably from overwork.*

than the depth charge. However, its twenty-four-bomb pattern required a direct hit to detonate a single 30-pound charge. It was recognized that the conventional depth-charge's 'big bang' was at once psychologically uplifting for the attackers and powerfully depressing for the attacked. Hedgehog's successor, 'Squid', therefore hefted three 200-pound bombs some 300 yards ahead of the ship. Depth-measuring Sonar automatically fused the bombs to detonate at the correct depth. New Castle-class corvettes shipped a single Squid, while Loch-class frigates carried a double Squid, which laid a three-dimensional pattern. Over the last two years of the war, analysis indicated that depth charges were lethal on one attack in sixteen, Hedgehog one in five, and Squid a devastating one in two.

In November 1942 Allied mercantile losses had hit a record 862,000 grt yet, just seven months later, U-boats had to be temporarily withdrawn from the Atlantic with unacceptable losses, exceeding forty in two months out of three. Almost one thousand Allied ships were now dedicated to AS operation, and new aircraft-deployed weapons included armour-piercing rockets and even 57mm anti-tank guns.

Long before the odds had thus deteriorated, the enemy had decided that submarines needed to remain submerged far longer, yet be able to operate at higher underwater speed to avoid a crippling loss of performance. The first requirement was met by reintroducing what was termed the Schnorkel, or Snort, a device first patented in Italy in the 1920s and actually installed in Dutch submarines captured by the Germans in 1940. When raised, the Snort provided an intake/exhaust tube which allowed a boat's diesel engines to be run while submerged. Battery charging no longer necessitated surfacing and an emergency programme was initiated to provide equipment for retro-fitting to existing boats.

*The Bristol Beaufighter, fitted with a variety of engines, served with both the Royal Air Force and the Fleet Air Arm as heavy fighter and 'ship buster'. This 1944 picture shows ground crew fusing rockets prior to take-off. These projectiles easily punched holes in U-boat pressure hulls.*

Dr Hellmuth Walter had been working on a closed propulsion system for a decade, using diesel fuel with hydrogen peroxide as an oxygen source. Unstable, it proved to be a design cul-de-sac, and there was a shift in emphasis to improving conventional engineering. There were two major objectives: to reduce hull resistance and to increase propulsive power. To achieve the first a new-style hull form was developed, optimized for smooth and quiet flow, and without the conventional multitude of protrusions. The hull needed to be large to float three times the usual battery capacity. With the Snort fitted as standard, the Type XXI, as it was termed, had a formidable performance.

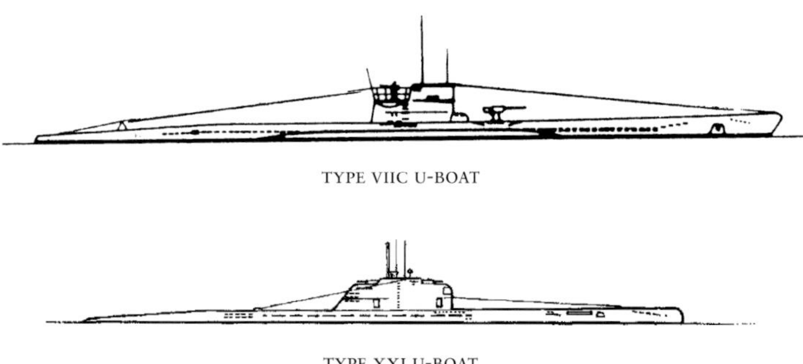

TYPE VIIC U-BOAT

TYPE XXI U-BOAT

GENESIS OF THE 'MODERN' SUBMARINE

*Scourge of Allied shipping, the VIIc had sleek looks that belied her deficiences of poor submerged speed and endurance. The XXI Elektroboot, in contrast, was optimized around hydrodynamic efficiency in the submerged condition. Speed, however, required large and heavy batteries and, in reality, she was 12 per cent longer than the VIIc.*

Prepared in good time, the design was ready for production by mid 1943. Allied attempts to destroy U-boats by bombing shipyards had enjoyed little success, but bombing was increasing in intensity. To realize a 290-boat programme, therefore, it was decided to prefabricate hulls in eight major sections at separate facilities. These would be transported by inland waterway to three bomb-proof assembly facilities. Although meticulously detailed, the plan suffered interminable delays through shortage of essential materials, and from the Allies targeting key points on the canal system and manufacturers of vital components.

In the event, the Type XXI and its near-water diminutive, the Type XXIII, began to work-up early in the final phase of the war, and even this was disrupted by aerial mining of their Baltic trials areas.

*6 May 1945. As the war ended, many U-boats attempted to escape from the Baltic to Norwegian bases. They suffered severely at the hands of marauding aircraft. Here, one of the few operational Type XXIs, probably U2534, is shot up in the Kattegat by RAF Mosquitoes.*

## The American submarine blockade of Japan

Japan's sequestration of most of South-east Asia was aimed largely at guaranteeing sources of essential raw materials. Such an action inevitably meant war with the established colonial powers but, in 1941, the Netherlands and France were themselves already subjugated, while the situation of Great Britain appeared little better. Only the United States posed a major threat, obliging the Japanese to take a huge gamble. This was to overrun the region rapidly with a meticulously planned campaign before seeking a negotiated peace based on the new order. It was reasoned that the Americans, an ocean away from their lost territories, would weigh their value against the cost of their recovery. A national tendency to isolationism would prevail and Japan, having made the odd minor concession, would be left unchallenged. All depended upon a campaign of limited duration. In achieving their territorial aims Japan's military leaders were brilliantly successful, but it was not in their gift to decide that the ensuing war would be short.

Following Japan's involvement in the First World War, she was given mandate over the great island groups of the western Pacific – the Marianas, Marshalls and Carolines. To these thousands of islands her conquests had added thousands more. The islands could provide the coveted raw materials but, beyond limited oil-refining capacity, they possessed virtually no heavy industry. All would require transport to Japan, conversion to a finished state and redistribution.

Herein lay the key to Japan's downfall for, in general freighting and in the support of her population and the many established garrisons, she needed merchant shipping. From Singapore to Yokohama is over 3,000 sea miles; from Yokohama to the Marianas is 1,250 sea miles and to the Gilberts, twice that. Passages were long and shipping was vulnerable.

In December 1941 Japan's mercantile marine aggregated a not-inconsiderable 6.1 million grt, to which conquest added a further 820,000 grt. Of this, 2.85 million grt was the minimum necessary to sustain the needs of the population. The remainder was requisitioned for military needs, with the army and the navy operating separate fleets, uninterchangable, totally inflexible.

Banking all on a short war, the Japanese had given little thought to the protection of mercantile assets, despite the recent and well-documented experience of the British in 1914–18. The Imperial Navy, earlier a protégé of the British Royal Navy, had inherited a philosophy of attack. Its submarines were designed to support warships and to sink warships, their personnel trained to it. By inference enemy submarines would operate similarly. No plans existed for convoying and the paper strength of about two hundred escorts included many vessels intended primarily for minesweeping and for the most part poorly equipped. In this island-studded theatre, land-based air power should have been a potent protective force but, in practice, it enjoyed low priority and was largely ineffective.

The United States' war plan against Japan ('Orange') was long established

Early R- and S-class boats, dating from 1918–22, served throughout the Second World War, first as operational boats then, with new construction, being retired as training or target craft. Without air conditioning, conditions aboard were unpleasant when operating in tropical waters.

and regularly updated. It assumed the indefensibility of territories in the western Pacific, their loss and eventual recovery. It assessed the issues involved and, in direct contrast to its Japanese equivalent, accepted that a war would be a long one. Japan would be defeated by a combination of blockade and bombardment. It would require time to create the means for bombardment; in the distant and enemy-dominated waters of the western Pacific, the submarine was the only practical instrument of blockade.

Signatory to the various inter-war conventions, the United States officially repudiated unrestricted submarine warfare. Adherence to the prize rules, however, effectively ruled out the submarine in the enforcement of blockade. In Europe, Germany had abandoned constraint virtually from the outset while Britain had done much the same, although less publicized. American policy, however, remained equivocal, referring possibly to unrestricted operations in specified areas, or universally 'if justified by events'. The opening 'event' as it happened, was on so brutal a scale that, just six hours after Nagumo's aircraft headed back from Pearl Harbor, the navy was ordered to 'execute unrestricted air and submarine war against Japan'.

The US Navy already had 111 submarines in commission and had seventy-three more under construction. Command areas were as follows:

a) Waters to the west of the Malayan peninsula and the island of Sumatra were the purlieu of British and Dutch submarines of the British Eastern Fleet, later based on Trincomalee.

b) The South-west Pacific Area (General of the Army Douglas MacArthur) embraced waters around Australia, the Philippines and South China Sea north to latitude 20 degrees North, Indonesia and New Guinea thence to the meridian of the central Solomons.

c) The Central Pacific Area (Admiral Chester W. Nimitz) included Japan, the East China Sea, the Sea of Japan and the mandates from the equator to latitude 40 degrees North.

Pacific Fleet (SubPac) submarines, initially twenty-two strong, were based on Pearl Harbor. The twenty-nine boats of the South west Pacific (SoWesPac) force, part of what had been the Asiatic Fleet, were stationed at Manila.

The major Japanese error in its Pearl Harbor attack plan was to concentrate on warships while leaving vital installations untouched. Thus the submarine base, with its specialized workshops, was unscathed. The command's six obsolescent S-class boats were all away, engaged mainly on training duties on the American west coast. Of the sixteen modern craft, only five were alongside in various states of repair. None was damaged. Three days after the Pearl Harbor raid the Cavite Navy Yard at Manila was seething with activity when it was devastated by bombing. Here, the submarine facilities were laid waste, one boat being destroyed.

*Many submarines were built at Manitowoc, on Lake Michigan. This entailed spectacular sideways launching into the narrow Manitowoc River. Here, the Gato-class* Robato *(SS273) hits the water on 9 May 1943. She was sunk on 26 July 1944 in Philippine waters, probably by mine. Four of her crew survived, only to perish in Japanese captivity.*

Allied naval forces were unable to affect seriously the course of the opening Japanese campaign. With the overrunning of the Philippines American submarines first fell back on Dutch facilities at Surabaya then, with the loss of the Malay Barrier, on Australia. By March 1942 they were based at Fremantle and Albany in the subcontinent's far south-west. There was criticism that this placed them some 3,000 miles distant from their most productive patrol areas but Port Darwin, the only practical alternative, was being heavily bombed by enemy formations based on Timor and a tender could not be risked there. An advanced refuelling base was eventually established on the inhospitable Exmouth Gulf.

Lacking facilities for extended tropical patrols, the surviving S-boats were sent around to Brisbane. Operating as Task Force 42, they were conveniently situated here to support MacArthur's campaign in New Guinea and the Solomons. They played a negligible role in blockade but, when deficiencies obliged their withdrawal late in 1942, the flotilla had to be made good from Fremantle.

Early operations were hampered not only by inexperience but also by the loss of most of the Fremantle force's stock of torpedoes, destroyed at Cavite. The boats were, therefore, much involved in minelaying. As the Japanese had not yet begun to exploit their gains, traffic was still sparse but American submarine availability was further eroded by an incessant call for fleet-related 'special missions'.

*Alongside a fleet tender a submarine crew tackles the ticklish yet repetitive task of striking down the torpedo outfit. For a considerable period American torpedoes were notoriously unreliable. The T-shaped object in the foreground is a trainable Sonar hydrophone.*

Such torpedoes as were available proved to be excessively unreliable. As with British and German experience, magnetic firing pistols were over-sensitive and had to be withdrawn. Contact exploders were found to actuate only with an acutely angled grazing hit. Many ran deep, others 'prematured', exploding at the end of their arming run. The problems resulted from insufficient pre-war testing, ten thousand-dollar torpedoes being deemed too expensive to expend; practice rounds did not exhibit the same characteristics. The torpedo question was morale-sapping to a degree, at a time when submarines were the only means of 'getting back' at a seemingly all-conquering enemy. It would be September 1943 before the faults were all rectified, by which time a German-based wakeless electric torpedo had also been introduced.

As the Americans did not copy the German's resupply system, the duration of a patrol depended greatly on torpedo expenditure. Many targets survived because skippers conserved rounds by firing ones and twos where a spread was required. Patrols varied between thirty and sixty days, with an average of forty-eight days, half of which were spent in transit. Older skippers, who tended towards excessive caution, gradually began to be replaced by younger and more aggressive commanders.

*The big American fleet boats had good endurance, clocking some extended patrols when their torpedoes were not quickly expended. Sixty-day voyages were much the norm, seventy not uncommon, even eighty not unknown. Compared with German skippers, Americans enjoyed less close control, operating usually in small groups.*

Compared with the standard German Types VII and IX, American submarines were large (1,570–2,415 tons against 769–871 and 1,051–1,178) as the duration of unresupplied patrols was a function of capacity. Operating more often in shallow water, their size increased vulnerability to counter-attack. They carried up to twenty-eight torpedoes, which did not compare favourably with the twenty-two of the far smaller Type IX. Deck guns were essential, increasing from a single 3-inch to two 5-inch weapons.

About eighty strong, American crews were nearly double those of the Germans but did not have to endure much of the cheerful squalor that was the lot of the U-boat men (S-boats excepted). Electronics were far superior, with air-and sea-search radars and even high-frequency Sonars capable of guidance through a moored minefield.

Submarine design was strictly standardized for series production. Three classes (Gato, Balao and Tench) represented phased improvements and, of a total of 339 ordered, 221 were completed.

Only about one-third of a force can be on station at any time and, for the first year, this averaged about twenty boats. Sinkings showed the enemy still observing a peacetime pattern, along the Malay Barrier, up through the China and Yellow Seas and off the Japanese coast. Ships that supplied the mandates also suffered. Advanced fleet bases at Truk (in the Carolines) and at Rabaul had little fuel storage capacity and their supply tankers were prized targets.

*A fine, modern Japanese freighter slips to a lonely grave. Destroying 'Marus', as the Americans termed them, was a mission equally important as that of Dönitz, as Japan depended absolutely upon her merchant marine to support her population and distant garrisons, and to import essential raw materials.*

The gathering momentum of the submarine campaign was complemented from early in 1943 by strategic minelaying, mainly by aircraft, including those carrier-based. A combination of bottom-laid influence mines and shallow water meant that many casualties could be salvaged. This was all to the good as these ships, all needing major repair, then cluttered shipyards that would have been better employed on new buildings. In addition, the Japanese were ill-prepared in mine countermeasures and responded by closing routes and ports for considerable periods.

During the first fifteen months the Japanese merchant fleet was reduced by some 400,000 grt. This was sustainable but ominously nearly 16 per cent of remaining tonnage was awaiting repair as military work took precedence for both skilled labour and materials.

With the Solomons campaign proceeding well, the Brisbane-based force could be reduced to add to the assault on the trade routes. By the autumn of 1943 the Americans had the valuable experience that Dönitz's 'wolf-pack' tactics had failed, much through being over-centralized. 'Section attack', using small groups of boats, had been practised by the Americans between the wars, but it was abandoned because of the need for better communications. This problem being resolved, the tactic was again introduced, as the enemy was beginning to run convoys.

Sections, usually comprising three boats, rejoiced in labels such as 'Roy's Rangers' or 'Shelby's Shellackers'. Having received his orders, the senior skipper was free to make his own tactical decisions, although Pearl kept him fully updated. Groups formed a search line and any boat making contact informed the others by radio phone. Each in turn would then act as 'flanker', attacking before falling back to be the 'trailer'. The usual lack of enemy aerial escort allowed the boats to use their 20-plus knot surface speed to make 'end runs' to repeat the process.

As Nimitz's forces began their amphibious leap-frog across the western Pacific, SubPac boats performed invaluable service in targeting the transports carrying troop reinforcements and *matériel*. Carrier aircraft joined American and Commonwealth land-based airpower to distress enemy shipping further. In all, aircraft accounted for nearly 30 per cent, and submarines about 57 per cent, of all losses. Submarines, however, had been committed from the outset, when air supremacy was but a distant dream.

In August 1943, faced with unacceptable casualty rates, the Japanese High Command ordered that all merchantmen be escorted. In November a dedicated Escort Command was established comprising two, later four, Surface Escort Divisions. A few light carriers were intermittently available and a building programme for frigates initiated. By July 1944 some fifty were in service; they looked austere to a degree but carried plenty of depth charges and were often handled effectively and aggressively. No less than six hundred aircraft were also allocated, organized in four air groups, but, with the navy's front-line carriers desperately short of qualified pilots, escort squadrons always received poor material and were always under strength.

Starting with the Singapore route, the Japanese had a general convoy system running by early 1944. It tended to small groups of five or eight ships, very uneconomical in terms of escort numbers. Of the original fifty routes, there was gradual enforced abandonment due both to Allied territorial gains and the unbearable pressure exerted by submarine and air attack. Abandoned garrisons at least did not require resupply.

Military success also enabled submarines to be forward-based, cutting transit times and increasing utilization. Having penetrated the difficult Sea of Japan and been disappointed at a relative paucity of targets there, the submarine force specifically targeted Japan's tanker traffic, routed between Sumatra or Borneo and the home islands. Even despite shipping oil back in drums, supplies became so short that the bulk of the battle fleet had to be based on Singapore to be near sources, albeit poorly refined.

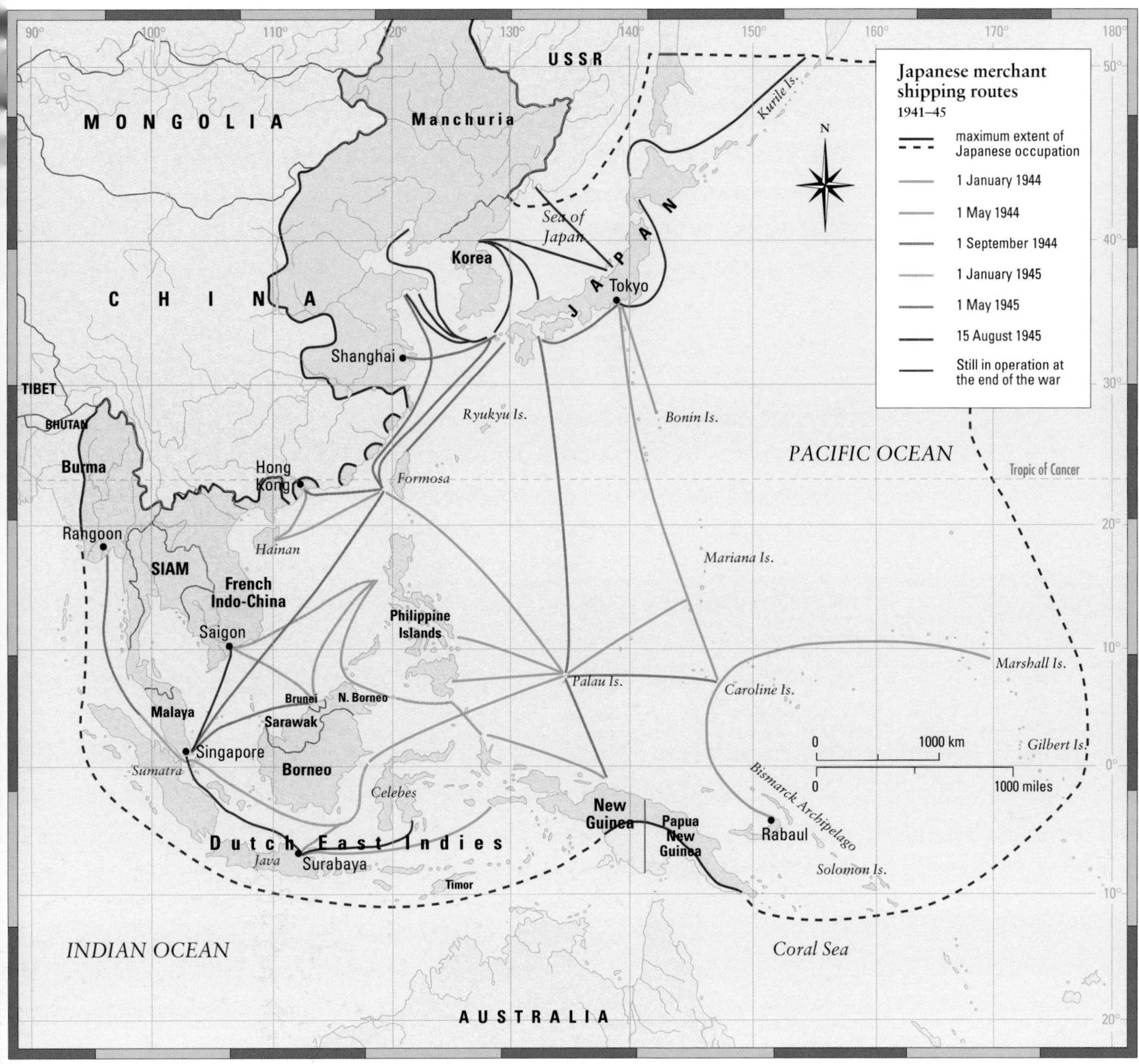


March 1945 saw the South China Sea so thoroughly covered by submarines and air power that convoys had to be discontinued. So few ships sailed that sinkings were confined to a few coast-huggers. From June, movements were almost all of coaster-sized ships and small wooden craft. Mines now accounted for the majority of casualties. Japan was now living on its own resources. No longer able to sustain the war nor the population, the High Command faced unconditional surrender even without the awful warning of two nuclear weapons.

Convoy failed the Japanese because of a lack of commitment. Availability of escorts failed to synchronize with the sailings of the convoy that required them while air support either did not materialize or was ineffective. When well organized, however, the opposition could be stiff, victory costing the Americans a total of fifty-two submarines. In August 1945 the Japanese had just 1.6 million grt left to them; of this, nearly 42 per cent was laid up awaiting repair.

JAPANESE MERCHANT SHIPPING ROUTES

*If it is remembered that the distance from Tokyo to Singapore is 2,900 nautical miles, equivalent to an Atlantic crossing, the scale of the Pacific theatre may be realized. Long-haul cargoes, such as oil from Borneo or rubber from Malaya, required much Japanese tonnage, all vulnerable to submarine and air attack.*

*The number of troops involved in a major landing required that they be shipped in properly equipped transports. For the actual landing they needed to be transferred overside into Landing Craft, Assault (LCA). This had to be done some distance offshore and was a vulnerable point of an operation.*

## Amphibious warfare

The use of naval vessels to mount and support military operations is a long-practised art. There is, of course, a wide variation in the scope of such operations, varying from raids or incursions to major invasions. Of these, the former are limited in their objectives, the forces involved being withdrawn on a prearranged schedule. Examples are St Nazaire, Dieppe or Tobruk. As the scope of this work is to concentrate on those aspects of the war at sea which had the greatest influence on its outcome, we must confine our narrative to invasions, operations designed to establish a beachhead through which military reinforcements may be passed with the objective of permanent occupation.

During 1940 the British Combined Operations Headquarters was established with the general brief 'to prepare the apparatus and plans for the invasion of the Continent'. For the moment, only raids were possible but were held to be useful in gaining experience and keeping the enemy off-balance. Small, élite formations were created for the purpose of raiding or for spearheading larger incursions. These took the name 'Commando', after the respected mobile Afrikaner groups of the South African wars.

For an invasion to succeed, air and sea superiority are esssential in order to ensure a continuous flow of supplies. For lack of such superiority the Germans failed to mount the anticipated invasion of the United Kingdom in 1940. After Dunkirk, a badly weakened Britain surveyed a hostile, occupied European coastline running from the North Cape to the Spanish border. At such a time it took a Churchill to ponder the problems of liberating the Continent, of the requirement for unorthodox means of putting personnel and transport ashore other than through an equipped port; in short, 'over the beach'.

The Dardanelles experience twenty-five years previously had convinced many that opposed landings were disasters in the making but, from 1924, the so-called Landing Craft Committee (subsumed in 1938 into the Inter-service Training and Development Centre) developed the parameters of a couple of useful beaching craft. Fitted with ramps forward, one could transport a 12-ton tank and the other, later known as an Assault Landing Craft, or ALC, carried a standard thirty-two-man army platoon. At 41.5 feet in length, the ALC was designed to be slung under standard ships' davits. Such ships, usually converted from passenger ships with adequate accommodation, were termed Landing Ships, Infantry, or LSI.

The boundary between the terms 'Landing Ships' and 'Landing Craft' is a little blurred, due to the bewildering range of vessels eventually developed. In general, 'craft' were held to operate from ship-to-shore, while 'ships' sailed from shore-to-shore. Only specific 'ships' could take the beach, however, while many 'craft' undertook ocean passages.

The small tank-carrying craft was refined into the Landing Craft, Mechanized, or LCM, capable of being carried under davits alongside what was now called the Landing Craft, Assault, or LCA.

The navy's constructive department, meanwhile, was tasked with producing a ship which could make an ocean passage with twenty tanks before landing them over an unprepared beach. As the necessary dimensions had to be combined with very shallow draught, three tankers of Shell Oil's Maracaibo fleet were selected for prototype conversion. Successful, if ungainly, the Maracaibos proved the basic features of bow ramps, beaching techniques and ventilation of vehicle decks. They were the first Landing Ships, Tank, or LST. Intermediate in size was the

*Gunfire support was maintained until the last possible moment to keep the defences neutralised until the first wave touched down. Here, LCAs approach the beach during the Hollandia landings, New Guinea, in 1944.*

Landing Craft, Tank, or LCT. Effectively an elongated LCM, with the usual engines aft and ramped bow, it differed from the LST primarily in having an open vehicle deck, capable of accommodating up to three heavy and six medium tanks.

With home construction facilities already stretched, the British sent a mission to the United States during 1941 to discuss procurement under Lend-Lease terms. An unexpected bonus was that, when shortly afterwards the Americans found themselves at war, amphibious craft production had already been initiated.

In the United States' armed forces, reponsibility for amphibious operations rested with the Marine Corps. Since 1921 it had been developing its role in daylight assault landings, identified as a necessary preface to the seizure of western Pacific islands for forward fleet bases. By 1935 it was able to produce what became, with successive revisions, the inter-service 'bible'. Entitled the *Tentative Landing Operations Manual*, this identified six key areas, namely command relationships, naval gunfire support, air support, ship-to-shore movement, securing the beachhead, and logistics.

Active co-operation benefited both Americans and British. The latter's drafts and requirements kick-started production of what would become a flood of craft of widely differing characteristics. The Americans' Higgins-type LCM proved to be inadequate but, farsightedly, they were already testing prototype LVTs (Landing Vehicles, Tracked). Spotting for naval fire support was not possible as

*Amphibious tracked vehicles were very necessary for the negotiation of offshore reefs, upon which conventional craft grounded. They could proceed directly from the flooded well of an LPD, or via the ramp of an LST, to a point safely beyond the beach. Here, on Eniwetok, the preliminary barrage has left its mark.*

specialist forward-based observation parties had not yet been trained. What had been identified, and had to be learned the hard way by the British, was the requirement for 'combat loading' of transports. Irrespective of its size and weight, what was needed ashore most urgently had to come ashore first.

The first practitioners of large-scale amphibious landings, however, were the Japanese. As their orthodox marine corps had been disbanded, they made the army the responsible authority for such operations, with the navy's role limited to transportation and protection. Assault battalions were trained for the role, as were assault engineer teams who crewed minor amphibious craft and organized beach activities.

During the highly successful campaign of December 1941 to April 1942, much reliance was placed on ships of the merchant marine, which had very little modification for their roles as troop carriers or attack transports. Landing craft were frequently carried on hatch covers and side decks, and handled by standard ship's gear. Known generally as *Daihatsus*, the landing craft looked rather like small fishing craft with a ramped bow. Diesel driven, they varied in length between about 10 to 15 metres and could transport a wide range of loads, including up to about one hundred personnel.

Night landings were preferred, with feints to unbalance the defences. Locations usually favoured the early seizure of an airfield, so that air cover could be extended to support each operation. From 1940 naval paratroops were trained for dropping from low altitude in the rear of defences. The overwhelming impression of the Japanese campaign is one of a bewildering succession of small-scale landings, possible only because defences were inadequate or non-existent.

From August 1942, when the Americans switched to the offensive, enemy amphibious operations were confined mainly to reinforcement and resupply of the many garrisons. For these duties the Japanese built many LSTs and LCTs, based closely on Allied design, and an original fast frigate type with a sloping stern, able to transport and launch either minor landing craft or miniature submarines.

In early landings particularly, the attrition rate in Allied minor landing craft proved to be very high, and ships were developed to transport small craft in bulk. In 1935 the Japanese had built an ungainly 8,000-tonner named *Shinshu Maru*, which was equipped with heavy gear to support twenty small craft and their loads. The ship had innovatory side ports and stern doors and her successful use in China may have been the inspiration for the British conversion in 1940 of two train ferries. These utilized their existing rails to accommodate thirteen trolley-mounted LCMs, launched and recovered over a stern ramp, assisted by an overhead gantry. The principle was extended to

*By transporting up to ten thousand troops at a time half way across the globe, the giant express liners represented the first link in a sequence that culminated for most on a bullet-swept beach. This is Cunard's* Queen Elizabeth *with what appear to be Clyde puffers alongside. Note the prominent degaussing girdle.*

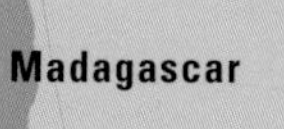


JAPANESE EXPANSION

*Retrospectively, the devastatingly successful Japanese overrunning of South-east Asia in 1942 looks very logical and straightforward. For the demoralized and bewildered ABDA forces at the time, however, the enemy seemed to appear from any and every direction.*

three auxiliary tankers, which functioned in their original role while stowing fifteen loaded LCMs on deck under heavy gantry davits.

Both of these were stopgaps, available as the concept of a submersible pontoon was being evaluated. Again, the British approached the Americans, with a draught requirement from which was developed the revolutionary Landing Ship, Dock, or LSD. Effectively a self-propelled floating dock, the LSD simply floats her cargo in and out of a floodable well. Even early examples could accommodate a mix of either two LCT(3), each loaded with twelve medium tanks, fourteen LCM (3), each with one medium tank, or forty-one LVTs.

Often referred to as Amtracks, LVTs first saw action on Guadalcanal. Early

examples weighed 7.5 tons and, with twenty equipped marines aboard, could negotiate an offshore reef and advance beyond the open beach. Subsequent variants acquired protection, some 17-tonners even taking a 75mm gun and acting as light armour.

The major amphibious landings of the Second World War marked the three major axes of Allied advance. Briefly, these were:

1. Admiral Nimitz: Gilbert Islands (November 1943); Marshall Islands (January–February 1944); Mariana Islands (June–July 1944); Palau Islands (September 1944); Iwo Jima (February 1945); Okinawa (April 1945).
2. General MacArthur: Solomon Islands (August 1942 – December 1943); Lae (September 1943); Hollandia (April 1944); Wakde–Biak (May 1944); Morotai (September 1944); Leyte (October 1944).
3. General Eisenhower: North Africa (November 1942); Sicily (July 1943); Salerno (September 1943); Anzio (January 1944); Normandy (June 1944); south of France (August 1944).

Techniques and experience varied for each sequence of operations. Admiral Nimitz headed the body known as the Fifth Fleet, whose tactical commander was Admiral Raymond A. Spruance. Within its structure was included the amphibious element, Task Force 51 (TF51), under the able Vice Admiral Richmond K. Turner, whose function was to put ashore V Amphibious Corps, led by Lieutenant General Holland M. Smith. Turner commanded all the major assaults, whose scale and ferocity increased as each came closer to the enemy's home islands.

*Correctly a Landing Ship, Medium (Rocket), or LSM (R), this is one of a dozen converted to clear a beach with a close-in salvo prior to a landing. She carries eighty-five rocket launchers, a 5-inch gun, two 40mm and three 20mm automatic weapons. This salvo was laid on Okinawa.*

At Tarawa and Makin in the Gilberts, and at Kwajalein and Eniwetok in the Marshalls, assaults were directed at reef-fringed islets on the edge of coral atolls. Defence in depth was not possible and the battle began at the water's edge. From Saipan on, land masses were larger and, excepting Iwo Jima, mountainous and with heavy vegetation.

Before June 1944, carrier-based aviation was not generally available for close air support and the choice of objectives needed to take account of airfields. Veteran battleships, some reclaimed from the mud of Pearl Harbor, found a major role in delivering ever-heavier pre-assault bombardments, supported by aircraft to almost the very moment of first touchdown. Destroyers, working close inshore, were found to be invaluable in delivering 5-inch and 40mm fire at point-blank range on demand.

Until LSDs became generally available, LVTs were launched from LST 'tractor flotillas'. On their final approach, amtracks would be subjected to a lashing fire, and a popular innovation was escort by LCIs (Landing Craft, Infantry or 'Elsie Items') converted to gunboats (LCI(G)). Some of these were fitted with batteries of nearly three hundred medium-calibre rockets. Firepower such as this saved many casualties in the initial wave but there was a high attrition rate among LVTs returning for the follow-up. As the shallow coral shelf within the reef was usually sown liberally with mines and obstructions, Underwater Demolition Teams (UDT), first used in the Marianas, were formed for their preliminary disposal.

General MacArthur's Seventh Fleet in the South-west Pacific was

*Naval gunfire is the key to success in amphibious warfare. Here, the veteran battleship* Warspite *engages targets in Normandy after D-Day. Field Marshal Rommel reported that 'the effects of naval bombardment are so powerful that an operation with infantry or armoured formations is impossible in an area commanded by (it)'.*

commanded by Vice Admiral Thomas C. Kinkaid. Rear Admiral Daniel E. Barbey's VII Amphibious Force ('VII Phib') was also known as Task Force 76 (TF76).

The campaign along the 1,500-mile northern coast of New Guinea involved numerous small landings, much influenced by mud, mangrove and jungle. Where offshore reefs required it, LVTs were employed but many such operations were spearheaded from APDs, or high speed transports, old destroyers modified with basic accommodation for about 160 troops and with four assault landing craft under davits. Many landing craft were crewed by the army's Engineer Special Brigades (ESB), who also manned shore parties, organizing the discharge and rapid distribution of stores.

First assault waves were followed up with LSD-launched LCMs with armour and heavy equipment, then LCIs, each with about 180 infantrymen. MacArthur's deliberate westerly progress kept the Japanese unsure as to whether the main threat came from him or from Nimitz.

In August 1942 a powerful British raid on Dieppe indicated that the seizure of even a small port would be impossible in the face of a resolute defence. This conclusion much influenced amphibious operations in the European theatre, for here an equipped port was necessary to exploit continental invasions.

The reconquest of Europe was presaged by the North African landings of November 1942. Simultaneous landings were made in the vicinity of Casablanca, Oran and Algiers. Casablanca was an all-American operation, mounted directly from the United States. No LSTs were yet available and the 350 minor landing craft suffered badly in the heavy Atlantic surf. Fortunately, Vichy French opposition to the landing was negligible, although the US Navy had a brisk task subduing some very hostile French naval units in the port. Casablanca itself was secured with the assistance of armour landed along the coast at Safi from a converted train ferry.

*Even as the assault troops consolidate the beach area, supplies and ammunition pour ashore. The rapid delivery of these to the points where they are immediately needed is of great importance and is the responsibility of specially trained units, who frequently find themselves engaged in the front line. This is Iwo Jima.*

Assaults at Oran and Algiers were staged directly from the United Kingdom with joint Anglo-American participation. Whereas initially Safi had been rushed successfully by two old destroyers, a similar British attempt at Oran was bloodily repulsed. The Maracaibo conversions were, however, very successful in putting essential armour ashore, the port being quickly secured.

At Algiers, the landing was marked by considerable confusion in the darkness and only the lack of real opposition avoided a costly failure. About 90 per cent of assault craft were wrecked. Here, only one of two British destroyers succeeded in breaking into the port and she received fatal damage.

Fortunately, it was a further eight months before the Axis forces could be defeated in North Africa and Sicily invaded, allowing time for improvement in procedures and training. Here two armies, the US Seventh and the British Eighth, were landed on the coasts flanking Cape Passero. Newly available LSTs could beach directly on to the sand. Only light air support was available and, as off

North Africa, the Luftwaffe mounted many damaging nuisance raids. The British airborne attack preceding the landing went badly awry when 50 per cent of the gliders involved were blown out to sea by contrary winds.

The ensuing slog up the long peninsula of Italy was deeply unpopular with the Americans who held that it was an irrelevant delay to an essential cross-Channel operation. As the terrain overwhelmingly favoured the defence, it is surprising, in view of Allied superiority in this area, that more use was not made of tactical amphibious landings to turn enemy defensive lines.

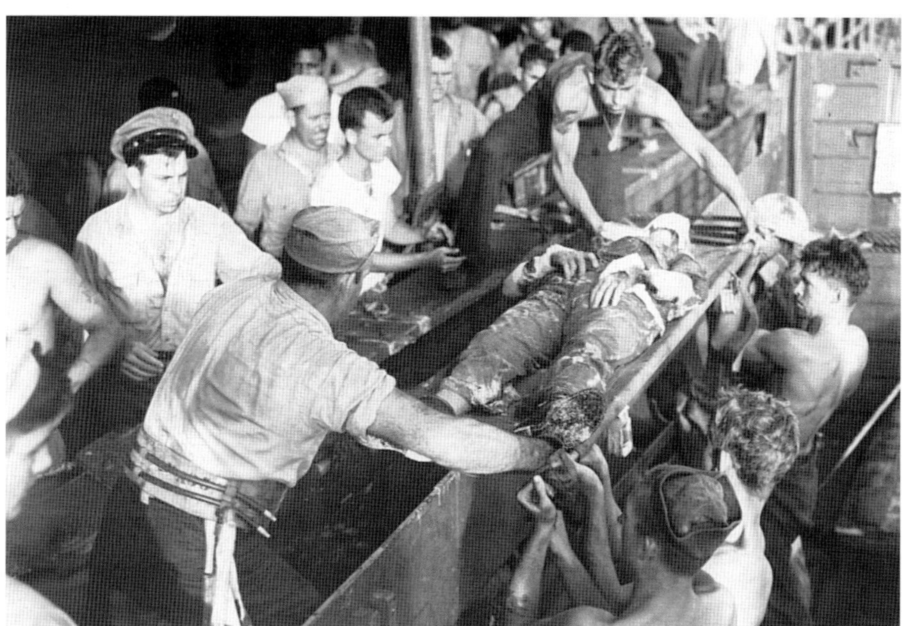

*Willing hands transfer a stretcher case to a hospital ship offshore. Front line medics work wonders but, in the early stages, before field hospitals can be established, fully equipped mobile shipboard facilities undertake the major work. The reassurance that they offer is beyond measurement.*

In the event, the landing of the American Fifth Army at Salerno in September 1943, to facilitate the capture of Naples, was so obvious a move that a fully prepared defence nearly succeeded in sweeping it back into the sea. Again, only light air cover was available and it was naval gunfire that saved the day by breaking up enemy attacks, although the ships themselves faced a new hazard in the enemy's air-launched, radio-controlled glider bombs.

In January 1944 a similar attempt was made at Anzio in order to speed the path to Rome. Many resources had already been withdrawn, however, for the coming Normandy invasion, and the operation was on too small a scale. It was immediately contained by the Germans and was unsuccessful in that it did not achieve its objectives, while absorbing more Allied resources than German ones.

The final large-scale Mediterranean operation, in the south of France, was technically unremarkable, although preceded by a large detachment of paratroops. Forces ashore were quickly built up to two armies, one of them French, which moved northward up the Rhône valley.

All experience to date was incorporated in the Normandy invasion of June

1944. The build-up in southern England could not be disguised, but an elaborate deception programme kept the enemy guessing as to its objective. Because of these doubts the Germans divided their resources between fixed coastal defences and a mobile reserve. A sustained Allied air offensive was then mounted to cut communications to the coast while virtually destroying the Luftwaffe's available strength. Pre-assault paratroop and glider drops were made to seize crossings vital to the operation. The landing itself was on a five-division front, preceded by a not entirely effective air and naval bombardment. Initial enemy resistance was agreeably light, except on the Americans' Omaha beach, where the wide stretches of sand became a killing ground.

*For success, the Normandy invasion depended upon a rapid and sustained build-up. Equipped French ports, however, were heavily defended by the enemy. The solution was the Mulberry harbour. Prefabricated in sections, towed across and sunk in position, it permitted ocean-going ships to discharge 'over the beach'.*

The unique answer to the lack of an equipped port was to construct two temporary harbours. These 'Mulberries' comprised linked concrete caissons, prefrabricated in England, towed across and sunk in position. They allowed seagoing ships to discharge directly to complement the efforts of the ubiquitous LSTs.

Within a month over one million Allied personnel were ashore and there began the breakout that marked the start of the long road to Berlin.

## THE RISE AND RISE OF THE AIRCRAFT CARRIER

Of the major fleets involved in the Second World War, only those of Japan and the United States had already begun to develop the potential of the aircraft carrier as a strike platform, as opposed to acting as an auxiliary to the heavy guns of the battle fleet. It is to their activities, therefore, that this section is mainly devoted.

British fleet carriers were always in desperately short supply during the period of the war when they could have made the greatest difference. Their aircraft were of low performance and striking forces pitifully small. The success at Matapan and the apprehension of the *Bismarck*, for instance, resulted from a handful of aircraft in either case. The attack on the Italian fleet at Taranto and the anti-shipping activities of *Eagle's* aircraft in 1941 showed that, given the resources, the

*Swordfish aircraft ranged on the flight deck of HMS* Victorious *before her strike against the Bismarck during the epic pursuit of May 1941. The antiquated Swordfish was one of the Second World War's success stories, its superb low-speed performance making it a deadly torpedo and AS aircraft.*

Royal Navy would probably have followed the same path as the Pacific fleets. It was only later in the struggle that groups of carriers became available to be deployed offensively as, for instance, against the *Tirpitz* and in the Far East.

During the whole inter-war period, Japan and the United States regarded each other as potential adversaries, and the vast geography of the Pacific shaped their thinking. The American war plan envisaged Japan overrunning the western Pacific and, in order to recover lost territories, a fleet would need to make resisted progress westward for 5,000 miles, self-sufficient in maintenance, supplies and air support. To the American strategists each of the mandated Japanese islands was a potential unsinkable airfield, although the same Washington Treaty that permitted both fleets to introduce large carriers from an early date also prohibited development of 'fortifications' on the islands. The Japanese had long

*Secure in the Kaa fjord, the* Tirpitz *was a threat to every convoy bound to or from northern Russia. On 3 April 1944 the Home Fleet's two carriers were joined by four CVEs, putting up an air strike of forty-two dive-bombers and eighty fighters. Fourteen hits were obtained, but the battleship survived.*

observed this and as a result also required their fleet to take along its own air support. Both fleets discovered the value of the largest possible air strike in overwhelming an enemy defence to achieve an objective.

Limited by treaty to a total of 135,000 tons of aircraft carriers, the US Navy had nearly half its allowance invested in the two giant hulls of the *Lexington* and *Saratoga*. Until rearmament started in 1936, therefore, ensuing ships were the smallest that would do the job. Japan, to her intense resentment, had been limited to only 81,000 tons of carriers. One reaction was to delegate the important reconnaissance function to floatplanes deployed from surface combatants, maximizing the strike potential of the carriers. Plans were also made, and quickly implemented, to convert mercantile and selected warship hulls to further, auxiliary, carriers.

HAWAII OPERATION: ROUTE OF JAPANESE ATTACK FORCES

*The Japanese Pearl Harbor striking force sailed from the desolate Kurile islands and followed a northerly track to avoid detection. For the same reason, its return to Japan was indirect. The distances involved were such that eight tankers and supply ships were in company.*

In Chuichi Nagumo the Japanese had a carrier admiral who welded the half-dozen available fleet carriers into a highly efficient homogeneous force. In December 1941 he was able to unleash two overwhelming air strikes, of 183 and 167 aircraft against a sleeping Pearl Harbor. In the British attack on the alert port of Taranto a year before, the strikes had been by twelve and nine aircraft respectively.

Nagumo did not stop with the attack on the Hawaiian Islands. In the course of the Japanese campaign to overrun South-east Asia, his carriers covered landings on Wake Island, the Bismarck Archipelago and Java, all beyond the reach of land-based aircraft. They also grouped for attacks on Darwin, Colombo and Trincomalee early in 1942.

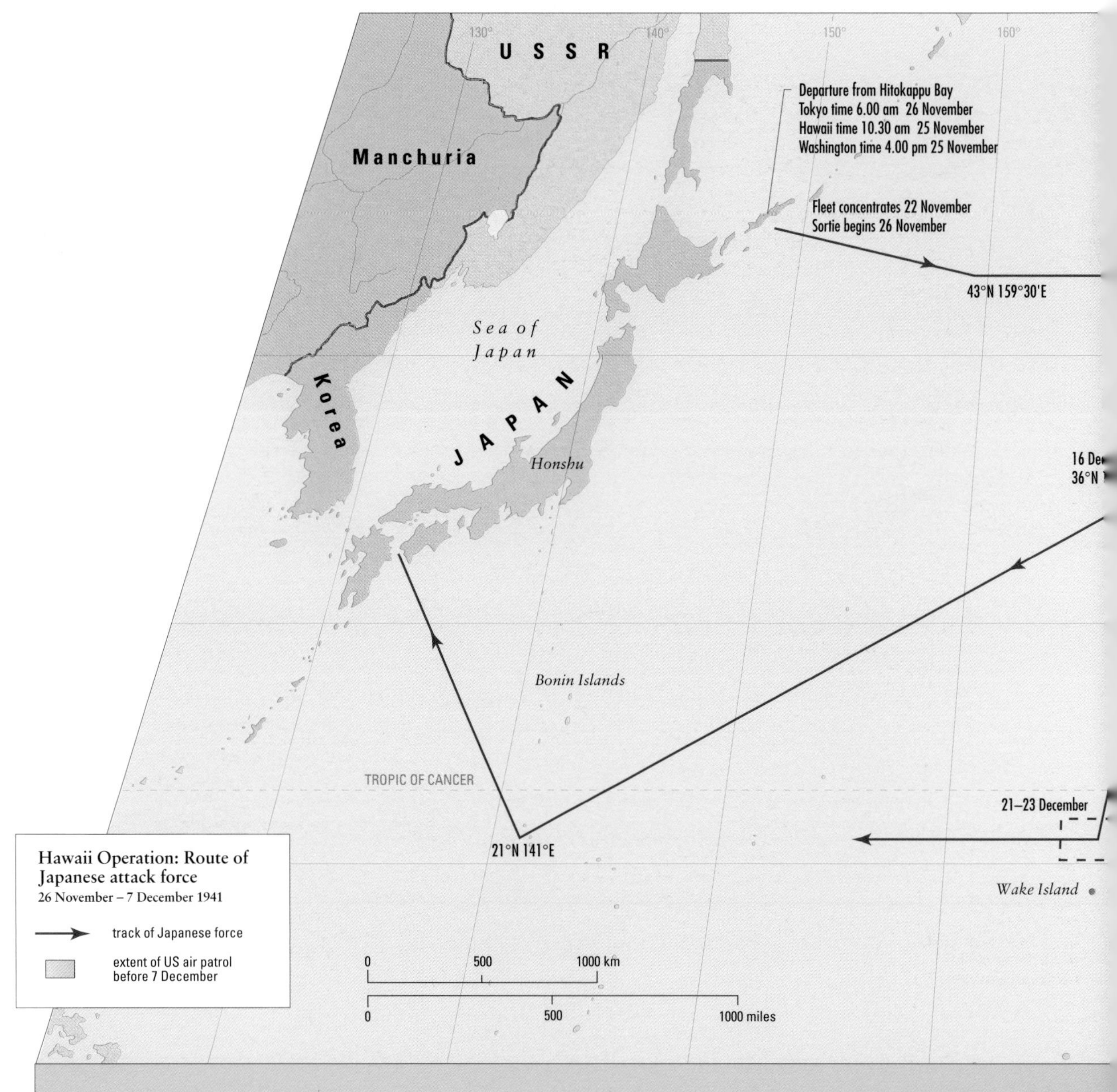

*Ford Island and 'Battleship Row' following the attack. At the head of the row the capsized* Oklahoma *lays outboard of the* Maryland. *Behind them* Tennessee *is inboard of* West Virginia. *At the bottom, the stricken* Arizona *streams bunker oil. Most were later salvaged.*

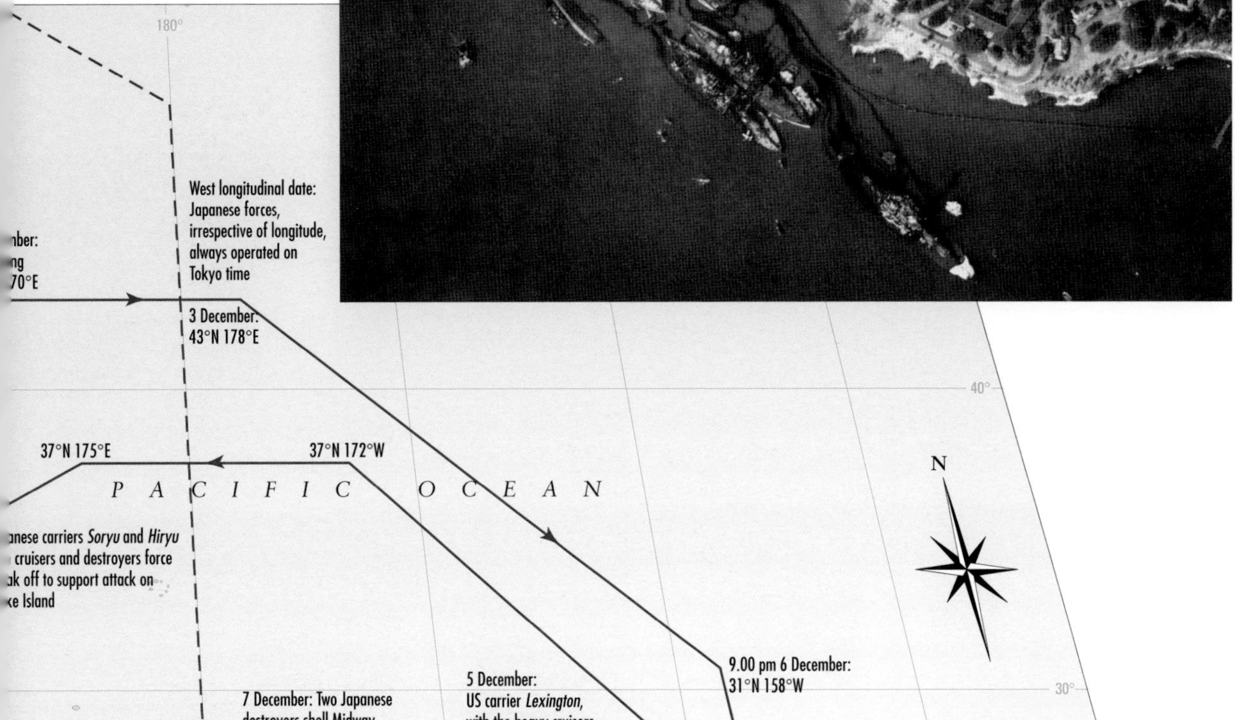

180°

West longitudinal date: Japanese forces, irrespective of longitude, always operated on Tokyo time

nber:
ng
70°E

3 December:
43°N 178°E

40°

37°N 175°E

37°N 172°W

P A C I F I C O C E A N

N

anese carriers *Soryu* and *Hiryu*
cruisers and destroyers force
ak off to support attack on
ke Island

9.00 pm 6 December:
31°N 158°W

30°

7 December: Two Japanese destroyers shell Midway

Midway

5 December:
US carrier *Lexington*, with the heavy cruisers *Astoria, Chicago* and *Portland* and the destroyers *Porter, Flusser, Drayton, Lamson*, and the *Mahan*, sailed from Pearl Harbor with aircraft for Midway

8 December (7 December east longitudinal date):
Attack launched 6.05–6.20 am local time

*Hawaiian Islands*

Oahu

4 December:
US carrier *Enterprise*, in the company of the heavy cruisers *Chester, Northampton* and the *Salt Lake City*, and the destroyers *Balch, Gridley, Craven, McCall, Maury, Dunlay, Fanning, Benham* and the *Ellet*, flew aircraft into Wake

5 December:
Heavy cruiser *Indianapolis* and the old destroyer-minesweepers *Dorsey, Elliot, Hopkins, Long* and the *Johnson*, sailed from Pearl Harbor for an amphibious exercise at Johnston Island

Attack on Pearl Harbor
Tokyo time 3.25 am 8 December
Hawaii time 7.55 am 7 December
Washington time 1.25 pm 7 December

20°

Johnston Island

7 December:
Heavy cruiser *Minneapolis* and the destroyer-minesweepers *Boggs, Chandler, Hovey* and the *Lamberton* were involved in gunnery exercises south of Oahu

## Pearl Harbor: the Japanese attack

*The enemy attack had been carefully worked out on a large- scale model, establishing the best over water routes for torpedo aircraft. Torpedoes had to be specially adapted to run in very shallow water. Extra heavy armour-piercing bombs were improvised from naval shells.*

**Pearl Harbor: The Japanese attack**
7 December 1941

1. Fifteen Kate high-level bombers from the *Akagi*, the first of forty-nine bombers to attack the four ships successively
2. Kate torpedo-bombers from the *Soryu*
3. Kate torpedo-bombers from the *Hiryu*
4. Lead Kate torpedo-bombers from the *Akagi* and *Kaga*
5. Follow-up Kate torpedo-bombers from the *Soryu* and *Hiryu*

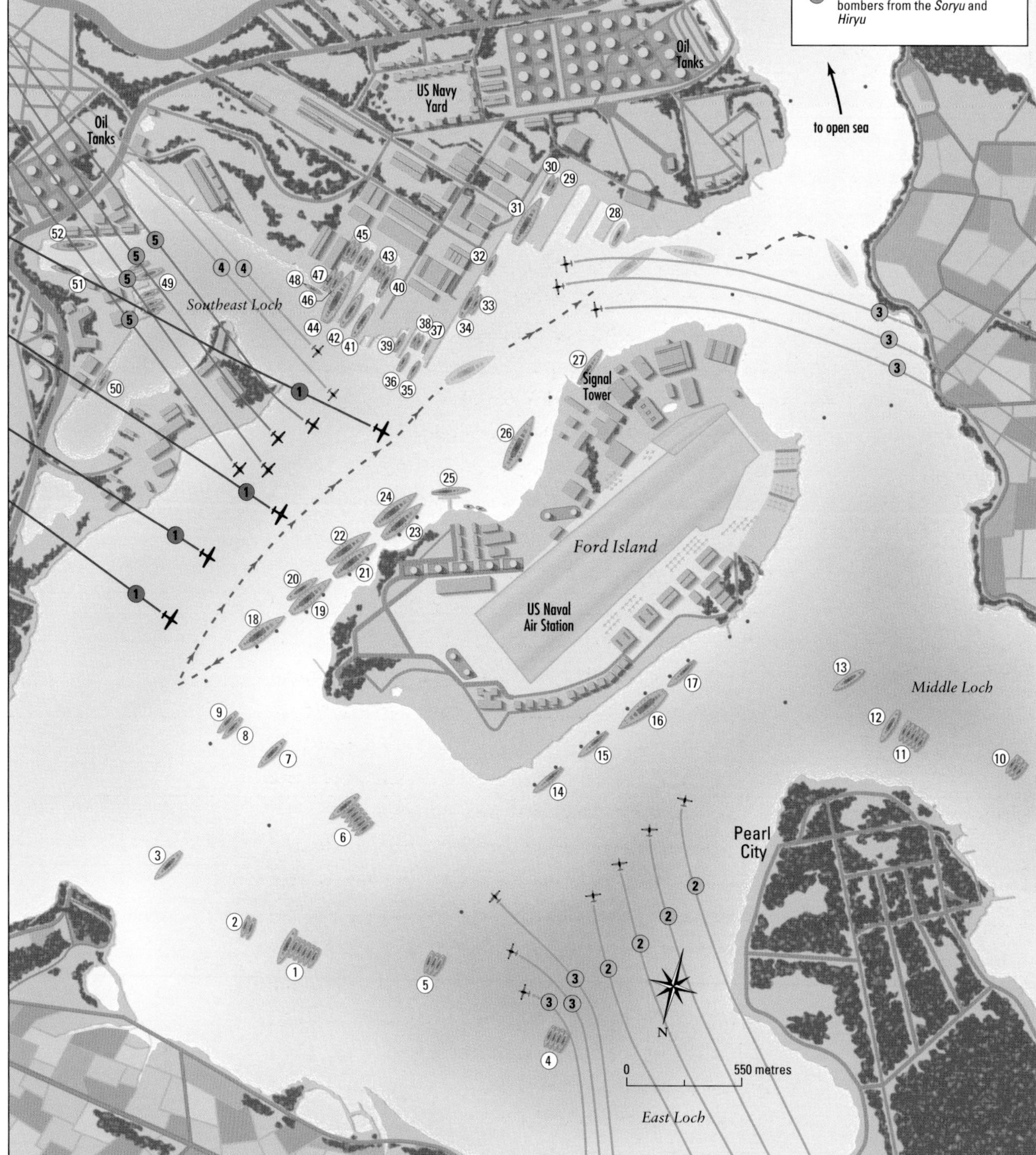

1. Tender *Whitney* and destroyers *Tucker, Conyngham, Reid, Case* and *Selfridge*
2. Destroyer *Blue*
3. Light cruiser *Phoenix*
4. Destroyers *Aylwin, Farragut, Dale* and *Monaghan*
5. Destroyers *Patterson, Ralph, Talbot* and *Henley*
6. Tender *Dobbin* and destroyers *Worden, Hull, Dewey, Phelps* and *Macdough*
7. Hospital Ship *Solace*
8. Destroyer *Allen*
9. Destroyer *Chew*
10. Destroyer-minesweepers *Gamble* and *Montgomery* and light-minelayer *Ramsey*
11. Destroyer-minesweepers *Trever, Breese, Zane, Perry* and *Wasmuth*
12. Repair vessel *Medusa*
13. Seaplane tender *Curtiss*
14. Light cruiser *Detroit*
15. Light cruiser *Raleigh*
16. Target battleship *Utah*
17. Seaplane tender *Tangier*
18. Battleship *Nevada*
19. Battleship *Arizona*
20. Repair vessel *Vestal*
21. Battleship *Tennessee*
22. Battleship *West Virginia*
23. Battleship *Maryland*
24. Battleship *Oklahoma*
25. Oiler *Neosho*
26. Battleship *California*
27. Seaplane tender *Avocet*
28. Destroyer *Shaw*
29. Destroyer *Downes*
30. Destroyer *Cassin*
31. Battleship *Pennsylvania*
32. Submarine *Cachalot*
33. Minelayer *Oglala*
34. Light cruiser *Helena*
35. Auxiliary vessel *Argonne*
36. Gunboat *Sacramento*
37. Destroyer *Jarvis*
38. Destroyer *Mugford*
39. Seaplane tender *Swan*
40. Repair vessel *Rigel*
41. Oiler *Ramapo*
42. Heavy cruiser *New Orleans*
43. Destroyer *Cummings* and light-minelayers *Preble* and *Tracy*
44. Heavy cruiser *San Francisco*
45. Destroyer-minesweeper *Grebe*, destroyer *Schley* and light-minelayers *Pruitt* and *Sicard*
46. Light cruiser *Honolulu*
47. Light cruiser *St. Louis*
48. Destroyer *Bagley*
49. Submarines *Narwhal, Dolphin* and *Tautog* and tenders *Thornton* and *Hulbert*
50. Submarine tender *Pelias*
51. Auxiliary vessel *Sumner*
52. Auxiliary vessel *Castor*

During the latter attacks the small British carrier *Hermes* was caught by dive-bombers which reputedly sank her with forty hits in ten minutes. Coming so soon after the destruction of the *Prince of Wales* and *Repulse* by enemy aircraft based in Thailand, it was realized that the British Eastern Fleet had no answer to Nagumo and it was withdrawn to East Africa, temporarily yielding control of the Indian Ocean.

Being able to read Japanese naval codes, the Americans had the huge advantage of knowing much of their enemy's intentions. Still advancing in May 1942, the Japanese sailed an invasion convoy against Port Moresby in New Guinea. Known to be providing distant cover were the enemy's two largest carriers under Rear Admiral Takagi. Against these, Admiral Nimitz dispatched his only two available carriers, *Yorktown* and *Lexington*, commanded by Rear Admiral Jack Fletcher.

Advertising his presence for no good reason by a passing raid on Tulagi, Fletcher became Takagi's quarry. Heavy frontal cloud made the reconnaissance sightings of both sides unreliable. Initially the Japanese expended a strike against an American oiler and her escort, then Fletcher launched ninety-three aircraft at what turned out to be not Takagi but the covering force for the invasion convoy. The strike sank the light carrier *Shoho*, but the convoy had already been diverted. Early the following morning Takagi and Fletcher located each other almost simultaneously. Eighty-two American aircraft struck first, a low-level torpedo attack diverting attention from the dive-bombers, which caused moderate damage to one carrier with three bomb hits.

The extra experience of the Japanese showed when they pressed home a torpedo attack from two directions, again to cover their dive-bombers. The American combat air patrol (CAP) was caught off-position, the *Yorktown* taking one bomb but the *Lexington* two bombs and two torpedoes. A large ship, she would have survived these structurally, but ruptured aviation fuel lines allowed pockets of explosive vapour to collect. A series of devastating explosions eventually destroyed the ship.

This, the battle of the Coral Sea, caused the Japanese to abandon their plans to invade the south coast of New Guinea. It was additionally significant that the battle was the first naval engagement in which the opposing sides did not sight each other.

The commander-in-chief of the Japanese combined fleet, Admiral Isoroku Yamamoto, sought to provoke a decisive action with the American Pacific Fleet

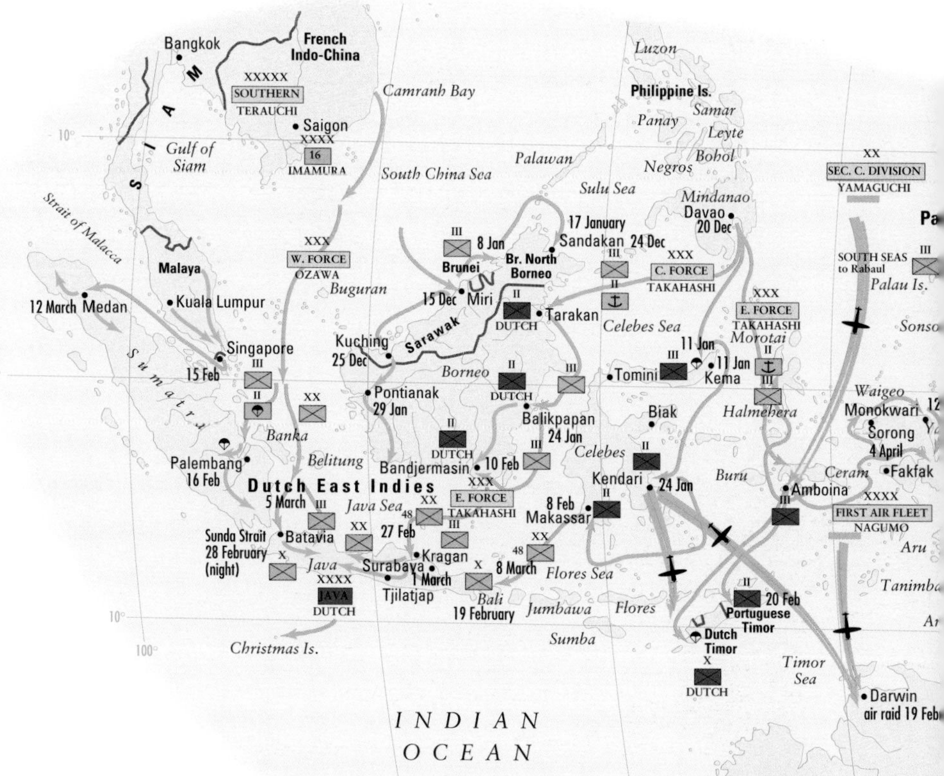


## Axes of Japanese advance and Allied response

*The raid on Darwin and the location of the Coral Sea action show just how closely the Japanese threatened Australia. Events, including the loss of Singapore and Hong Kong, exposed British imperial defence plans for the political sham that they were.The Coral Sea action, although a* matériel *victory for the Japanese, shocked them in being the first real opposition that they had faced. They read from it that they had advanced far enough and faced over-attenuated lines of communication.*

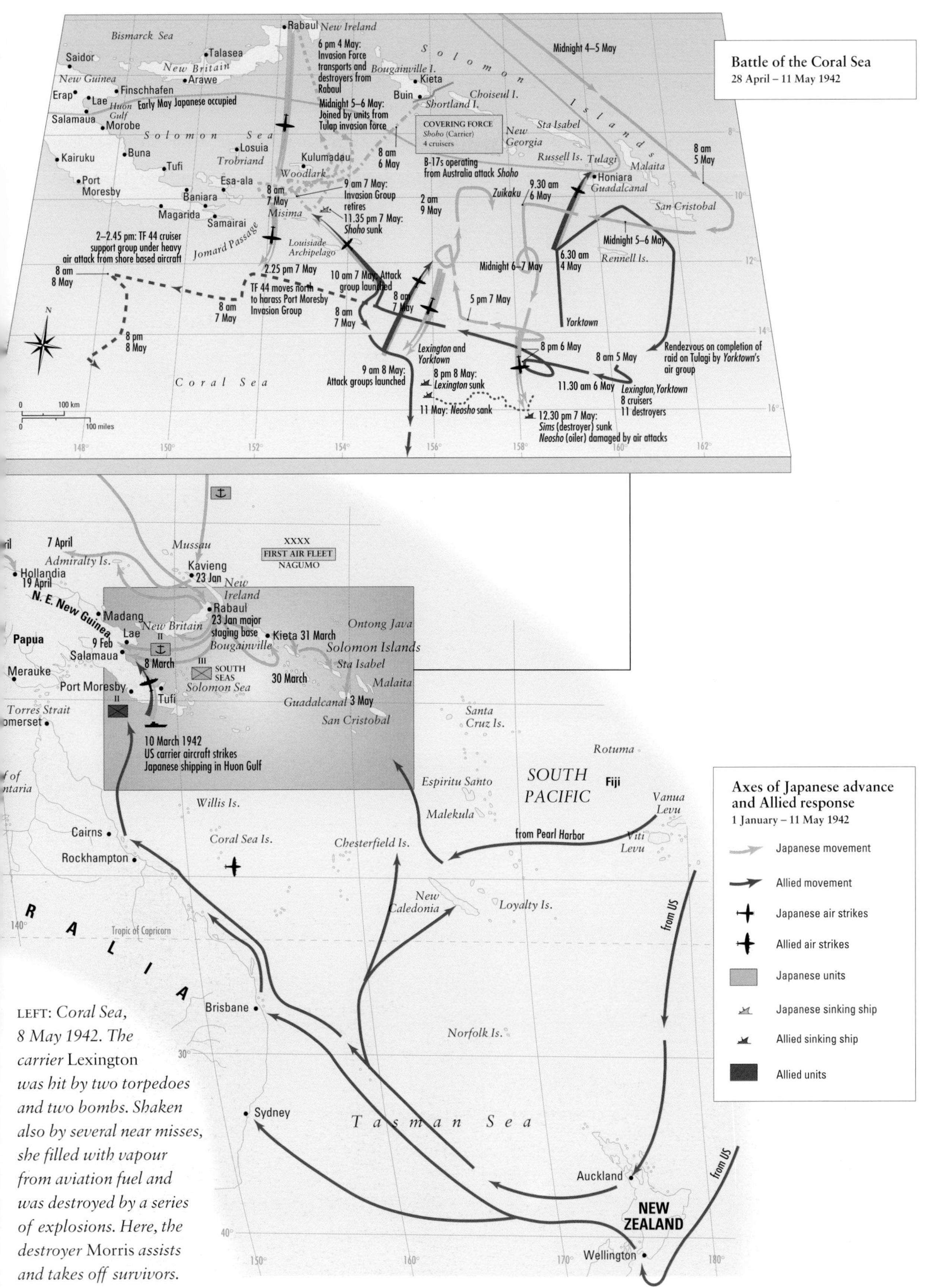


LEFT: *Coral Sea, 8 May 1942. The carrier* Lexington *was hit by two torpedoes and two bombs. Shaken also by several near misses, she filled with vapour from aviation fuel and was destroyed by a series of explosions. Here, the destroyer* Morris *assists and takes off survivors.*

before its inevitable reinforcement. He reasoned that the capture of Midway Island would elicit the required American response but his plan fragmented his forces. Nagumo, with four carriers (two were being repaired following the Coral Sea action), would reduce the island's defences sufficiently to allow a separate assault force to land. The main body of the Japanese fleet would stay to the west, awaiting American intervention. A fourth force would attack the Aleutian Islands, far to the north, to confuse the Americans and, it was hoped, split their forces. American intelligence, however, accurately predicted Yamamoto's intentions and Nimitz, in great secrecy, located Rear Admiral Raymond A. Spruance, with three carriers, to the north-east of the island.

On 4 June 1942 Nagumo hit Midway with 144 aircraft but the alerted garrison shot down thirty-eight and damaged many more. Intent on his main task, Nagumo neglected to fly adequate reconnaissance missions and Spruance, now superior in

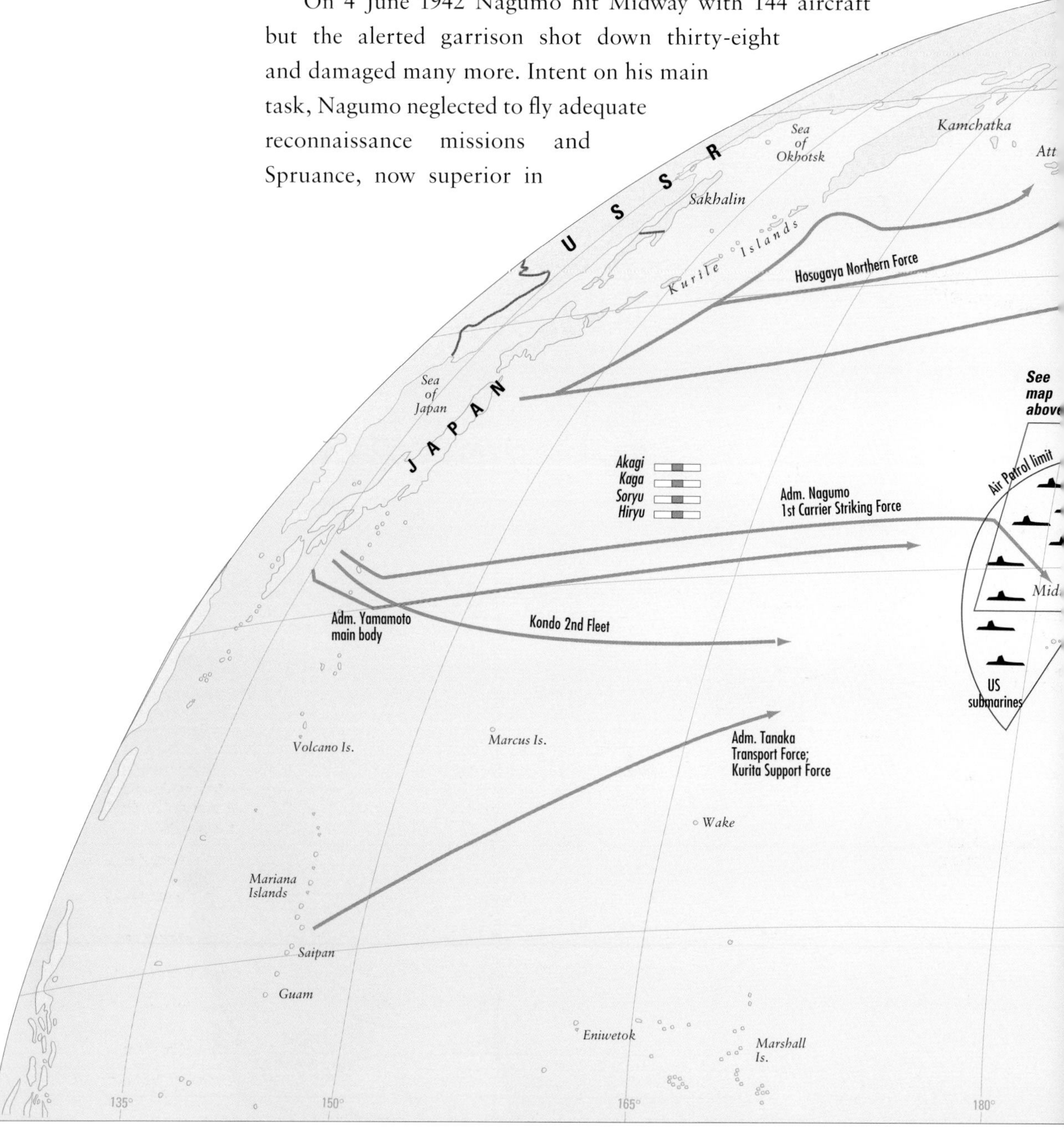

## Battle of Midway

*The decisive American victory at Midway was based on a combination of exploitation of good intelligence and the weakness of the over-complicated Japanese strategy, which relied on deception rather than the concentration of power at the critical location.*

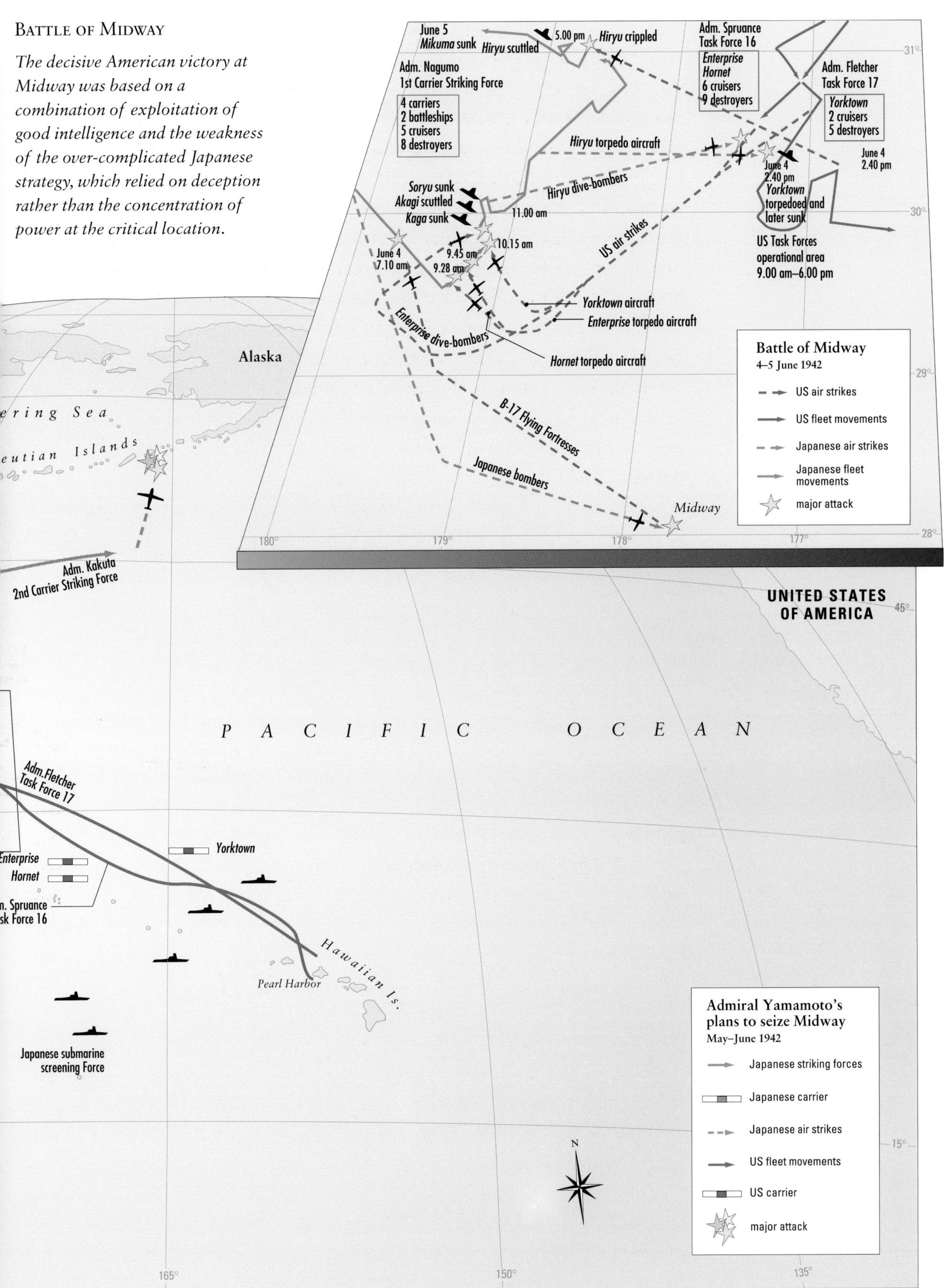

aircraft strength, remained undetected. As insufficient damage had been inflicted on the island, a second air strike was decided upon. On the two largest carriers, aircraft ready armed to meet the American fleet now had to be rearmed. While this was being effected, the first strike aircraft were being recovered. The carriers were thus in a vulnerable state of disorder when Spruance's strike arrived.

The Japanese CAP dealt severely with the American torpedo aircraft, which attacked first and without cover. In the process, however, its fighters were brought down to surface level and, in manoeuvring to avoid torpeodes, the carrier formation had lost its cohesion. Almost unopposed, the following American dive-bombers were able to hit hard at three of Nagumo's carriers, all of which succumbed to uncontrollable fires. Aircraft from the fourth Japanese carrier, *Hiryu*, struck back at the *Yorktown*, damaging her to the extent that she was eventually lost. *Hiryu*, in turn, was then destroyed by a further Spruance strike.

Despite the enormous firepower of Yamamoto's waiting fleet, it no longer enjoyed air superiority and the whole enterprise had to be abandoned. Midway, the first Japanese naval defeat, was for them a disaster.

Soon after, in August 1942, Nagumo provided distant cover for a Japanese convoy sent to reinforce Guadalcanal. He had his two large carriers *Zuikaku* and

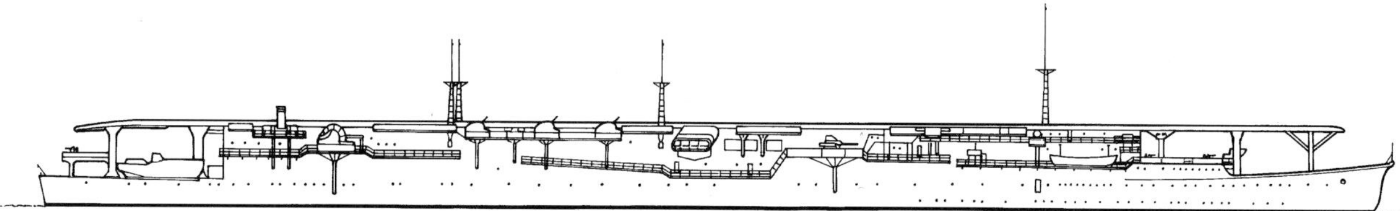

ZUIHO 1941

*The Japanese carrier* Zuiho *and her sister* Shoho *(sunk at the Coral Sea) were launched in 1935/6 as submarine depot ships. To circumvent Washington Treaty limits on carrier tonnage, they were designed for later convertion to lightcarriers.* Zuiho *was expended at Leyte Gulf in 1944 as a unit of* Ozawa's *diversionary force.*

*Shokaku*, repaired following damage at the Coral Sea. Opposing him, Rear Admiral Fletcher had good intelligence and three carriers but with poor timing detached one to refuel. In attacking the convoy, Fletcher's aircraft sank the light carrier *Ryujo*, whose own air group was away hitting the island. With his own first strike absent, Fletcher himself was then hit by Nagumo and was lucky to escape with a heavily damaged *Enterprise*. The action, known as the battle of the Eastern Solomons, then petered out with both commanders excessively nervous of losing another carrier.

The gritty, see-saw struggle for Guadalcanal brought about a further clash in October 1942 when Yamamoto sought to destroy American naval forces supporting the island. He steamed in two groups, a van (including the large auxiliary carrier *Junyo*) upon which a riposte was expected to fall, followed at a distance by another force, built around Nagumo's two large carriers and the smaller, converted *Zuiho*.

For his part, the pugnacious and impetuous Vice Admiral William F. Halsey had just two carriers, the scarred *Enterprise* and the newly arrived *Hornet*. True to her name, the *Enterprise* dispatched early reconnaissance aircraft armed with 500-pound bombs. Finding and reporting Nagumo, they also put the *Zuiho* out of the impending action with a single destructive hit. *Zuiho*, however, had already launched her share of a sixty-two-plane strike, which was followed within the hour by a second of seventy-three aircraft. En route these passed Halsey's response, also of seventy-three aircraft.

The American carriers and their screens manoeuvred independently, but no defence could withstand blows on this scale. Within ten minutes the *Hornet* had taken four bombs and two torpedo hits, together with two crashing aircraft. The *Enterprise* suffered two hits and a near miss. The protracted and ultimately unsuccessful efforts to save the *Hornet* left the *Enterprise* as the only serviceable American carrier in the theatre.

As Yamamoto had hoped, most of the American effort had fallen upon his surface ships, his big carrier *Shokaku* surviving four bomb hits. He should have struck again to finish off the *Enterprise* (and indeed the still-floating *Hornet*) but the newly introduced American proximity-fused AA ammunition had simply caused him too many losses.

This, the battle of Santa Cruz, had reduced American fortunes to a low ebb. The *Wasp* had been lost to submarine torpedoes in the previous month, leaving the *Enterprise* as the only carrier capable of flying urgently required replacement

*Years of planning against war in the western Pacific resulted in the US Navy having ships of long endurance, extended by re-supply from an adequate fleet train. In contrast, the British fleet was designed around operation from fixed bases, and was adversely affected when these were lost.*

aircraft into Guadalcanal. Tenacity finally paid off, however, with the Japanese evacuating the island in February 1943. Two months later, the course of the Pacific war was changed when good intelligence led to the ambushing and destruction of Admiral Yamamoto's aircraft over Bougainville.

The 1938 supplement to the 1934 Vinson-Trammell Act had provided for an extra 40,000 tons of carriers. These became the short-lived *Hornet* and the rather larger *Essex*. Although the latter's design was subsequent to the relaxation of treaty conditions, it was really only a 27,500-ton extrapolation of earlier work. Protection against shellfire had been reworked to meet the greater threat of bombing, but she was effectively unarmoured. With war came the urgent need to build rapidly. As there was no time to develop a new ship, the *Essex* became the lead for the protracted class that proved crucial to success in the Pacific.

In repairing heavily bombed British armoured carriers, the Americans had been impressed by their ability to survive. Their resultant closed design, however, made them cramped and allowed them much smaller aircraft capacity, which was counter to US naval doctrine, with its emphasis on large air wings and well-ordered flight deck operations.

Despite high priority, it took until the end of 1942 to complete the *Essex* and, with the navy desperately short of flight-decks, the President himself overrode professional detractors to insist on the conversion of cruiser hulls to light carriers. Nine of these useful little ships, the Independence-class CVLs, were completed during 1943 to complement the first seven Essex-class CVs. At a displacement of 14,200 tons they could accommodate thirty-one aircraft and maintain fleet speed of 31.5 knots.

The United States froze standard designs to facilitate rapid series production but, except for a single (and too late) class of light carriers, the Japanese had a haphazard approach, producing mainly one-offs and mercantile conversions.

From the last day of 1942, when the *Essex* commissioned, the Japanese fleet was effectively facing annihilation as American production got into its stride. The following table, listing completions per quarter, shows by just how much the Japanese were out-built.

In parallel with their ambitious carrier construction programme, the

*Observance of Washington Treaty limitations left the major fleets with insufficient carriers. Early losses thus left the US Navy very short of decks while the Essex-class fleet carriers were being built. As an interim measure, therefore, nine Independence-class CVLs were converted from cruiser hulls. This is the USS Langley (CVL.27).*

*Simpson Harbour, at Rabaul in New Britain, became the major Japanese fleet base for operations in the Solomons. Remorseless strikes from growing American carrier air power exposed its vulnerability and brought about its abandonment.*

Americans thoroughly trained enormous numbers of aircrew, an issue addressed by the Japanese, to their cost, with nothing like the same urgency

It took time to work-up new carriers to combat efficiency and it was November 1943 before they went again on the offensive. Two strikes were made on the enemy's fleet base at Rabaul. The second of these involved two new CVs and a CVL which collectively could muster 46 Avenger torpedo bombers, 69 Dauntless and Helldiver dive-bombers, and 120 Corsair and Hellcat fighters. Two Japanese ships were sunk and 6 heavily damaged, while 40 out of 108 defending fighters were shot down. The important result was that the Japanese High Command reassessed Rabaul as being too exposed to be used further as a fleet anchorage.

| | 1942 | | | | 1943 | | | | 1944 | | | | 1945 | | |
|---|---|---|---|---|---|---|---|---|---|---|---|---|---|---|---|
| | 1st | 2nd | 3rd | 4th | 1st | 2nd | 3rd | 4th | 1st | 2nd | 3rd | 4th | 1st | 2nd | 3rd |
| **American** | | | | | | | | | | | | | | | |
| Essex (CV) | – | – | – | 1 | 1 | 2 | 1 | 2 | 1 | 2 | 1 | 2 | – | 3 | – |
| Independence (CVL) | – | – | – | – | 3 | 2 | 2 | 2 | – | – | – | – | – | – | – |
| Escort carriers (CVE) | 2 | – | 8 | 5 | 3 | 10 | 14 | 21 | 18 | 16 | 2 | 2 | 2 | 6 | – |
| **Japanese** | | | | | | | | | | | | | | | |
| Fleet carriers | – | – | – | – | – | – | – | – | 1 | – | – | 1 | – | – | – |
| Light fleet carriers | – | – | – | – | – | – | – | 1 | 1 | – | 2 | 1 | – | – | – |
| Auxiliary carriers | 1 | 2 | 1 | 1 | – | – | – | 2 | – | – | – | – | 2 | – | – |

Admiral Nimitz's naval forces were reorganized as the Fifth Fleet, under the tactical control of Vice Admiral Spruance. Within its structure, the carrier force was styled Task Force 50 (TF50), first under Rear Admiral Pownall then, from January 1944, Rear Admiral Marc A. Mitscher. By November 1943 it could already deploy eleven carriers, the much-experienced *Saratoga* and *Enterprise*, four Essex-class CVs and five CVLs. These operated in four separate Task Groups (TG 50.1 to TG50.4), each with its dedicated surface and AA escort. This included battleships which, so long the yardstick of naval power, had yielded place to the new-style capital ship, with her ability to strike hammer blows at a distance of 200 miles and more.

Combined or separately, task groups were used to mount extended offensives against the enemy prior to any major amphibious assault. Japanese aerial opposition was virtually extinguished while, consequently lacking cover, their naval forces kept their distance. American combat sorties might exceed one thousand on such an operation but, due to the overwhelming nature of the attacks, losses were relatively light. Replacement aircraft were continuously ferried-in by attached CVEs.

*Loaded with ordnance and aviation fuel, carriers proved to be very vulnerable to dive-bombing. The US Navy's SB2C Helldiver replaced an earlier aircraft of the same name and could carry a 2000-pound bomb load. Two Helldivers here overfly the Essex-class* Hornet.

The alternative Japanese major fleet anchorage was at Truk in the eastern Carolines. Prior to the Eniwetok landings of February 1944, Spruance scourged Truk for two days with the combined air wings of 6 CVs and 4 CVLs, later supported by heavy naval firepower. Out of 350 Japanese aircraft, 300 were destroyed for the loss of just 25 American. Seven warships, several auxiliaries and about 28 merchantmen were sunk. Like Rabaul, Truk was effectively abandoned by the enemy as now being too vulnerable.

Relentlessly increasing in severity, similar blows were inflicted on the Marianas in February 1944, the Palaus in April and, in June, the Bonins and Truk and the Marianas again. Reacting powerfully to the threat against the Marianas, the Japanese mustered their whole fleet. This included the still-formidable total of 5 large and 4 small carriers, with a total of about 430 aircraft. Mitscher, however, now faced these with 7 CVs, 8 CVLs and 890 aircraft.

Covering the June landings on Saipan, Spruance cruised westward, interposed between the likely approach of the enemy and the islands. His opponent, Vice Admiral Jisaburo Ozawa, remained further to the west, just beyond the range of the American aircraft. His plan was to fly an outward leg,

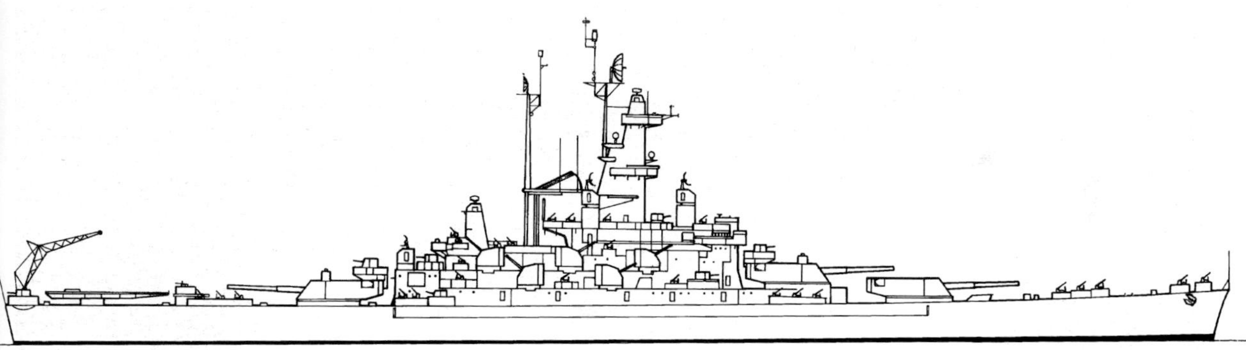

*MASSACHUSETTS*

*The American battleship* Massachusetts *(BB59) had an unlikely baptism of fire in duelling with the Vichy French battleship* Jean Bart *at Casablanca in November 1942. She was then present at all the major Pacific actions. One of the four South Dakota class, she is now preserved by her home state at Fall River.*

attacking Spruance and landing his aircraft on the islands to refuel and rearm, prior to a second attack as they returned to their carriers. They would be supported by land-based air power already in the islands, although Ozawa was never appraised by how much this had already been reduced by Mitscher's fliers.

As was customary, the American carriers were organized in four heavily escorted groups. Between them and Ozawa was a 'gun-line' of Rear Admiral Willis A. Lee's seven battleships and supporting ships. Mitscher could mount a rotating cover from his 450 fighters but, even before they met these, the Japanese suffered at the hands of Lee. Sinking nothing, four waves of Japanese aircraft were greatly reduced as they flew on to the islands, only to find intruder squadrons awaiting them over their airfields.

Ozawa, meanwhile, had run into submarine country and lost both the big Pearl Harbor veteran *Shokaku* and the new, armoured *Taiho*, which succumbed to a devastating Avgas vapour explosion following a hit by a single torpedo. Late in the afternoon Mitscher located Ozawa's force and, despite the hour, dispatched over 200 aircraft at the very limit of their range. They found and destroyed the large auxiliary carrier *Hiyo* but, while the attack cost only 20 aircraft, a further 80 ditched as their fuel ran out. So ended the battle of the Philippine Sea, a body-blow for the Japanese, who lost 3 carriers, 50 land-based and nearly 400 carrier aircraft, with most of the latter's crews. Whereas the Americans were organized to make good their not-inconsiderable losses, the Japanese were not. Their fleet was now vulnerable, its carriers possessing aircraft but few trained aircrew.

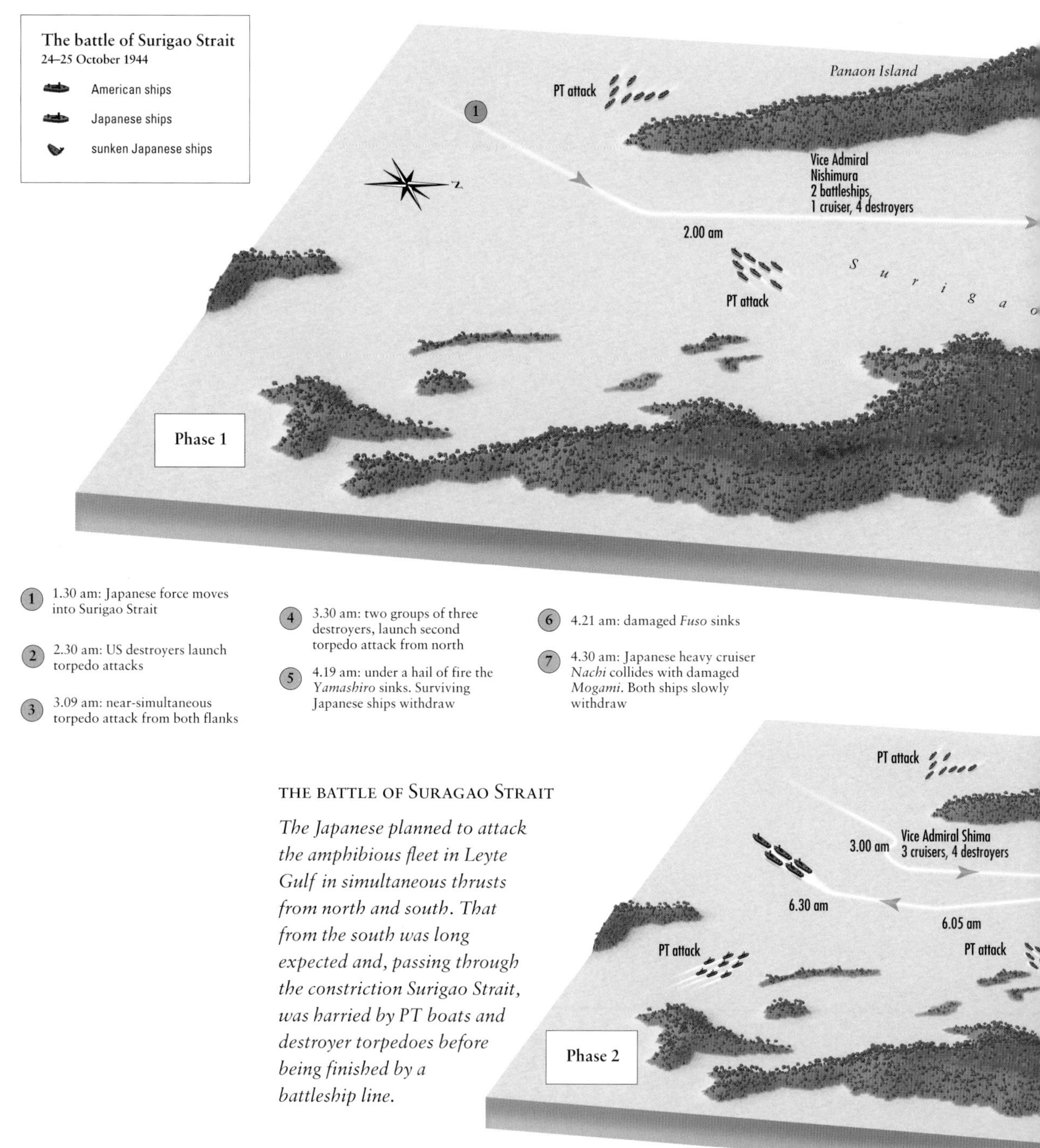


THE BATTLE OF SURAGAO STRAIT

*The Japanese planned to attack the amphibious fleet in Leyte Gulf in simultaneous thrusts from north and south. That from the south was long expected and, passing through the constriction Surigao Strait, was harried by PT boats and destroyer torpedoes before being finished by a battleship line.*

Landings at Leyte Gulf in the Philippines were planned for October 1944, and Mitscher's fliers had three months to scour these islands and the staging airfields on Formosa. The deteriorating standards of the enemy air force is evident in that about 1,360 Japanese planes were claimed for the loss of 115 American aircraft.

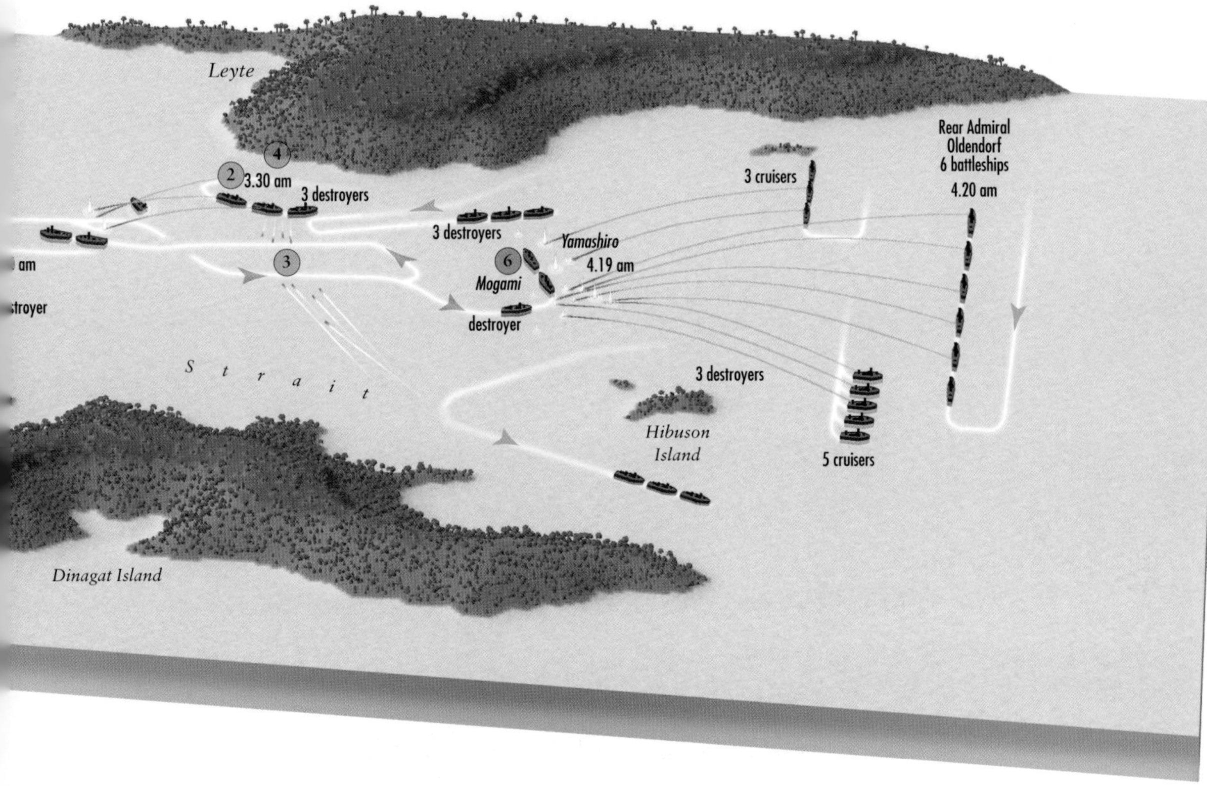

MacArthur's landings on 20 October triggered the 'decisive battle' that the Imperial Navy had long sought but was no longer in a condition to fight. Greatly



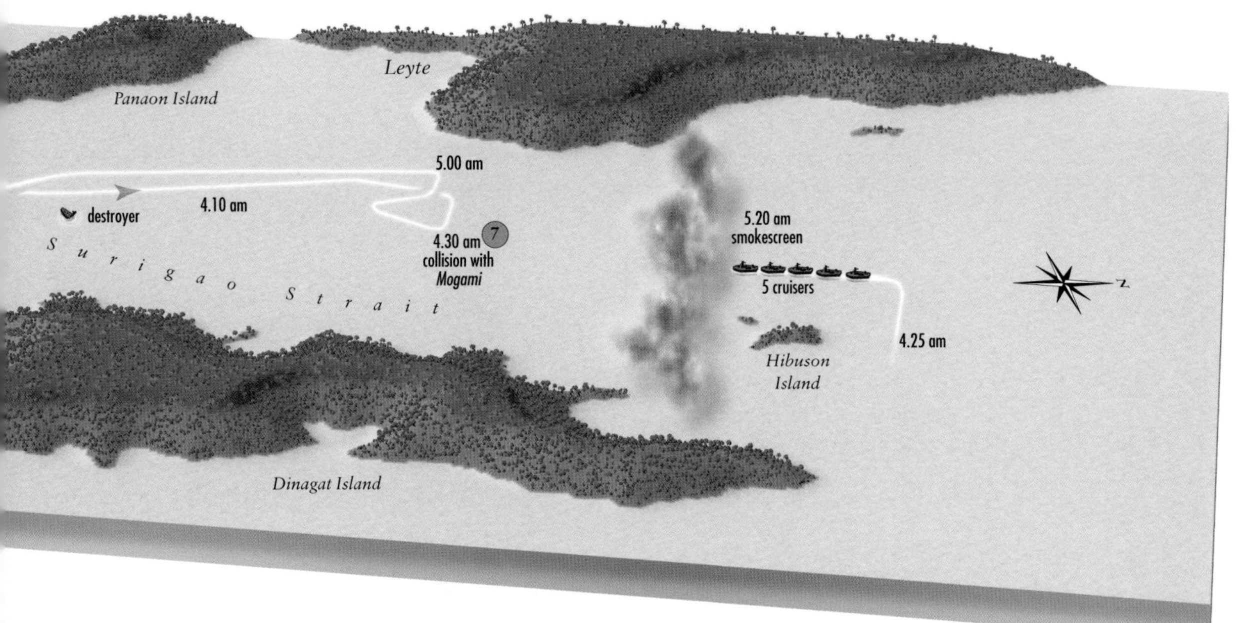

reduced land-based air could give little support or cover, while Ozawa's remaining four carriers, with barely one hundred aircraft between them, were fit only to be used as live bait to successfully lure fleet commander Halsey dangerously out of position.

In sacrificing itself, Ozawa's force opened the way for a powerful Japanese surface group to attack the amphibious forces directly. The only obstacle was Rear Admiral Thomas Sprague's eighteen CVEs, providing close air support for forces ashore. Packing thirty-plus aircraft apiece, the little carriers responded like heroes, with fliers and surface escort fighting desperately. Unnerved, the Japanese admiral, Kurita, retired, less three heavy cruisers.

The battles for Leyte Gulf collectively finished Japanese sea power as a serious threat but a worrying development emerged as Sprague's carriers were deliberately crashed by enemy aircraft. The kamikaze had arrived.

February and April 1945 brought the bitter struggle for Iwo Jima and Okinawa. Mitscher's force, now of 10 CVs and 6 CVLs with 1200 aircraft, were reinforced by the 4 armoured carriers of the reconstituted British Eastern Fleet, with a further 220 aircraft. This latter was effectively no more than an extra task

*This dramatic damage was not caused by enemy action but by wave impact. As designed, the Essex-class carriers had very light flightdecks, carried forward on pillars above an open forecastle, and vulnerable to severe pitching. The British style 'hurricane bow' was later adopted, continuing the shellplating to the underside of the flight deck.*

group, whose poor endurance meant frequent absences for replenishment from American sources, while being covered by American CVEs.

British carriers, however, were able to withstand kamikaze impacts that took American CVs out of the line, but this was only at the cost of capacity. With roughly the same displacement, an Essex could deploy 95 to 100 aircraft, while from the British squadron, *Formidable* accommodated just 43 aircraft, the *Indefatigable* 69. To detect the approach of the kamikaze, each carrier now deployed an Airborne Early Warning (AEW) aircraft which was fitted with specialist radar.

In August 1945, the detonation of the first nuclear weapons opened a new debate regarding the continuing viability of concentrated task groups of high-value units such as carriers or amphibious ships.

## The invasion of Norway, 1940

Senior officers of the German navy could well recall how, in the previous war, the presence of the British Grand Fleet in its northern bases prevented any effective access to the open ocean. They recalled, too, how in 1918 British political pressure caused Norway to install a minefield in her own territorial waters, completing the great Anglo-American mine barrier and forcing mercantile shipping into international waters where it could be regulated.

With the British economic blockade of Germany again tightening its grip early in 1940, the thousand-mile long conduit of the Norwegian inner leads was a safe route for German shipping, as long as Norway remained neutral. This was particularly important with respect to iron-ore imports from Sweden when, for five months per year, ice closed off the Baltic route.

While the British had as yet made no move to re-create the Northern Barrage, the then First Lord, Winston Churchill, was keen to choke the German ore movements by again mining Norwegian territorial waters. The pretext for this was that Germany, particularly with the Altmark incident, was already violating them. Operation Wilfred was thus planned to block the leads at three points. Any

*Following the destruction of the raider* Graf Spee *her supply ship,* Altmark, *tried to return to Germany with 300 British merchant seamen prisoners on board. She was intercepted by British destroyers and boarded within Norwegian territorial waters. In this memorable incident all captives were successfully liberated.*

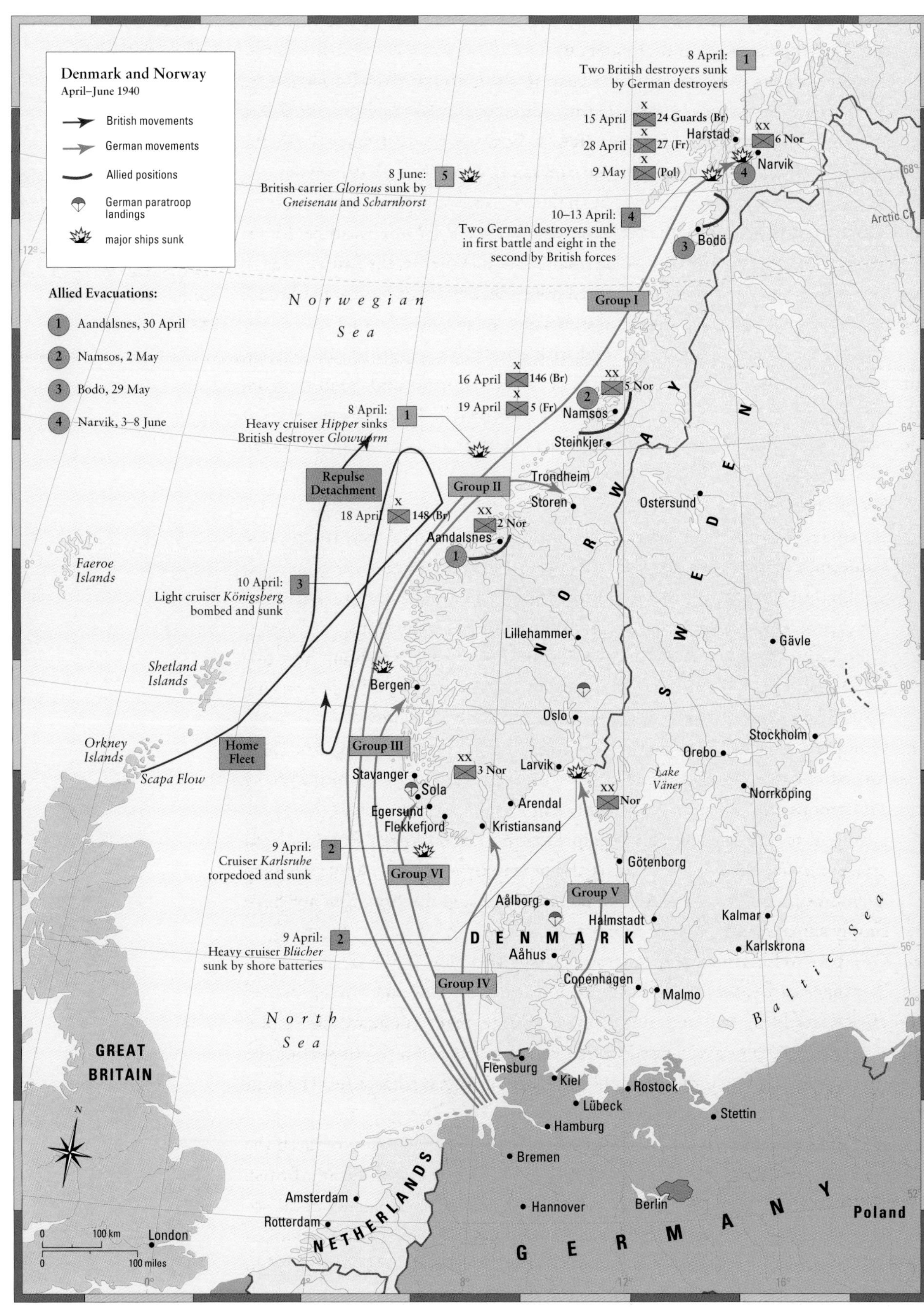
Denmark and Norway
April–June 1940
British movements
German movements
Allied positions
German paratroop landings
major ships sunk
Allied Evacuations:
1 Aandalsnes, 30 April
2 Namsos, 2 May
3 Bodö, 29 May
4 Narvik, 3–8 June
8 April: Two British destroyers sunk by German destroyers
15 April 24 Guards (Br)
28 April 27 (Fr)
9 May (Pol)
6 Nor
Harstad
Narvik
8 June: British carrier Glorious sunk by Gneisenau and Scharnhorst
10–13 April: Two German destroyers sunk in first battle and eight in the second by British forces
Bodö
Arctic Ci
Norwegian Sea
Group I
16 April 146 (Br)
19 April 5 (Fr)
5 Nor
Namsos
8 April: Heavy cruiser Hipper sinks British destroyer Glowworm
Steinkjer
Repulse Detachment
Group II
Trondheim
Storen
Ostersund
18 April 148 (Br)
2 Nor
Aandalsnes
Faeroe Islands
10 April: Light cruiser Königsberg bombed and sunk
NORWAY
SWEDEN
Lillehammer
Gävle
Shetland Islands
Bergen
Oslo
Orkney Islands
Scapa Flow
Home Fleet
Group III
Stockholm
Orebo
3 Nor
Larvik
Stavanger
Sola
Lake Väner
Nor
Norrköping
Egersund
Flekkefjord
Arendal
Kristiansand
9 April: Cruiser Karlsruhe torpedoed and sunk
Group VI
Götenborg
Group V
Aålborg
Halmstadt
Kalmar
9 April: Heavy cruiser Blücher sunk by shore batteries
DENMARK
Aåhus
Karlskrona
Group IV
Copenhagen
Malmo
Baltic Sea
North Sea
GREAT BRITAIN
Flensburg
Kiel
Rostock
Lübeck
Hamburg
Stettin
Bremen
NETHERLANDS
Amsterdam
Hannover
Berlin
Rotterdam
London
GERMANY
Poland
0 100 km
0 100 miles
N

military response by the enemy would be met by a landing of Allied troops at Bergen, Narvik, Stavanger and Trondheim.

Such ambitions were transparently clear to the German High Command, as the British in Norway could throttle the winter ore traffic and put the Baltic within range of the Royal Air Force (RAF). Beginning in February 1940, the Germans therefore planned a pre-emptive invasion, codenamed *Weserübung*.

Norway's mountainous geography makes for sparse communications, with most centres of population situated on the deeply indented fjord coastline. Major links are maintained by sea and the German plan, like that of the British, was to use surprise to come alongside at selected ports, secure the port area and hold it pending the rapid arrival of support vessels sailed in advance.

For the Germans it was a very high-risk enterprise, requiring the services of every available warship, working in small groups and remote from their bases, in a North Sea dominated by the British Home Fleet. Success depended upon total surprise but subsequent withdrawal of the ships looked problematical.

Six groups would be sailed at appropriate intervals against Norway:

1. Group I to Narvik. Ten destroyers, carrying two thousand Alpine troops. Fast battleships *Scharnhorst* and *Gneisenau* to give distant cover.
2. Group II to Trondheim. Heavy cruiser *Hipper* and four destroyers with seven hundred troops. Follow-up by one tanker and three supply ships.
3. Group III to Bergen. Light cruisers *Köln* and *Königsberg*, a training ship, two torpedo boats and an E-boat flotilla with its parent ship, all told carrying 1,900 troops. Follow-up by one tanker and three supply ships.
4. Group IV to Christiansand and Arendal. Light cruiser *Karlsruhe*, three torpedo boats and an E-boat flotilla with its parent ship, all told carrying 1100 troops. Follow-up by four supply ships.
5. Group V to Oslo. Pocket battleship *Lützow*, heavy cruiser *Blücher*, light cruiser *Emden*, three torpedo boats and ten minor warships, all told carrying 2,000 troops. Follow-up by two tankers and fire supply ships. Twenty-three supply ships would follow within days.
6. Group VI to Egersund. Four minesweepers with a motor-cycle detachment.

Stavanger airfield would be seized by a Luftwaffe landing force, tactical minefields would be laid and almost every operational U-boat would be pre-positioned to intercept anticipated British response. Five Danish ports would be taken simultaneously, mainly with minor warships acting as transports. The hour was fixed for 5 a.m. on 9 April 1940.

Had Wilfred commenced on 5 April, as planned, it would have reduced the British to total confusion but, unfortunately, it was delayed until the 8th. British codebreakers were still in the early stages of mastering Naval Enigma but the so-called 'traffic analysis' studied the general pattern of transmissions and looked for any variations that might indicate enemy activity. An upsurge was noted in early April and the Admiralty's Operational Intelligence Centre (OIC) notified.

Denmark and Norway April–June 1940

*This map well illustrates the boldness of the German plan to invade Norway. All but the smallest group was open to flank attack by the British Home Fleet. Surprise was relied upon, and achieved, but this still left the Germans the problem of getting their ships home again.*

The prompt, however, was too imprecise to cause the Admiralty to order any precautionary dispositions.

Having furthest to travel, German Groups I and II and various supply ships were sailed early, and sightings caused the Home Fleet to sail from Scapa late on the 7th, though it steered north-eastward to guard against a possible Atlantic breakout.

Three British minelaying groups sailed as scheduled, two towards the Norwegian coast between Bergen and Trondheim, the third towards the Narvik approach in Vestfjord. To counter expected opposition, the Narvik group was covered by the battlecruiser *Renown* and a destroyer group. One of the latter, *Glowworm*, lost a man overboard. Searching, she became detached and blundered into enemy Groups I and II, still in company. Having exchanged fire

with two of their destroyers, she was heavily hit by the 8-inch main battery of the *Hipper*. With no chance of escape, her captain, G. B. Roope, turned and rammed the cruiser, an action for which he was awarded the Victoria Cross.

British submarines and reconnaissance aircraft were by now reporting so many enemy groups at sea that the overall picture became one of confusion, not helped by Group II being sighted marking time off Trondheim as Group I held on towards Narvik in a full gale.

The British commander-in-chief, Admiral of the Fleet Sir Charles Forbes, sent the *Repulse* to reinforce the *Renown*. Cruisers, ready loaded with combat troops, disembarked them and proceeded to sea. Group IV overcame resistance easily, but Group V, approaching Oslo via the Drobak narrows, was engaged by the Oskarsborg fort, whose ancient Krupp guns immobilized the *Blücher* with two 28cm shells. Drifting, the ship was then torpedoed twice, capsizing with heavy loss of life. This, however, did not affect the outcome at Oslo which, once seized, became the enemy's main port of entry.

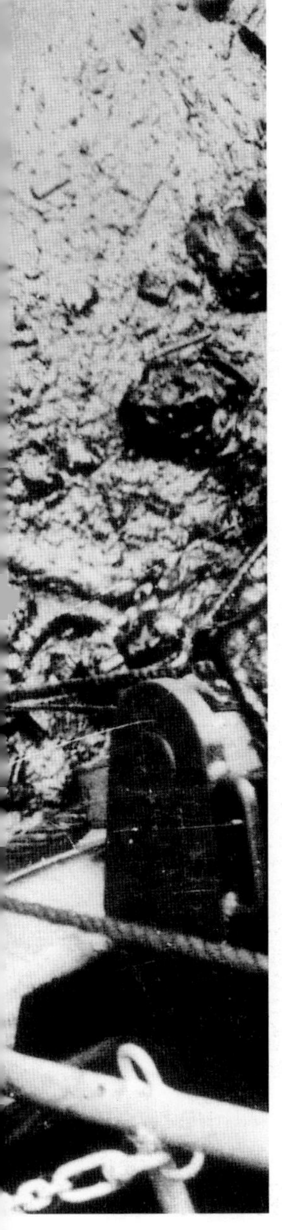

*In gallantly fighting the heavy cruiser Admiral Hipper and her escort the captain of the British destroyer* Glowworm *earned a Victoria Cross. Rescued by the enemy, the survivors in their oil-soaked wretchedness could be survivors of either side, anywhere.*

At Trondheim the *Hipper* bought vital minutes in confusing the Norwegians by signalling in English. Her destroyers quickly landed assault troops who occupied batteries from the land side. The defences at Bergen were less easily misled and damaged both the *Königsberg* and the returning *Bremse*. Here, Group III forces were accessible from the sea and four British cruisers were ordered to intervene. A fine opportunity was lost with the countermanding of the instruction. The situation was redeemed somewhat by sixteen Skua dive-bombers of the Fleet Air Arm which, flying at extreme range from their Orkney base, sank the *Königsberg* at her berth. She was the first major warship to be sunk by dive-bomber in combat.

As Group I's destroyers steamed into Narvik their heavy cover remained at sea where, early on 9 April, it encountered the *Renown*. The German commander failed to exploit his two-ship advantage and, in an indecisive exchange of fire, the *Gneisenau* received three 15-inch hits in exchange for two 11-inch.

Before entering Narvik the enemy destroyers had landed detachments to seize key points, and had torpedoed and sunk two Norwegian coast-defence ships. They were still much scattered and needing to refuel when, out of the snowy gloom of the following dawn, they were surprised by five British destroyers. In an exceedingly fierce mêlée each force lost two ships. The attackers also intercepted support ships carrying all the invader's ammunition and motor transport.

The port of Narvik lies at the head of a long cul-de-sac and it was unwise of the German commander to remain, although refuelling was painfully slow and action damage needed to be repaired. Early on 13 April the British returned with the battleship *Warspite* and nine destroyers. Every last enemy was hounded into dead ends and destroyed. Although 50 per cent of the German navy's large destroyers had been thus eliminated, Narvik remained in German hands.

In support of *Weserübung*, Admiral Dönitz involved no less than twenty of his twenty-three commissioned ocean-going U-boats and all but four of his twenty-six coastal boats. The Germans were also freely reading British naval codes, an advantage offset somewhat by the British having learned their dispositions; they achieved little because of chronic torpedo problems. Like the Americans, the Germans had economized too far on pre-war live firings and now suffered from unrectified depth-keeping problems and over-sensitive magnetic firing pistols.

British (and, indeed, one Polish) boats, in contrast, made good practice, sinking twenty-one supply ships totalling 112,000 grt, a German loss rate of about 9 per cent. The light cruiser *Karlsruhe* and training ship *Brummer* were also sunk by torpedo, with severe damage inflicted on the *Gneisenau* and *Lützow*. Three British submarines were lost.

*On 8 June 1940 the British aircraft carrier* Glorious *was returning from Norway when she was intercepted by the German* Gneisenau *(seen here firing on her) and her sister,* Scharnhorst. *With no reconnaissance aircraft aloft, the* Glorious *was surprised and, with no strike at readiness, quickly sunk.*

With the seizure of the major port of Oslo, the Germans were able rapidly to extend their hold over the whole country. Allied military forces were landed in the north, but it was always a matter of too little too late and the campaign was a failure.

The Luftwaffe was quickly established and, lacking air superiority, Allied navies soon discovered that daylight operations were consequently hazardous. For instance, the heavy cruiser *Suffolk* was directed to bombard the strategic airfield at Sola, near Stavanger at dawn on 17 April. Orders prevented her from withdrawing in good time and, with designated RAF cover failing to materialize, she suffered thirty-three separate air attacks over the space of seven hours. She survived, but returned with half her main battery inoperative following a 1,000-pound bomb hit that also admitted some 2,500 tons of water aft.

Supporting the campaign and conducting the June evacuation proved expensive to the Royal Navy, mainly in minor warships, although the light cruiser *Curlew*

*At 7.22 p.m. on 23 May 1941 HMS* Suffolk *sighted the* Bismarck *and* Prinz Eugen *in the Denmark Strait, putting in train a fateful sequence of events. Note the quarterdeck, cut down one level to save topweight, the Walrus amphibian and the curious 'whited-out' funnel tops.*

and valuable carrier *Glorious* were also lost, the latter totally unncessarily. Her escort destroyers did, however, succeed in torpedoing the *Scharnhorst* in return.

Acting with great boldness, the numerically inferior German fleet achieved its objectives in the invasion of Norway, assisted by an extraordinary reluctance on the part of the British to react to preceding indicators. In relation to its size, the losses suffered by the German navy were severe and inevitably exerted a negative effect on subsequent undertakings. The strategic importance of an occupied Norway also diminished for the enemy with the unexpectedly rapid acquisition of bases on the French Biscay coast. It came back into its own, however, when in September 1941, the Allies commenced the convoy cycle to North Russia.

Journey's end. *Charles Pears's painting depicts the arrival of a convoy at Murmansk. Having survived enemy and weather to get there, personnel found conditions ashore so unremittingly bleak as to make the prospect of the return trip almost welcome.*

## The Mediterranean convoy war 1940–43

The long barrier of Italy and Sicily divides the Mediterranean into an eastern and western basin, the resulting central narrows being only 75 miles in width. This central section is totally dominated by Italy, yet here is located Malta, then the main base of the British Mediterranean Fleet. About 1,000 miles to the west and 800 to the east lie Gibraltar and Alexandria, with their lesser facilities. Their function was to safeguard the route via the Suez canal to India and the Far East.

Of the North African coastline, 750 miles comprises Italian Libya, where a quarter of a million troops under Marshal Rodolfo Graziani were stationed. To the west are Tunisia and Algeria. Their initial strategic value was not recognized by the overstretched Germans who placed them under an armistice commission when France capitulated in June 1940.

Italian military ambitions looked eastward to Egypt and the canal zone, protected by just 36,000 British and Commonwealth (hereafter referred to as 'British' for the sake of simplicity) troops under General Archibald Wavell.

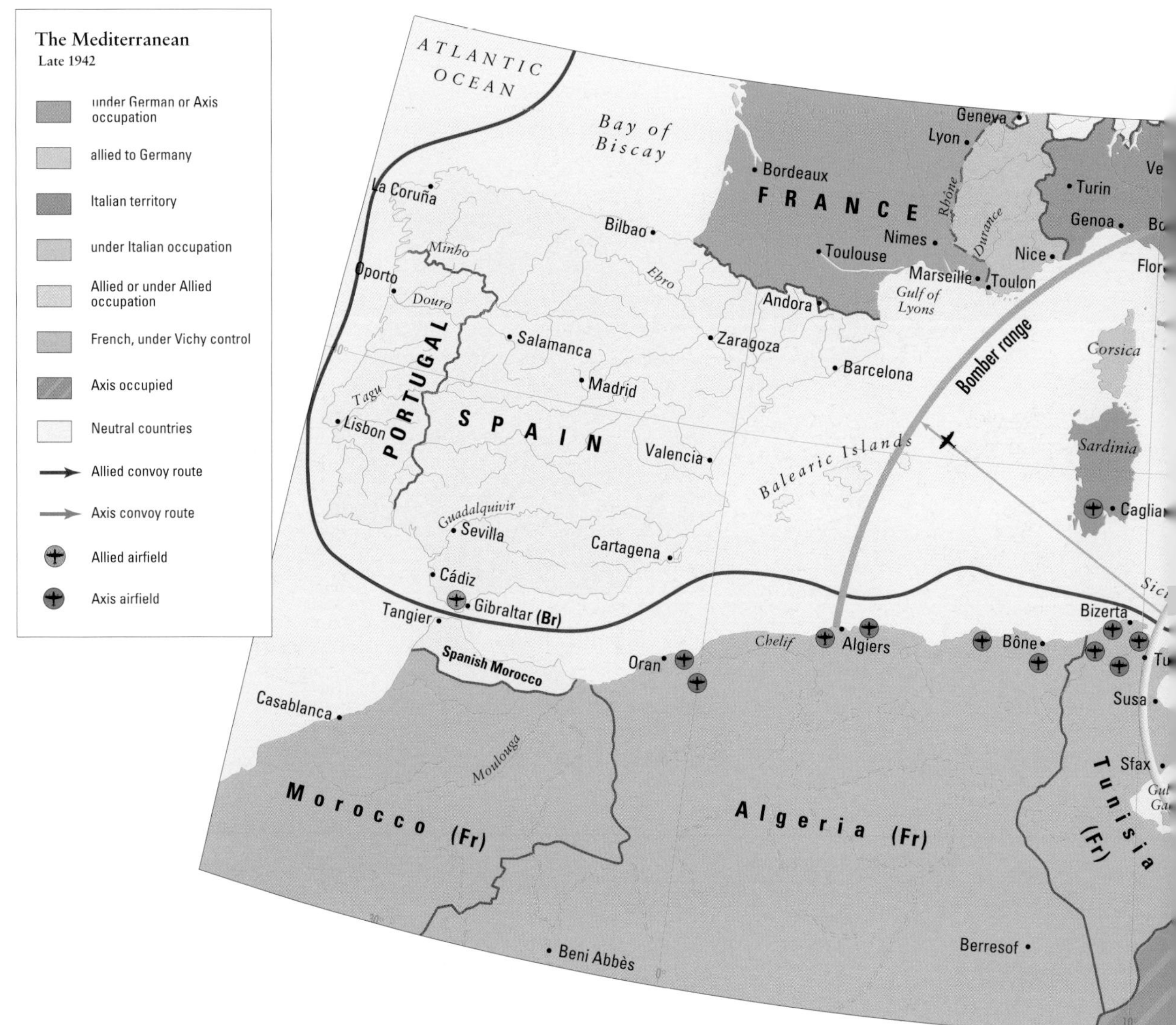

Despite Mussolini's posturing, Italy was ill-prepared for war: equipment was poor, inadequate stockpiles of bunker fuel existed for the fleet, few supplies had already been shipped to North Africa and, when she declared war in June 1940, one-third of her merchant fleet (about 218 ships of 1.2 million grt)were caught beyond Mediterranean limits and unable to get home.

This momentous month saw the Royal Navy lose the ally of the powerful French fleet and gain an enemy in the Italian. Italy's strength was considerable, including 2 new and 4 well-modernized battleships by the end of 1940, 7 heavy and 12 light cruisers, 60 fleet and 60 light destroyers, and over 100 submarines. The fleet's weakness was the lack of aircraft carriers, its chief of naval staff, Admiral Cavagnari, believing that both reconnaissance and attack could best be undertaken by land-based air, leaving the naval budget free for the acquisition of further heavy-gunned warships. Pilots, however, had little or no training in working over water.

Pre-war British planning had assumed that, with the powerful Italian air force

THE MEDITERRANEAN 1942

*Contrasting with the earlier Mediterranean map (see page 92/3) a hostile Italy effectively divides the sea into two basins. With most of the North African coast, together with Greece, occupied and France neutralized, the difficulties of keeping Malta functioning are obvious. The island's situation with respect to Italian convoy routes will also be apparent.*

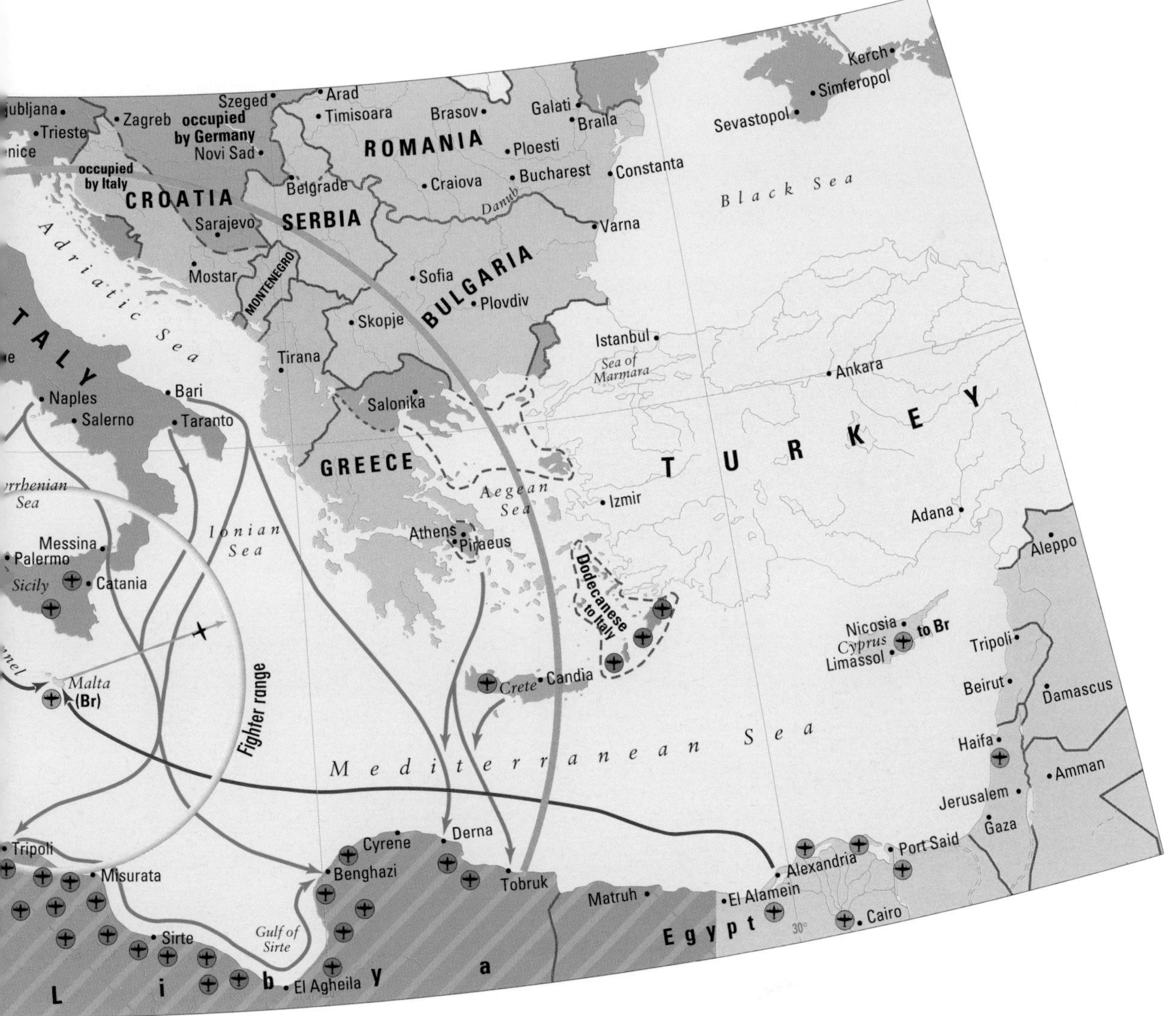

only 60 miles distant in Sicily, Malta would be indefensible, the Mediterranean Fleet needing to be based on Alexandria. Cavagnari, however, had been conditioned to look at an Anglo-French alliance that would always be superior to his own forces and, despite the French collapse, he still thought defensively. His failure to secure Malta and to seize French North African naval bases at the very outset would ultimately prove disastrous.

Pressed by the Germans to attack the British in Egypt, Mussolini willingly complied, only to dismay his ally by dissipating his strength in invading Albania and Greece, insisting on sending thirty submarines to work in the Atlantic, and gathering an air group to fly against England.

Supporting the Italian army in North Africa required an immediate and huge increase in shipments. Convoys ran mainly between Genoa–Naples and Tripoli–Benghazi, passing east or west of Sicily. The Italian port of Taranto was also important. Malta was well placed to interdict such movements, but although these were predictable thanks to the British ability to decrypt Italian naval codes, the island as yet lacked the means. Veteran O-class boats from the China station and Porpoise-class minelayers were ill-suited to these shallow and constricted waters, several being quickly lost to surprisingly efficient Italian AS measures.

At Alexandria, Admiral Sir Andrew Cunningham's Mediterranean Fleet included 4 battleships, of which only one, the flagship *Warspite*, had been modernized. There was the veteran carrier *Eagle*, 5 modern light cruisers, 16 destroyers and 10 submarines.

*Based on the battlecruiser* Renown *and carrier* Ark Royal, *Force H was formed at Gibraltar in June 1940. Under Vice Admiral Sir James Somerville it operated in both Mediterranean and Atlantic as a 'detached squadron' of Admiral Cunningham's Mediterranean Fleet.*

At Gibraltar, a new squadron, Force H, was established under Vice Admiral Sir James Somerville. It included the modern carrier *Ark Royal*, the battlecruiser *Hood* and, initially, two old battleships, one modernized.

Cunningham's policy was to hit hard and hit early in order to establish a moral ascendancy. The Italian fleet, while potentially dangerous, was found to be irresolutely led. Its air support limited itself in the early stages to spectacular but usually ineffective high-level bombing. It was decided that Malta could, after all, be defended and the first of many such carrier ferry trips flew fighter aircraft to the island. Some 40,000 tons of supplies arrived, its convoy undetected by the Italian fleet's poor reconnaissance service. Similarly undisturbed, the Italians shipped 150,000 tons to Libya without loss between June and the end of September 1940. Graziani's North African offensive began on 13 September but quickly came to a halt. His overland supply route from Benghazi was over-extended and insufficient use was made of small forward ports.

Meanwhile, as merchant ships, escorts and some 650 aircraft were diverted to the disastrous Italian adventure in Greece, Malta built up aerial resources for AS and reconnaissance, bombing and torpedo strikes.

Malta convoys were entirely different from ocean convoys. The enemy almost inevitably observed their passage past Gibraltar or Suez, and their progress was contested by serial air and submarine attack with the threat of heavy surface attack in the wings. A convoy thus became a fleet operation, with a small number of 15-knot merchantmen covered by as large an escort as could be mustered.

*Threatening to attack the Pedestal convoy of August 1942, the Italian cruisers* Bolzano *and* Attendolo *were torpedoed near the Lipari islands by the British submarine* Unbroken. *Put aground on Panarea in a sinking condition, the* Bolzano *was eventually salvaged and taken to la Spezia for repair. Here she was destroyed by British 'human torpedoes'.*

Although, in the special conditions of the Mediterranean, 'independents' could often be slipped through with lower loss rates than ships in convoy (only 40 per cent against 68 per cent respectively), during November 1940 eight more supply ships arrived in convoy MW3 and Operation Collar.

Perturbed at Graziani's faltering and the obvious build-up in Malta, the Germans transferred 330 aircraft of the specialist Fliegerkorps X to Sicily in December 1940. The British army had already counter-attacked, however, bundling the Italians out of Cyrenaica and as far west as Agheila. Tobruk and Benghazi were in British hands and the RAF could reach Malta from North African airstrips.

In January 1941 Operation Excess attempted to run in four supply ships from the west simultaneously with two from the east. Both movements were heavily contested, only 10,000 tons of supplies reaching the island, the carrier *Illustrious* being nearly sunk by dive-bombing and one cruiser lost. Only light surface units would henceforth be sent through the central narrows.

The rapid establishment of Axis air superiority saw a massive build-up in their supplies and also the virtually unopposed transport of the German Afrika Korps (DAK) to North Africa during February 1941. Wavell had never taken Tripoli, his advance halted by Churchill's obsession with sending his best forces to Greece, where the Germans again looked set to come to the aid of their wayward ally. British gains remained so weakly held that an eastward

*Following severe damage from enemy dive-bombing in January 1941, HMS* Illustrious *was temporarily patched up in Malta. For twelve days she endured every attempt to finish her off, eventually sailing for Alexandria and thence, via the Cape, for full repair in the United States.*

reconnaissance by the DAK's commander, Erwin Rommel, turned into an advance that pushed Wavell back to the Egyptian frontier by April. Deliberately left invested at Tobruk, however, was a powerful garrison, whose occupation of the port left Rommel unable to advance to a point that would have left the canal zone within Luftwaffe range.

In the four months to January 1941 almost 200,000 tons were followed by about 450,000 tons to June as the Italians continued to exploit Malta's discomfiture under continuous bombing. During March, in contrast, Admiral Cunningham's full force covered the four ships of convoy MC.9, which delivered 45,000 tons to the island.

At this time, too, a light striking force (Force K) was established at Malta. Consisting initially of four powerfully gun-armed destroyers, the group immediately exploited Ultra intelligence to annihilate a five-ship enemy convoy and its three escorts at the cost of one destroyer. So anxious was the War Cabinet to halt the flow of supplies to the Germans in North Africa that Cunningham had been instructed to block Tripoli by scuttling the battleship *Barham* and a light cruiser in the port. The success of Force K and a fleet bombardment of the port allowed Cunningham to circumvent the order. The need to evacuate the remnants of Wavell's once-victorious army from Crete to Alexandria, following the ill-advised intervention in Greece, was now to result in extensive loss and damage to Cunningham's warships. Inevitably, this filtered down to further relieve the pressure on the Axis link to Libya.

Ceaseless bombing made the situation of surface ships in Malta virtually untenable and submarines remained the navy's only strike weapon. Porpoise-class minelayers, together with the fast Manxman-class layers, ran in essential stores and personnel, but attack was now mainly the responsibility of the little U-class boats. These were well suited to the conditions, contributing greatly to the Axis loss of 115 ships of 250,000 grt in the first five months of 1941. The Axis forces needed 60,000–70,000 tons of supplies per month and, despite a loss rate of over 25 per cent, this was being delivered to Benghazi. Moving it forward to the front line, however, proved difficult as the Desert Air Force targeted road and coastal traffic. Rommel was obliged to pull back to the strong position at Agheila, whence his lines of communication were shorter.

In July and September 1941 the British ran the very successful Substance and Halberd convoys, delivering a total of 150,000 tons to Malta at small loss. The Italian fleet continued to be deterred by carrier air attack, while lacking the reconnaissance support necessary to exploit its superior strength and speed. Torpedo bombers were now a very real threat, to meet which carrier fighters were essential. Malta-based Swordfish and Albacore torpedo droppers worked effectively by night while the RAF hit enemy ships from Cyrenaican airstrips using alternative routes from the Dodecanese.

Following the German invasion of Russia in June 1941, much of Fliegerkorps X was transferred and, with the resultant reduction of air attack, Malta's own

OVERLEAF: *Enemy aircraft frequently attempted to close the Suez canal by sowing magnetic mines. This mine-spotting post is manned by Egyptian personnel. Passing through is HMS* Euryalus, *one of the hard-worked Dido-class anti-aircraft cruisers. She distinguished herself at Second Sirte and in Force K, the Malta strike force.*

aerial strike forces prospered, extending their raids both to the Italian ports of origin and to the congested destination of Tripoli.

In September 1941 British 'U-boats' sank two 19,500-ton liners out of a three-ship troop convoy, and two destroyers during the night of 8/9 November. Sixty thousand tons of supplies were thus destroyed under the noses of two Italian heavy cruisers, which did not have the benefit of radar.

Later the same month Force K repeated the experience on a smaller convoy only to run into a minefield off Tripoli shortly afterwards, losing a cruiser and a destroyer, with two further cruisers severely damaged.

There followed a sequence of disaster for the Royal Navy. Ten German U-boats had been dispatched to the Mediterranean and these sank the carrier *Ark Royal* (13 November), the *Barham* (25 November) and a light cruiser (14/15 December). Neatly avenging Taranto, Italian frogmen attached limpet mines to the battleships *Queen Elizabeth* and *Valiant*, putting them on the bottom in Alexandria harbour (14 December). This was the time of Pearl Harbor and the Admiralty was seeking to reduce Cunningham's strength further in order to send a modern force to the Far East.

Despite British tribulation, Rommel's fuel situation had reached crisis point. The Italians resorted to the desperate solution of transporting cased petrol aboard fast light cruisers. Following a single successful experiment, they dispatched a pair of ships which encountered four Allied destroyers off Cape Bon on 13 December. Within two minutes each was an inferno. Over nine hundred Italian seamen died.

Two battle-hardened Australian divisions had been withdrawn to meet the new Japanese threat. When two shiploads of armour arrived safely at Benghazi in mid December, Rommel saw an opportunity and went unexpectedly on the offensive, pushing the British back to Gazala. Here he paused, built up strength, and attacked again. By July 1942 the British were back in the El Alamein position.

Meanwhile Kesselring's Luftwaffe forces blitzed Malta to the extent that even the submarines had to be evacuated. In the six months to June 1942, over 440,000 tons of supplies were sent over to Libya at a loss rate of only 6 per cent. On the other hand, the British loss of Cyrenaican airfields made running convoys from Alexandria very risky. A four-ship convoy, MG.1, went through in March 1942 in the face of direct opposition from an Italian battle-group but, ultimately, every merchantman was lost and little cargo landed. Rommel's capture of Tobruk in June 1942 won him huge quantities of fuel. German plans were to supply the DAK through the port, via Crete, for the final push to the canal zone. Malta's capture, if then necessary at all, could be delayed until Cairo had been taken. British airpower, however, continued to target the enemy's long desert supply lines and Rommel dissipated his resources beating futilely at the strong Alamein positions.

Having received no real supplies during the first six months of 1942, Malta's situation was becoming desperate. Cunningham's successor, Admiral Sir Henry

*The successful British raid on Taranto in November 1940 was neatly offset by the Italians themselves thirteen months later when three 'human torpedoes' penetrated Alexandria harbour. Static charges were positioned below the flagship* Queen Elizabeth, *her sister,* Valiant, *and a tanker, putting all three on the bottom.*

Harwood, resolved to run in convoys from east and west simultaneously. Eleven ships (Vigorous) and six ships (Harpoon) were heavily escorted but faced their sternest test yet under every type of enemy assault. Only 25,000 tons managed to get through.

An August convoy was essential now to the island's very survival. Fourteen merchantmen, with about 140,000 tons of supplies, were supported by a massive force, supplemented by Home Fleet units. It included 2 battleships, 4 carriers, 7 cruisers and 33 destroyers. Forewarned, the enemy assembled some 780 aircraft on adjacent airfields, deployed 20 submarines, laid temporary minefields and formed torpedo craft and cruiser groups to attack on the final leg.

The result, Operation Pedestal, was a sheer trial of strength. A carrier and 2 cruisers were lost, together with 9 cargo ships. Predictably, the enemy claimed a significant victory but wiser heads knew that the 55,000 tons that had been delivered meant that Malta's future was reasonably secured. Nevertheless, during 1942, 38 merchantmen had so far been dispatched to Malta. Only 10 had arrived and, of these, 3 had been sunk following their arrival.

As General Bernard Montgomery, the new British commander, amassed men and *matériel* behind the Alamein defences, Rommel received 36,000 personnel, mainly by air, but a barely sustainable level of supplies. While the British had the benefit of the long Suez canal route, the Italians enjoyed no such advantage. By September 1942 they had less than one million grt of merchant shipping remaining. Meanwhile a late onslaught by Kesselring failed to subdue Malta's strike potential despite inflicting considerable losses.

When Montgomery launched his Alamein offensive on 23/24 October 1942, it was with such a preponderance of resources that no skill on the part of the enemy made any appreciable difference.

On 8 November the Anglo-American landings commenced in Morocco and Algeria (Operation Torch), but it would be a futher six months before the Axis presence in North Africa was squeezed out of existence. Malta received a

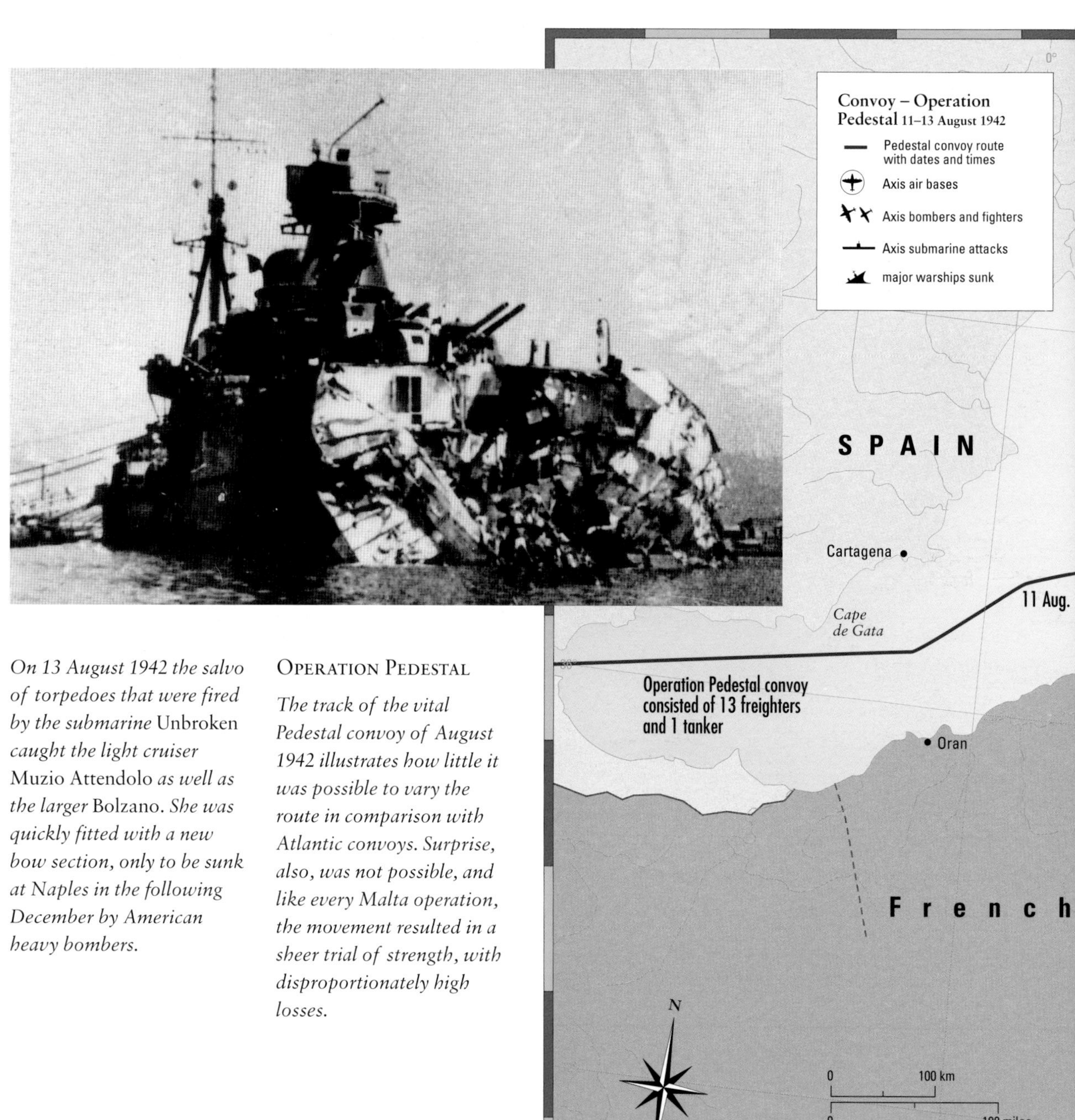


*On 13 August 1942 the salvo of torpedoes that were fired by the submarine* Unbroken *caught the light cruiser* Muzio Attendolo *as well as the larger* Bolzano. *She was quickly fitted with a new bow section, only to be sunk at Naples in the following December by American heavy bombers.*

Operation Pedestal

*The track of the vital Pedestal convoy of August 1942 illustrates how little it was possible to vary the route in comparison with Atlantic convoys. Surprise, also, was not possible, and like every Malta operation, the movement resulted in a sheer trial of strength, with disproportionately high losses.*

convoy (Stoneage) in this month without loss, while further striking forces now worked out of Algerian ports. Despite this, the Italians doggedly persevered, delivering 300,000 tons mainly through Tunisian ports between November 1942 and April 1943.

In all, Axis shipping loaded some 2.7 million tons of *matériel* for North Africa, of which 435,000 tons were lost. The effort cost 1,324 merchantmen, aggregating 2.1 million grt. A total of over 11,400 Italians were killed while engaged on the service.

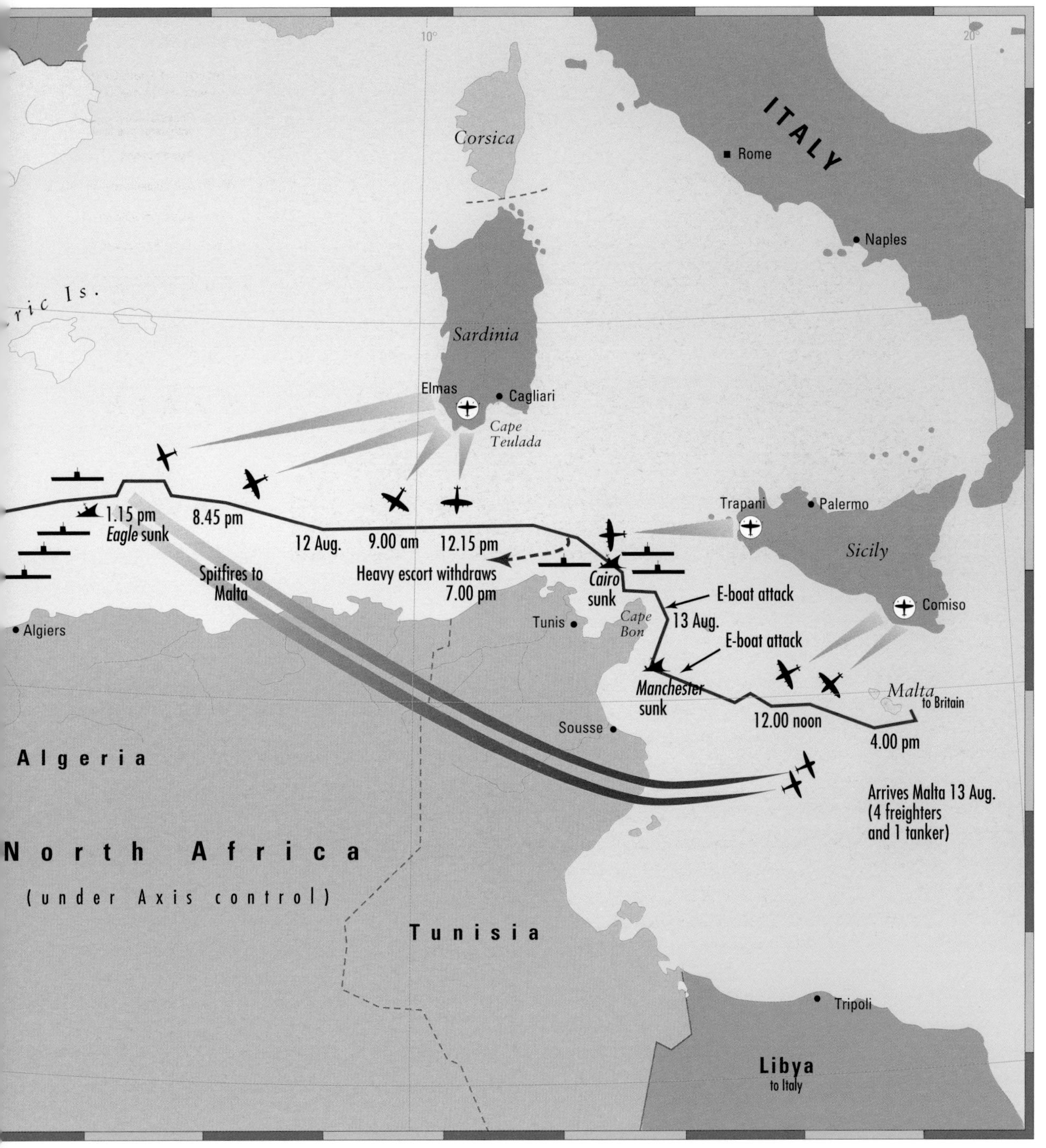

# EPILOGUE

As the echoes of victory celebration died and weather-scarred ships returned for paying-off and to an uncertain future, naval staffs already had much to ponder. Exigencies of war had made the western democracies unlikely allies of Stalin's Soviet Russia, a régime every bit as vile as the one with which they were at war. Victory in the west was soured by the immediate division of Europe, the growth of the Cold War, and the creation of the Warsaw Pact and NATO.

*Sunday, 2 September 1945, USS* Missouri, *Tokyo Bay. Nemesis of the Japanese, Fleet Admiral Chester Nimitz signs the surrender document. Behind him stand General of the Army Douglas MacArthur, Admiral William Halsey and Rear-Admiral Forrest Sherman. Vice Admiral Charles Lockwood is lost in the crowd beyond.*

The technologically backward Soviet Union of 1941 had been transformed by equipment gifted from the West and through know-how freely acquired from Germany as spoils of war. With particular reference to the war at sea the Germans had, since 1943, considerably progressed the technology for air-to-surface missiles and, more spectacularly, had developed the high-speed, snort-equipped submarine. Being more sea-dependent, the West was more threatened by such developments than was the Soviet Union.

Even as President Wilson had urged, thirty years before, the US Navy was now established as 'incomparably' the world's greatest sea power. Its recent triumph in the Pacific had been founded on the twin pillars of carrier and amphibious groups, the essence of 'force projection', yet their continuing validity was already in question. The unleashing of nuclear power over Japanese cities had done no more than demonstrate to an already beaten foe the futility of further resistance. The controlled experiments beginning at Bikini atoll less than a year later were probably more significant in showing that high-value task groups were vulnerable to nuclear bursts.

The Soviets, in victory, had acquired sufficient technology to build their own large and crude missiles, both air- and surface-launched, together with the long-range maritime patrol aircraft and small, high-speed warships necessary for their delivery.

The air threat had indeed developed rapidly. From October 1944, when the first kamikazes crashed their victims, it was no longer sufficient just to shoot down an attacking aircraft – it had to be disintegrated. Hundreds of 20mm and 40mm weapons were landed in favour of 3-inch radar-laid guns, but this programme was still incomplete when the arrival of the stand-off air-to-surface missile demanded the development of surface-to-air missile systems, capable of knocking down a missile-carrying aircraft at a safe range.

In the event of a new shooting war an impoverished Europe would be dependent for its defence on American resupply convoys. Against these, the Soviets' extensive fleet of fast submarines, based on captured German Elektroboot technology, posed a major threat. A first response, fast AS frigates converted from destroyers, was inadequate in itself because, whereas a surface ship's performance is degraded by weather conditions, a submarine's is not. Developments thus moved quickly in the direction of rapid-deployment stand-off systems based on organic shipboard helicopters, early examples of which had been flown at sea by both sides during the recent hostilities.

Huge numbers of superfluous warships were available after 1945. Many, including carriers, were transferred to friendly fleets; others began years of lay-up, in various degrees of maintenance, pending ultimate scrapping. The remainder formed the backbone of the major fleets although, in truth, most were already obsolescent in a new era where the electronics engineer was as important as the naval architect.

*Nuclear tests conducted at Bikini and Eniwetok in 1946 brought the major navies face to face with a threat on a scale not hitherto comprehended. They posed questions on the continued viability of fleets that yet remain unanswered.*

# BIOGRAPHIES

**BEATTY, ADMIRAL OF THE FLEET SIR DAVID** (1871–1936)
Personality, dash and courage complemented the ability which saw Beatty made a full captain at only 29 years of age. In 1914, as rear admiral, he was appointed to command the Grand Fleet's battlecruisers. His willingness to take risks resulted in the catastrophic loss of several of these flawed beauties. Succeeding Jellicoe after Jutland he was, despite his reputation, obliged to follow the same policies.

**CHURCHILL, SIR WINSTON S.** (1874–1965)
Inspirational wartime leader, Churchill was First Lord of the Admiralty at the outset of both world wars. Given to bold initiatives and intervening with commanders on the spot, his Dardanelles operation was strategically brilliant but poorly directed. Later schemes – Norway, Greece/Crete, *Repulse/Prince of Wales*, cost the navy dear. Involved in the dissolution of the RNAS and the adoption of the Ten Year Rule, his popularity in the service remains a mystery.

**CUNNINGHAM, ADMIRAL OF THE FLEET SIR ANDREW B.** (1883–1963)
During the First World War, Cunningham saw action at the Dardanelles, in the Zeebrugge raid and in the Baltic. He commanded the Mediterranean Fleet until 1942, achieving much against great odds. Following a year in Washington he returned to command, under Eisenhower, all Allied naval forces in the Mediterranean. In October 1943 he was appointed First Sea Lord. A difficult personality, he was an excellent delegator.

**DÖNITZ, GRAND ADMIRAL KARL** (1891–1980)
A U-boat commander during the First World War, Dönitz trained a nucleus of new personnel until 1936, when he was appointed commander of U-boats. With war, he was single-minded in his conviction that sinking merchant ships would secure victory. He succeeded Raeder as commander-in-chief of the German navy early in 1943, retaining control of U-boats, and managed to maintain morale among crews to the end. He was nominated leader following Hitler's suicide.

**FISHER, ADMIRAL OF THE FLEET SIR JOHN A.** (1841–1920)
Charismatic but ruthless, Fisher was one of the navy's greatest-ever reformers and administrators. Associated with the introduction of the destroyer, the water-tube boiler and oil-firing, and with improved gunnery. He championed the submarine, scrapped obsolete tonnage, redistributed the fleet and oversaw the dreadnought revolution. With Churchill as First Lord and Fisher First Sea Lord, direction was dynamic but, inevitably, ended in a clash of personalities, with Fisher resigning over the Dardanelles fiasco. Then aged 74, he made little further contribution.

**HALSEY, FLEET ADMIRAL WILLIAM F. JR.** (1882–1959)
A destroyer man, Halsey possessed an aggressive drive that was both his strength and his weakness. He qualified as an aviator in 1935 and, thereafter, was associated with carrier warfare, but missed Midway through sickness. As Commander South Pacific he over-risked his forces at Santa Cruz but was made Commander, Third Fleet in 1944. He showed poor judgement at Leyte Gulf and in exposing the fleet to two typhoons.

**HIPPER, ADMIRAL FRANZ RITTER VON** (1836–1932)
Rated 'the outstanding sea officer of the war' by Marder, Hipper came from a non-naval background. 'Energetic and impulsive', he never

held a senior staff appointment ashore and spent most of the First World War commanding the High Seas Fleet's scouting groups, i.e. its battlecruisers and associated light forces. He succeeded Scheer as commander-in-chief in August 1918 but was unable to prevent the general fleet mutiny, by which he was devastated.

**HORTON, ADMIRAL SIR MAX K.** (1883–1951)
Horton made his name in the First World War as a submarine commander. Following ten years in surface ships, he was appointed Flag Officer, Submarines in January 1940. Appointed Commander-in-Chief, Western Approaches in November 1942, he brilliantly oversaw British involvement in the Battle of the Atlantic, championing large convoys and formation of support groups. He made a major contribution in keeping Normandy landings U-boat free.

**JELLICOE, ADMIRAL OF THE FLEET SIR JOHN R.** (1859–1935)
A gunnery specialist, Jellicoe had an eventful early career in the navy. He was a Fisher protégé, and was appointed to the command of the Grand Fleet in August 1914. He was a recognized tactician, and his patient policy of containing the High Seas Fleet while strangling the enemy economy by blockade was correct, although widely unpopular. Succeeded by Beatty after Jutland, he became First Sea Lord, but his pessimism about the U-boat war saw him dismissed at the end of 1917.

**KING, FLEET ADMIRAL ERNEST J.** (1878–1956)
A carrier man, King held the dual post of Chief of Naval Operations and Commander-in-Chief, US Navy from March 1942 for the remainder of the war. Unarguably of outstanding ability, the austere King engendered respect but not devotion. His reputed antagonism to a British Eastern Fleet in 1945 was based largely on a personal agenda aimed at further, and unnecessary, enlargement of the US Navy.

**MACARTHUR, GENERAL OF THE ARMY DOUGLAS A.** (1880–1964)
MacArthur's almost viceregal stature in the Philippines survived the islands' lacklustre defence mainly by virtue of the heroism of the final stand. Despite his unpopularity and self-promotional image, he went on to direct the highly successful South-west Pacific campaign. His later conduct, during the Korean War, brought about his dismissal by the president.

**MAHAN, REAR ADMIRAL ALFRED T.** (1840–1914)
Mahan's general interest in history became more sharply focused when he was appointed lecturer at the Naval War College, of which he became president in 1886. He wrote several hugely successful books on sea power as a factor in world greatness, and *inter alia*, the value of the 'fleet-in-being' to a weaker power. Kaiser Wilhelm II was reputedly among the many who were greatly influenced by Mahan's theories.

**MITSCHER, VICE ADMIRAL MARC A.** (1887–1947)
One of the US Navy's earliest qualified aviators, Mitscher commanded the carrier *Hornet* at Midway, earning promotion to rear admiral. Following shore air appointments, he was again promoted and made Commander Fast Carrier Forces Pacific Fleet. Slight and unassuming, his 'wizened face usually seen under a long-visored lobsterman's cap', Mitscher excelled in deploying his naval air power. He declined post-war appointment as Chief of Naval Operations and died 'in harness' as Commander-in-Chief Atlantic Fleets.

**NAGUMO, VICE ADMIRAL CHUICHI** (1887–1944)
Commander-in-Chief of the First Air Fleet, Nagumo had no background in naval aviation. 'Gruff and uncommunicative', he did not get on with Yamamoto and had no faith in the Pearl Harbor attack. The enormous cumulative damage inflicted by his carrier force was due more to uncoordinated opposition than to inspired

leadership. Having failed to follow up his advantage at Santa Cruz, he was relieved. He committed suicide following the loss of Saipan.

**Nimitz, Fleet Admiral Chester W.** (1885–1966)
An experienced sea commander, Nimitz was appointed Commander-in-Chief Pacific Fleet following Pearl Harbor. Flying his flag ashore, his major responsibility was the Pacific Ocean Area, across which his amphibious forces closed on Japan. Courteous and calm in demeanour, he inspired confidence in his subordinates, who broke the power of the Japanese navy in a series of decisive encounters. Post-war, Nimitz became Chief of Naval Operations.

**Pound, Admiral of the Fleet Sir A. Dudley** (1877–1943)
A torpedo specialist, Pound commanded the battleship *Colossus* at Jutland. Commander-in-Chief, Mediterranean Fleet during the crisis years 1936–9, he was appointed First Sea Lord and Chief of the Naval Staff shortly before the outbreak of war. Quiet-mannered but determined, Pound was not overawed by Churchill although, like him, he tended to intervene directly. His control was unspectacular but sure. He died in office, being succeeded by Cunningham.

**Raeder, Grand Admiral Erich** (1876–1960)
Until late 1917, Raeder served as chief of staff to Admiral Hipper in the High Seas Fleet scouting forces. Of monarchist leaning, but maintaining a neutral stance, he prospered during the Weimar Republic, being appointed naval commander-in-chief in 1928. His master-plan for a new German fleet was confounded by Hitler's precipitating war at an unexpectedly early date. He resigned early in 1943 following criticism of poor showing by major fleet units.

**Scheer, Admiral Reinhard** (1863–1928)
Until early 1916 commander of a single battle squadron, Scheer succeeded as commander-in-chief through the illness of Pohl. He immediately imparted a more offensive edge to fleet activity, although his tactical competence at Jutland was questionable. Failure to better the Grand Fleet led him to support resumption of unrestricted submarine warfare. In August 1918 he succeeded as Chief of the Admiralty Staff.

**Scott, Admiral Sir Percy** (1853–1924)
Through his belief in training gun crews practically, rather than theoretically, Scott more than doubled the navy's average rate of hitting at the turn of the century. Fisher (First Sea Lord) and Jellicoe (Director of Naval Ordnance) were able to build on this improvement. Hugely unpopular through outspokenness, Scott was memorably defended by Fisher: 'I don't care if he drinks, gambles and womanizes; he hits the target!'

**Sims, Admiral William S.** (1858–1936)
Sims met Scott in the Far East when the latter was commanding HMS *Terrible*. Impressed by Scott's gunnery training methods, Sims successfully persuaded the president to have them introduced in the US Navy. In 1917, with the United States still neutral, Sims was posted to London as liaison officer. Thence he became Commander US Naval Forces Operating in European Waters. His Anglophilia was not widely appreciated elsewhere in the US Navy.

**Somerville, Admiral of the Fleet Sir James F.** (1882–1949)
As Commander-in-Chief, East Indies, Somerville was invalided from the service in 1939. Recalled, he was appointed to command the newly formed Force H. Working from Gibraltar, this participated in the action at Mers-el-Kebir, in the pursuit of the *Bismarck* and in escorting east-bound Malta convoys. From early 1942 he supervised the slow build-up of the Eastern Fleet then, from August 1944, headed the British Military Mission in Washington.

**SPRUANCE, ADMIRAL RAYMOND A.** (1886–1969)
Best known for his brilliant tactical instinct while commanding the American carrier force at Midway, Spruance went on, as Commander Fifth Fleet, to draw heavy criticism at the Philippine Sea, where his strict observance of priorities let the Japanese 'off the hook'. He then commanded naval support at Iwo Jima and Okinawa. Modest and quiet-mannered, he succeeded Nimitz in the command of the Pacific Fleet.

**SUETER, REAR ADMIRAL SIR MURRAY** (1872–1960)
Highly innovative, Sueter was involved in the early development of wireless telegraphy and the submarine. Connected with the RNAS from its inception he became Inspecting Captain of Airships, then Director of the Admiralty Air Department and Superintendent of Aircraft Construction, building up the force and championing the torpedo aircraft. Over-critical of policy, he was banished to a Mediterranean command and, in 1920, retired into politics.

**TIRPITZ, GRAND ADMIRAL ALFRED VON** (1849–1930)
A fortuitous proposal for an ambitious fleet expansion led Tirpitz to be made rear admiral by the sea-minded Kaiser and appointed Secretary of State at the Navy Office. From 1897 he created the Imperial German Navy according to his 'risk theory'; designed to deter action by the numerically superior Royal Navy through the likelihood of its incurring unacceptable loss. He resigned in March 1916 after being increasingly sidelined in decision making.

**TYRWHITT, ADMIRAL OF THE FLEET SIR REGINALD Y.** (1890–1951)
Known invariably as 'Com. (T)', Tyrwhitt led the Harwich Force throughout the war with great dash and aggression. His light cruisers tangled with the enemy at the Heligoland Bight, the Dogger Bank and at various of Hipper's tip-and-run forays. The force missed Jutland because the Admiralty initially ordered it to cover the English Channel approaches as a precaution. Surprisingly, Tyrwhitt was not promoted to full flag rank until 1919.

**WILHELM II, KAISER UND KÖNIG** (1895–1941)
Ambivalent in his attitude to Britain, Wilhelm created his fleet as a means of strengthening Germany's standing in the world, and to make her more attractive as an ally. Arrogant, yet weak-willed and vacillating, Wilhelm courted opprobrium in Britain, dispensed with the moderating influence of Bismarck, and sidelined Tirpitz, the creator of the fleet which he then proved over-reluctant to risk. He abdicated at close of hostilities.

**YAMAMOTO, ADMIRAL ISOROKU** (1884–1943)
Commander-in-chief of the Imperial Japanese Navy, Yamamoto master-minded naval support for the army campaign that overran South-east Asia. Unpretentious, and with a warm personality, Yamamoto was a skilled poker player. Opposed to war with the West and frequently at odds with the army, he none the less committed himself fully once the die was cast. His complex battle plans were largely ruined by American code-breaking.

# Further Reading

As a subject, Naval History exists on a variety of planes, from Grand Strategy through Technology to the Rattling Good Yarn. Here, we will need to confine ourselves to the general area covered by the book. The range of secondary sources available is so vast that no list could be described as definitive, but the aspiring student could do much worse than run through the following titles.

Thorough and very readable are Arthur J. Marder's five volumes *From the Dreadnought to Scapa Flow* (Oxford University Press, 1961–70). Very strong on background and personalities from 1905 to 1919, his three volumes on the Fisher papers, *Fear God and Dread Nought* (Cape, 1952–9) make a useful complement.

Of the war itself, a concise and comprehensive modern treatment is Paul G. Halpern's *A Naval History of World War I* (UCL Press, 1994). For those requiring fuller detail there is the five-volume official history by Corbett and Newbolt. *Their History of the Great War: Naval Operations* (Longmans, 1920–31) is measured and unstuffy, but not very exciting.

While the above give overall coverage, major areas of the naval war are separately treated. Admiral Sir Reginald Bacon's two-volume *The Dover Patrol 1915–17* (Hutchinson, 1919) is highly detailed and recommended. For a full understanding of how merchant shipping was managed during years of crisis, try C. Ernest Fayle's three-volume *Seaborne Trade* (John Murray, 1920–4).

For the Grand Fleet's day-to-day operations, Admiral Jellicoe's *The Grand Fleet 1914–16* (Cassell, 1919) covers the period until his effective dismissal. Dated, but valuable (and with excellent appendices), is Gibson and Prendergast's *The German Submarine War, 1914–18* (Constable, 1931).

Norman Friedman's *British Naval Aviation: The Evolution of the Ships and their Aircraft* (Conway, 1988) is good value in carrying the story to modern times, but is heavy reading.

To understand the Grand Fleet's particular bogey, Douglas Robinson's *The Zeppelin in Combat* (Foulis, 1962) is essential reading, nicely complemented by C. F. Snowden Gamble's classic *The Story of a North Sea Air Station* (Oxford, 1928).

HMSO's *A History of the Blockade of Germany,* edited by A .C. Bell, is the definitive work but a good, readable account is E. Keble Chatterton's *Big Blockade* (Hurst & Blackett, 1932).

To add to the accounts of the Dardanelles operations in the above major histories, try Arthur J. Marder's essay, 'The Dardanelles Revisited', in *From the Dardanelles to Oran* (Oxford, 1974). The senior naval officer, Admiral Wilfred Nunn, produced the best account of the navy's Mesopotamian operations in *Tigris Gunboats* (Andrew Melrose, 1932). For the Baltic operations, 1918–21, the best, though rather dry, source is Geoffrey Bennett's *Cowan's War* (Collins, 1964).

For the American view of co-operation with the Grand Fleet, Admiral Hugh Rodman's *Yarns of a Kentucky Admiral* (Hopkinson, 1929) is not very informative, but Admiral William S. Sims's *The Victory at Sea* (John Murray, 1920) is excellent. What is truly enlightening, however, is the Navy Records Society 1991 publication *Anglo-American Naval Relations 1917–19,* edited by Michael Simpson.

An informative but self-justifying German viewpoint is given by Admiral Scheer's *Germany's High Sea Fleet in the World War* (Cassell, 1920). Also useful is

Captain Hugo Waldeyer-Hartz's biography *Admiral Hipper* (Rich & Cowan, 1933).

Essential background on both people and policies is given by other Navy Records Society publications, notably Paul Halpern's two-volume *Keyes Papers* (1972–80), A. Temple Patterson's *Jellicoe Papers* (1966–8) and B. M. Ranft's *Beatty Papers* (1989).

Unfortunately, most of the fighting leaders, who could have added so much, proved disappointing autobiographers, but try Admiral Goodenough's *A Rough Record* (Hutchinson, 1943) and Admiral Lewis Bayly's *Pull Together!* (Harrap, 1939). Patrick Beesly's *Room 40: British Naval Intelligence 1914–18* (Hamish Hamilton, 1982) gives a valuable insight into behind-the-scenes work at the Admiralty.

Between-the-wars material is duller stuff. Stephen Roskill's two-volume *Naval Policy between the Wars* (Collins, 1968–76) is scholarly but essential. Painfully partisan, but with useful appendices, is Harlow A. Hyde's *Scraps of Paper* (Media Publishing, Lincoln, Nebraska, 1988), dealing with the disarmament treaties. Rather opaque, but valuable for a full understanding of the growth of American naval aviation, is Turnbull and Lord's *History of United States Naval Aviation* (Yale University Press, 1949). Edward S. Miller's *War Plan Orange* (Naval Institute Press, Annapolis, 1991) gives insight into American war strategy in the Pacific.

From the other side of the hill, both Admiral Dönitz's Memoirs, *Ten Years and Twenty Days* (Weidenfeld & Nicholson, 1959) and Admiral Raeder 's *Struggle for the Sea* (William Kimber, 1959) are valuable, if unenlightening.

Another Arthur Marder work, his part-posthumous two-volume *Old Friends, New Enemies* (Clarendon Press, Oxford, 1981–90) explains growing Anglo-Japanese antagonism between the wars, then the difficulties of the Royal Navy, both in fighting the Japanese and in co-operating with 'Ernie' King's US Navy. In conjunction, see HMSO's six-volume *War with Japan*, a staff history released for publication in 1995. Statistics are its strong feature.

Both major histories of the naval side of the Second World War – Stephen Roskill's three-volume-in-four *The War at Sea* (HMSO, 1954–61) and Samuel Eliot Morison's epic fifteen-volume *History of US Naval Operations in World War II* (Oxford, 1947–62) were written before the acknowledged existence of Ultra and are in need of revision. Roskill is austere and over-concise: Morison lavish in detail but given to purple passages. Roskill's account of British operations, particularly in the Mediterranean, is very usefully expanded by its two-volume equivalent, *Royal Australian Navy 1939–42 and 1942–5* (Collins, 1957 and 1968). Canada's immense and under-recognized contribution is well related in Joseph Schull's official account *The Far Distant Ships* (Ottawa, 1952).

Indispensible detail is available from two other publications of the Navy Records Society, *The Somerville Papers* (1995) and *The Cunningham Papers* (1999).

Clay Blair's monumental *Silent Victory* (Lippincott, 1975) and *Hitler's U-boat War 1939–42 and 1942–5* (Random House, 1996–9) are deservedly standard works on the American submarine war against Japan and the war against the U-boat. Again, the admirals who directed these campaigns are disappointing as writers. Admiral Charles A. Lockwood's *Down to the Sea in Subs* (Norton, 1967) is useful on personalities, otherwise superficial. Admiral Chalmers' account of *Max Horton and the Western Approaches* (Hodder & Stoughton, 1954) is far too concise to do justice to its subject.

Good reading!

# INDEX

Figures in *italic* refer to captions

# Picture credits

Every effort has been made to contact the copyright holders for images reproduced in this book. The publishers would welcome any errors or omissions being brought to their attention.

Imperial War Museum/Norman Wilkinson, Endpapers, pp. 14 Sir John Lavery, 20 (SP3127), 23 (Q39769), 33 (FL14444), 38 (Q18040), 47 (Q46155), 51 Glyn Philpot (top), 53 W. L.Wyllie, 58 (Q19890), 64 (Q27510 top), 64–5 (Q20638), 77 (Q19386), 81 (Q52993 top), (SP413 centre), 84 (Q27501), 86 (SP114), 87 (Q19279 top), (Q20640 bottom), 88 (Q54433), 95 (Q20375), 96–7 Norman Wilkinson, 97 (Q22839), 98 (Q13259), 102 (Q67088), 102 (Q27320A), 104–5 (Q69748), 106 (Q61738A), 107 L. Campbell Taylor, 108–9 (SP2335), 114 (Q17879), 118 (MH6204), 121 (HU2671), 125 (A10296), 126 (A5627), 132–3 Charles Pears, 134 (A6), p136–7 (HU3275), 143 (A22031), 144, 146–7 John Hamilton, 148–9 (A5449), 149 (C3393), 152 (CH13180), 153 (C5338), 163 (NYF52687), 164 (NYF23240), 165 (EN19866), 168 (NYF64407), 169 (A23916), 170 (NYF58682), 174 (A4090), 187 (NYFP645), 193 (HU27803), 198 (HU3287), 199 (A6093), 204 (MH4624), 206–7 (A13496), 209 (MH6748);
Bridgeman Art Library: p. 17 Wyllie Gallery; pp. 92–3 Topham Picture Point; Heeresgeschichtliches Museum in Arsenal pp 18–9 August Ramberg; AKG, London: pp 22, 25, 26–7, 28, 29, 30, 35, 42–3, 44, 54, 56, 57, 62–3, 66–7, 70, 80, 82, 89, 115, 120–1, 131, 196–7; National Maritime Museum: pp 24–5 Carl Saltzmann, 74 Herbert Barnard John Everett, 116 (P39119), 166 (N36622), 175, 199 Charles Pears (bottom), 202 Lieutenant-Commander Rowland John Robb Langmaid; Hulton Archive: pp 31, 51(bottom), 119, 130, 133, 151, 173, 213; Corbis: pp 37, 110, 192; Hulton-Deutsch Collection, pp. 72–3, 122, 128, 141, 145, 148, 156, 157, 158, 159, 172, 177, 180, 185, 188, 212; National Archives, pp. 113, 186; Bettmann, 117; The Mariners' Museum, 139 Acme, 155 Underwood & Underwood; Bibliothek Fur Zeitgeschichte: pp 45, 46, 69, 112, 203, 210; Royal Naval Air Service: pp 85; John Kingsmill Gardiner: p. 135.

Drawings on the title page and on pages 34, 68, 71, 126–7, 137, 140–41, 142, 145, 153, 184, 189 are by Peter Smith and Malcolm Swanston of Arcadia Editions Ltd.

ENDPAPER: *Operation Pedestal, August 1942. Bombed, torpedoed and hit by a crashing aircraft, the tanker* Ohio *battles on to Malta's relief. American-owned but British-crewed, the ship was towed into Valletta a constructive total loss but with much of her cargo intact. Her ordeal was symbolic of the tenacity of naval and mercantile services alike.*